# THE CAUDILLO OF THE ANDES

Born in La Paz in 1792, Andrés de Santa Cruz lived through the turbulent times that led to independence across Latin America. He fought to shape the newly established republics, and between 1836 and 1839 he created the Peru-Bolivia Confederation. The epitome of an Andean *caudillo*, with armed forces at the center of his ideas of governance, he was a state builder whose ambition ensured a strong and well-administered country. But the ultimate failure of the Confederation had far-reaching consequences that still have an impact today. The story of his life introduces students to broader questions of nationality and identity during this turbulent transition from Spanish colonial rule to the founding of Peru and Bolivia.

Natalia Sobrevilla Perea is Lecturer in Hispanic Studies at the University of Kent. She has published widely on the political, social, and intellectual history of Peru and the Andes and is currently leading a project to digitize nineteenth-century newspapers in regional archives in Peru, funded by the British Library. Dr. Sobrevilla Perea was previously a predoctoral Fellow and then lecturer at Yale University.

D1598616

NEW APPROACHES TO THE AMERICAS

Edited by Stuart Schwartz, *Yale University*

Also Published in the series:

# THE CAUDILLO OF
# THE ANDES

---

## ANDRÉS DE SANTA CRUZ

### NATALIA SOBREVILLA PEREA
*University of Kent*

Para Enrique y Lidia
por el cariño y el
apoyo por que saliez
este libro. gracias

**CAMBRIDGE**
UNIVERSITY PRESS

Londres, febrero 2012

CAMBRIDGE UNIVERSITY PRESS
Cambridge, New York, Melbourne, Madrid, Cape Town, Singapore,
São Paulo, Delhi, Dubai, Tokyo, Mexico City

Cambridge University Press
32 Avenue of the Americas, New York, NY 10013-2473, USA

www.cambridge.org
Information on this title: www.cambridge.org/9780521719964

First published 2011

Printed in the United States of America

*A catalog record for this publication is available from the British Library.*

*Library of Congress Cataloging in Publication data*
Sobrevilla Perea, Natalia.
The caudillo of the Andes : Andrés de Santa Cruz / Natalia Sobrevilla Perea.
p.  cm. – (New approaches to the Americas)
Includes bibliographical references and index.
ISBN 978-0-521-89567-5 (hardback) – ISBN 978-0-521-71996-4 (paperback)
1. Santa Cruz, Andrés, 1792–1865.  2. Caudillos – Bolivia – Biography.
3. Marshals – Bolivia – Biography.  4. Presidents – Bolivia – Biography.  5. Presidents –
Peru – Biography.  6. Peru-Bolivian Confederation – History.  7. South America –
History – Wars of Independence, 1806–1830.  8. South America – History – Autonomy and
independence movements.  9. Bolivia – Politics and government – 1825–1879.  10. Peru –
Politics and government – 1829–1919.  I. Title.  II. Series.
F3324.S26S68   2011
984'.04092–dc22[B]       2010049862

ISBN 978-0-521-89567-5 Hardback
ISBN 978-0-521-71996-4 Paperback

# Contents

# List of Maps and Illustrations

# Timeline for Santa Cruz

| | |
|---|---|
| 1717 | Creation of the Viceroyalty of New Granada |
| 1729 | Viceroyalty of New Granada suspended for financial difficulties |
| 1739 | Viceroyalty of New Granada is reinstated |
| 1767 | Expulsion of the Jesuits |
| 1776 | Creation of the Viceroyalty of Río de la Plata |
| 1780 | Túpac Amaru rebellion |
| 1781 | January – death of Tomas Katari |
| | March – First siege of La Paz |
| | April – Death of Túpac Amaru |
| | October – Second siege of La Paz |
| 1783 | Defeat of Túpaj Katari |
| 1786 | Joseph de Santa Cruz is sent to Caupolicán |
| 1788 | 3 May – creation of the Audiencia of Cuzco |
| | 27 August – Agustín Gamarra is born in Cuzco |
| 1792 | 5 December – Andrés de Santa Cruz is born in La Paz |
| 1801 | Intendant of Potosí proposes that Cuzco should become the capital of a viceroyalty |
| 1804 | Napoleon is crowned emperor in Paris |
| 1805 | Rebellion in Cuzco |
| 1806 | 25 June – first British invasion of Buenos Aires |
| 1807 | 5 June – second British invasion of Buenos Aires |
| 1808 | Napoleon takes over the Spanish Peninsula |
| 1809 | 25 May – junta set up in Chuquisaca |
| | 16 July – junta set up in La Paz |
| | 10 August – junta set up in Quito |
| 1810 | 9 April – junta set up in Caracas |
| | 25 May – junta set up in Buenos Aires |

20 July – junta set up in Santa Fe de Bogotá

18 September – junta set up in Santiago de Chile

1811    20 June – battle of Guaqui

1812    19 March – Cádiz constitution enacted

1813    20 February – capitulation of Salta

1 October – battle of Vilcapuquio

14 November – battle of Ayohuma

1814    2 August – revolution erupts in Cuzco

September – barracks in La Paz set alight; Santa Cruz's father dies

1815    March – Ramirez takes Cuzco from rebels

29 November – battle of Viluma

1816    9 July – independence of United Provinces of the River Plate in Congress of Tucumán

1817    12 February – battle of Chacabuco

April – Santa Cruz is captured and taken as prisoner to Buenos Aires

1818    5 April – battle of Maipú, independence of Chile

1819    January – blockade of Peruvian coast

7 August – battle of Boyacá independence of Colombia

1820    January – Santa Cruz arrives in Lima

10 March – Trienio Liberal begins in Spain with return of Cádiz Constitution

4 September – Cádiz Constitution is reinstated in Peru

8 September – San Martín disembarks in Peru

November – Tarma and Jauja declare for independence

6 December – Battle of Cerro de Pasco – Arenales wins; Santa Cruz changes sides

20 December – independence of Trujillo and northern Peru

1821    29 January – mutiny in Aznapuquio – Pezuela is deposed, La Serna made viceroy

24 June 1821 – battle of Carabobo, independence of Venezuela

28 July – declaration of independence in Peru

September – José La Mar relinquishes Real Felipe in Callao

1822    April – battle of Mamacona

24 May – battle of Pichincha – Santa Cruz excels in the battlefield

26 July – interview in Guayaquil between San Martín and Bolívar

22 September – first Peruvian Congress is sworn in

1823    January – first campaign of *intermedios* disembarks in Moquegua

26 February – mutiny at Balconcillo Santa Cruz leads group that calls for the fall of the triumvirate and presidency of José de la Riva Agüero

March – second campaign of intermedios sails south

April – end of Trienio liberal in Spain

June – royalists retake Lima for a month

July – Riva Agüero establishes government in Trujillo with some representatives

25 August – battle of Zepita, triumph for Santa Cruz

October – Santa Cruz is forced to abandon Upper Peru

12 November – Peruvian Constitution is enacted

25 November – Riva Agüero is captured and sent into exile

December – Bolívar arrives in Peru

1824   24 February – mutiny at Real Felipe; the fort returns to royalist hands

March – Pedro Antonio de Olañeta declares loyalty to the king, not the constitution

April – Bolívar organizes his troops in the northern Andes

6 August – battle of Junín

9 December – battle of Ayacucho

1825   February – Sucre crosses the Desaguadero and arrives in La Paz

6 August – assembly declares independence of Upper Provinces

25 October – Bolívar arrives back in Peru

December – tribute is abolished

1826   23 January – capitulation at Real Felipe in Callao

February – Bolívar returns to Lima; discussions over possible federation

July – Santa Cruz arrives in Lima and takes over government in the name of Bolívar

October – negotiations on possible federation with Bolivia

9 December – lifelong constitution is enacted in Lima

1827   31 January – mutiny in army barracks calling for return of 1823 Charter

April – José La Mar is elected president

1828   Santa Cruz sent on official mission to Buenos Aires

April – Santa Cruz arrives in Santiago; uprising in Bolivia where Sucre is shot

August – Santa Cruz is elected to the presidency of Bolivia

December – Santa Cruz accepts presidency of Bolivia

1829   April – Santa Cruz is confirmed as president by electoral colleges

June – Gamarra strikes against La Mar in northern Peru, La Fuente in Lima

August – alleged plot by Santa Cruz in southern Peru

1830   17 December – death of Bolívar in Santa Marta, Colombia

1831    New constitution is enacted and new tax codes introduced;
        France recognizes independence of Bolivia
1833    National Convention elected in Peru to review constitution
1834    January – Luís José de Orbegoso is elected in Peru to replace
        Gamarra
        24 April – embrace of Maquinguayo
        May – Gamarra and Santa Cruz meet in Cochabamba
        June – peace is restored in Peru
        November – Orbegoso leaves Lima for Arequipa
1835    23 February – Felipe Santiago Salaverry takes power in Lima
        April – Cuzco and Puno declare independence from Peru
        June – Peace in Peru, co-operation agreement signed between
        Santa Cruz and Orbegoso
        July – Santa Cruz is reelected president of Bolivia
        13 August – battle of Yanacocha, Santa Cruz defeats Gamarra
        September – Santa Cruz enters Cuzco to great acclaim
        December – Lima proclaims its adhesion to Orbegoso and Santa
        Cruz
1836    7 February – battle of Socabaya; Salaverry is defeated by Santa
        Cruz
        19 February – Salaverry is shot by firing squad
        17 March – Congress of Sicuani – Southern Peru is created
        10 April – Santa Cruz made Supreme Protector by Congress of
        Sicuani
        28 July – Congress is set up in Huaura
        11 August – Congress of Huaura accepts Southern Peru and the
        Confederation
        15 August – Santa Cruz enters Lima to great acclaim
        October – Confederation created by decree
        November – Congress of Tapacarí meets and accepts
        Confederation
1837    1 May – Pact of Tacna between the three states
        6 June – Portales is killed in an army uprising
        June – treaty signed between Confederation and Great Britain
        August – war between the Peru-Bolivia Confederation and the
        Argentine Confederation
        September – Blanco Ecalada sails from Valparaiso
        17 November – Treaty of Paucarpata is signed
1838    Gamarra arrives in Chile
        May – Bolivian Congress meets in Cochabamba
        21 August – battle of Guía

1839  30 January – Battle of Yungay
1840  Santa Cruz is exiled in Quito with all his family
1841  February – Santa Cruz is proclaimed president in La Paz
      July – Gamarra given powers by Congress to invade Bolivia
      27 September – Ballivián declared president of Bolivia
      18 November – Battle of Ingavi; Gamarra is killed
1842  Anarchy in Peru
1843  October – Santa Cruz is captured off the coast of Peru trying to
      return to Bolivia
1845  Santa Cruz is sent from his prison in Chillán, Chile, to exile in
      France
1848  Ballivián is ousted from power by Manuel Isidoro Belzú
      Santa Cruz is appointed Minister to the courts of France, Great
      Britain, and the Vatican
1851  Santa Cruz signs concordat with the Vatican
1855  Santa Cruz returns to America, settles briefly in Salta, and runs for
      presidency of Bolivia
1865  25 September – Santa Cruz dies in France
1965  Santa Cruz's body is returned to La Paz

# ACKNOWLEDGMENTS

This book came to being thanks to Stuart Schwartz who, knowing of my work on *caudillismo* and my interest in biography, asked me if I would like to write about Santa Cruz. James Dunkerley and his unrivaled knowledge of Bolivia made the task more possible and rewarding, but I doubt I would have managed without the constant encouragement of my father Luís Sobrevilla. I am also very grateful to the two anonymous readers who backed this project from its very inception and who provided insightful comments from the proposal to the final draft. I am particularly indebted to Scott Eastman and Matthew Brown for reading the entire manuscript and improving its content with their questions and comments. Thanks are also due to my sister Julia Sobrevilla, who made it more readable.

A grant from the University of Kent enabled me to travel to gather important documents, and the support of the Hispanic Studies section made writing possible. In Bolivia I am particularly grateful to Carlos Mesa Gisbert, who kindly allowed me to use many of the images from his book and arranged for his mother Teresa Gisbert to grant permission to use the rare 1830s portrait held in her private collection that graces this book's cover. In Sucre I am indebted to Marcela Inch, Director of the National Archive and Library of Bolivia, and to all her staff. In Lima, I thank the staff of the Instituto Riva Agüero; Ada Arrieta, Marta Solano, and in particular Rossana Pozzi Escot at the Colección Félix Denegri Luna. Special thanks are due to Claudia Castillo Cantelli at Pontificia Universidad Católica for ensuring that all materials reached me.

At Yale University, I would like to thank Enrique Mayer for all his support and Latin American curator Cesar Rodriguez for his help in navigating the Peruvian collection. I am also grateful to the staff of the John Carter Brown Library, who assisted me in locating further documents and provided me with an ideal space to review the final manuscript. In Madrid, Víctor Peralta Ruiz shared his contacts and vast knowledge of the topic. Alejandra Irigoin helped me understand money in the period, and Pablo Ortemberg sent me papers from Paris and Buenos Aires, and in Lima Marina and Domingo García Belaunde lent me crucial books at a late stage. The maps were drawn by Ana Lía Suarez and made it to this book thanks to the invaluable help of Lara Gómez and Roberto Gargarella. Further cartographical advice was provided by Rodrigo Sarria.

Many colleagues listened along the way and helped me with their observations. I would particularly like to thank Carlos Aguirre, Cristóbal Aljovín, Beatriz Bragoni, Amy Chazkel, Steffen Davies, Will Fowler, Paul Gootenberg, Iñigo García-Bryce, Pedro Guibovich, Sara Mata, Carmen McEvoy, Mauricio Novoa, Elías Palti, José Ragas, Claudia Rosas, Hilda Sabato, Ana María Stuven, Marcela Ternavasio, Marcel Velásquez, and Charles Walker. Friends made the task more enjoyable, and for their companionship I would like to thank Rosa María Alfaro, Diego Arbaiza, Luís Carlos Arias Schreiber, José Gabriel Chueca, Gonzalo Escalante, Flavia Fiorucci, Daniel Hahn, Sian Lazar, Katja Montagne, Verónica Mujica, Karen Paz, Marcela Pizarro, Sybille Prinz, Ernesto Soto, and Fernando Velásquez. Thanks are also due to my extended family, who supported me in countless ways: Marie Arana, Hortensia Muñoz, Helen Perea, and Soledad and David Sobrevilla. The undertaking would have been impossible, however, without my husband Ottokar Rosenberger, who believes in me, even when I begin to doubt, and it would have been much less fun without our three boys Sebastian, Nicolas, and Matias. This book is dedicated to them and to my mother Isabel Sobrevilla Perea, who taught me to never give up.

# INTRODUCTION

Andrés de Santa Cruz y Calahumana was born in the city of La Paz in the Viceroyalty of Río de la Plata in 1792 at the very end of the colonial period, when the Andes were still firmly under the control of the Spanish monarchy. He grew up in the aftermath of the greatest indigenous rebellion seen in 300 years and lived through the convulsed times that led to independence. Santa Cruz was an important participant during this time of change. He had the opportunity to lead and fought to shape the newly established republics in the Andes.

This is the story of a man, but it is also the story of a time and a place. Indeed, this life story is an entry point into the world in which this particular man lived. It is much more the story of the place he inhabited than a tale of the man as an individual. It does not attempt to reconstruct his personal life in detail; rather, it focuses on the politics of his time and the part he played in the process by which the countries we now know as Peru and Bolivia came into being.

Santa Cruz is often overlooked in history books when the wars of independence and the early national periods are studied because little attention is paid to the complicated events that took place in this region. His life, however, provides an excellent illustration to help us understand the process by which new nations were created once the Spanish Empire began to unravel. It provides an opportunity to look at the long-term consequences of these processes. The region where Santa Cruz spent most of his life, and where he left his largest mark, is seldom regarded as a unit. This is to a large degree because Peru and Bolivia are now two very different republics, and studies have tended to favor the national unit. Santa Cruz felt closely bound to both countries that emerged from independence, and he had to come to terms with them becoming different nation-states. He had to deal with being considered as a foreigner in Peru, a land he believed to be his own. During his lifetime, he saw many different administrative divisions in these regions, and this made it possible for him to imagine a union between these two countries. Between 1836 and 1839, he was, albeit briefly, able to put this idea into practice and create a Peru-Bolivia Confederation.

Santa Cruz was a man bound to the military; he trained from a young age with the Spanish militias, and first encountered war at the age of seventeen. He learned everything he knew about campaigning in the Andes under the command of men from southern Peru, who were fiercely loyal to the King of Spain. These men were convinced the area around Lake Titicaca should remain a political union, even after it was divided between two viceroyalties with the creation of the Viceroyalty of the Río de la Plata in 1776. When the main cities in this viceroyalty (Chuquisaca, La Paz, and later Buenos Aires) created Juntas to govern in the name of the King of Spain in 1809 and 1810, the people of southern Peru organized armies to prevent the provinces close to the lake from separating from the viceroyalty of Peru. To a large degree this is what Santa Cruz attempted throughout his career: to keep these provinces united. He was convinced that the linkages between them were so strong that they should remain together. What he learned in his youth from the men of Arequipa and Cuzco, who led the first armies organized in the southern Andes to fight against the Juntas, inspired his thinking. In addition, Santa Cruz learned the best ways of conducting war in this area.

Even after changing sides and joining those fighting for independence in 1820, his desire to keep these provinces united remained unchanged. The military was the backbone of his project. During the years of fighting for independence, he was instrumental in creating a national army, and he was one of the people in charge of transferring knowledge and experience from the colonial army to the first embryonic national army of Peru. Santa Cruz had the opportunity to further widen his understanding of tactics and strategy after coming in contact with men who had experience in guerrilla warfare, as well as with those who fought alongside with freed slaves. After meeting Antonio José de Sucre and Simón Bolívar, Santa Cruz became more accustomed to using the rhetoric of freedom, to the need to foster feelings of belonging among his followers, and to the idea of establishing constitutions to create nations and federations. We know very little of his thoughts from before then, because previously he had no need to use this language to seek support.

We do not know to what degree these were ideas he really believed in, or how much his thinking had moved on from former ideas. He was not in a position of command, and the main argument put forward by those loyal to the crown was the importance of remaining faithful to the king, who was the legitimate authority.

Once Santa Cruz did start using the discourse of freedom, he combined it with all the knowledge he had acquired throughout his career, mastering these rhetorical devices and combining them with an excellent grasp of practical matters. Wars in the early nineteenth century were, among other things, about keeping control of troops – making sure men were clothed, fed, paid, and kept happy enough that they would not desert en masse.

The army and the militia were at the center of Santa Cruz's idea of governance. His letters clearly show his view that a successful government must dominate the armed forces. This included having loyal and committed militias in urban areas, as well as rural auxiliary forces that could be called on to provide further support. His strategy, however, went beyond controlling the military; it also involved competent management of the economy and the development of modern legislation. Clear legislation and incentives for trade and economic growth encouraged the most affluent members of society to contribute to his project. Santa Cruz was a state builder, whose ambition was to ensure a strong and well-administered country. He wanted to create a viable state that would become embodied in an innovative union: the Confederation of Peru and Bolivia.

## THE CAUDILLO OF THE ANDES

Santa Cruz epitomized a Spanish-American *caudillo*. This book is an attempt to come to terms with what exactly a *caudillo* was within the context of the nineteenth-century Andean world. The word originates in Spanish from *cabeza* – head – and traditionally referred simply to a leader. In colonial times it was sometimes used to describe a member of the military and on some occasions, even viceroys. *Caudillo* could be employed positively or negatively. It was the word used to portray Túpac Amaru and the leaders of the Indian uprising that ravaged the southern Andes in the 1780s. A positive use of the term became popular when the port of Buenos Aires was invaded by the British in 1806 and 1807; the leaders of the local militias who fought against the invaders were also called *caudillos*.

Napoleon was called by this term as well. Initially this had a positive slant, because the French were Spanish allies. But after Napoleon invaded the Spanish peninsula, *caudillo* was used increasingly with pejorative connotations. When fighting erupted in the Americas, the revolutionary leaders were referred to as *caudillos* or *insurgentes* by those who remained loyal to the king. After independence, the term continued to be used as shorthand for "leader." But with time it became a term of derision. This was due in large part to its association with the Argentine context in which *caudillos* were described by most prominent literary figures of the nineteenth century as barbarous.

Domingo Faustino Sarmiento was the first person to use the term to characterize what he considered to be a typically Argentine phenomenon. He linked it to the geographical space of the pampas that, inhabited by *gauchos*, could only be governed by *caudillos*.[1] His book *Facundo* describes the life and times of a provincial leader who ruled through terror. In reality, the book was a commentary on the Argentine leader Juan Manuel de Rosas, who controlled the province of Buenos Aires through violent means and who eschewed the notion of becoming president of the whole of Argentina or creating a constitution.

In the second half of the nineteenth century, Sarmiento began the discussion of *caudillismo* as an explanation for the social development of Spanish America. The debate continues to resonate to this day. Some contend that in the Latin American context, because of the legacy of *caudillismo*, only strong leaders can prevail. At the heart of this discussion is the dichotomy Sarmiento established between civilization and barbarism. He contended that civilization could be found in the city and legal government. Barbarism, on the other hand, was embodied by the rural areas and the *caudillo*. The discussion of *caudillismo* became central to the debate over the difficulties of unifying Argentina as a nation. Subsequently, *caudillos* have been portrayed as heroes and villains by opposing sides of an intensely political debate that still rages in Argentina and beyond.

It is important, however, to ask what is understood by *caudillismo* in the region more generally. It is also necessary to question how useful this term is in places like the Andes that are so different from the Argentine pampas. Although the discussion of *caudillismo* has not been as pervasive throughout the continent as it has been in Argentina, it was used to understand Bolivia by one of its most prominent

---

[1]   Domingo Faustino Sarmiento, *Facundo o Civilización y Barbarie*, Buenos Aires: Ed. Huemul, [1845] 1978.

twentieth-century writers. Alcides Arguedas published *Los caudillos letrados* in 1922 and *Los caudillos barbaros* in 1929.[2] He included Santa Cruz among the former and argued that *caudillos* were part of the fabric of government in Bolivia. Arguedas noted how the *caudillos* had gone from being literate to being barbarous. This, in itself, was a commentary on Sarmiento.[3]

In the English language, *caudillismo* has been often used as shorthand for Latin American leaders who are sometimes described as "men on horseback." Such leaders, according to early twentieth-century writers such as Charles Chapman, governed with the support of wealthy land-owning Creoles as long as they could offer peace and security in exchange. Although Chapman believed that revolutions could be fought in the name of principles, some considered that the only substantive change was of person and ritual, while laws and constitutions remained virtually unaltered.[4] This vision of *caudillismo* prevailed until the 1960s, when it began to be understood as a Latin American variant of patronage. The idea was that relationships were structured around the exchange of benefits and protection. The patron, a word associated in its origin with Rome, provided for the client, who in return would remain bound to the patron.

*Caudillos* have been interpreted by most scholars writing in English as charismatic leaders who were able to attain power because they had a large following of clients. Charisma, understood following Max Weber as the ability of one person to rule others by sheer strength of personality, remains one of the most popular explanations of *caudillismo*, even though many of the leaders were not really that charismatic. Another widely accepted explanation correlates local Spanish-American culture and the legacy of the colonial period with the development of *caudillos*. Nineteenth-century accounts focused strongly on personality, whereas Richard Morse was one of the preeminent advocates of a culturalist explanation for *caudillismo*.[5]

[2]  Alcides Arguedas, "Los Caudillos Letrados" in *Historia General de Bolivia (El proceso de la nacionalidad) 1809–1921*, La Paz, Arnó editores, 1922; *Caudillos bárbaros, historia – resurrección. – La tragedia de un pueblo (Melgarejo–Morales) 1864–1872*, Barcelona: Viuda de L. Tasso, 1929.

[3]  The negative connotation of the term *caudillo* is indeed so strong that Carlos Mesa Gisbert, Bolivian ex-president and devoted *crucista*, asked me to reconsider whether Santa Cruz was really a *caudillo*. Personal communication, March 2010.

[4]  Charles Chapman, "The Age of Caudillos: A Chapter in Hispanic American History," *Hispanic American Historical Review (HAHR)*, vol. 12, 1932, pp. 292–3.

[5]  Richard Morse "Towards a Theory of Spanish American Government," *Journal of the History of Ideas*, vol. 15, 1954, pp. 71–93.

Others, such as Tulio Halperín Donghi, have traced *caudillismo* to what they describe as structural issues that resulted from the wars of independence.[6] Among the structuralists, there are three main interpretations, and most authors accept a combination of them.[7] The "political vacuum" interpretation, described by Charles Walker, is one of the most widely accepted structuralist explanations. It rests on the assumption that there were no able governing classes in the aftermath of independence, whereas there was an abundance of military men, so these *caudillos* came to control the governments. Walker criticizes this view for not considering the real mechanics of politics by reducing the whole issue to the relationship between patrons and clients.[8] Another structural explanation is based on the economic fragility that plagued most of the newly founded republics. However, as Paul Gootenberg has shown in his study of the financing of *caudillos* in Peru and Donald Stevens in his for the case of Mexico, it is hard to distinguish whether economic difficulties led to *caudillismo* or vice versa.[9] Regional conflict has also been seen as a structural cause for the development of *caudillos*, as leaders from regions fought against the center. John Lynch, who has written extensively about the cases of Argentina and Venezuela, asserts that the *caudillo* "first emerged as a local hero, a strong man of his region, whose authority derived from ownership of land, access to men and resources and achievements."[10]

Lynch has done much to unravel the meaning of *caudillismo* and describe these leaders in greater detail. His work moved away from traditional interpretations of *caudillos* and concentrated on a structural

---

[6]  Tulio Halperín Donghi, *Hispanoamérica Después de la Independencia*, Buenos Aires: Paidós, 1972.

[7]  In "Peasants, Caudillos, and the State in Peru: Cuzco in the Transition from Colony to Republic, 1780–1840," PhD dissertation, University of Chicago, 1992, p. 18, Charles Walker presents a useful review of the literature drawing mainly from the work of Frank Safford, "Politics, Ideology and Society in Post-Independence Spanish America," *Cambridge History of Latin America*, vol. III, pp. 347–421.

[8]  Walker, "Peasants, Caudillos, and the State," p. 23.

[9]  Paul Gootenberg, "Paying for Caudillos: The Politics of Emergency Finance in Peru, 1820–1845," in Peloso and Tenenbaum, *Liberals, Politics and Power*, state formation in nineteenth-century Latin America, Athens GA: University of Georgia Press, 1996, pp. 134–165; Donald F. Stevens, *Origins of Inestability in Early Republican Mexico*, Durham, NC: Duke University Press, 1991.

[10]  John Lynch, *Caudillos in Spanish America 1800–1850*, Oxford: Clarendon, 1992, p. 4.

analysis. Lynch sought to create a model for the whole region based on meticulous studies. His conclusions, however, are problematic when they are generalized. After concentrating on the prairie regions, Lynch concluded that *caudillos* emerged when there was an institutional vacuum, where formal rules were absent and political confrontation was resolved through conflict. These were agrarian societies where the relationship between landowner and peasants was that between a patron and a client. According to Lynch, a *caudillo* had to be both "autonomous in that he owed obedience to no one beyond him" and "absolute in that he shared his power with no other person or institution."[11] All this gave significant specificity to the existing description of *caudillos*, in the English-speaking context, but did little to dispel the assumption that it was little more than a very specific form of patron-client relationships, centered in this case in the large landholdings typical of this geographical area.

Andrés de Santa Cruz's life blows apart many of the long-held assumptions on *caudillismo*. As long as the term remains short-hand for patron-client relationships of a certain type, and not much effort is made to understand the nuances between different leaders, the term will not be very useful. In the case of Andrés de Santa Cruz, some of the elements described by Lynch are present. But none of them completely capture the complex reasons for his rise to power and his ability to govern. To conclude that he did so because he could provide his clients with patronage would certainly not be an accurate reflection of the richness of his character or the time in which he lived. He was no doubt a man of a certain charisma, although not in comparison to Bolívar's famed persona. Moreover, most of his contemporaries thought he was a successful administrator, rather than a leader of multitudes. Bolívar's Irish aide-de-camp, Daniel O'Leary, described him as having a "Jesuit's character" and considered him to be obsessed with money and the ambition to lead.[12] These were indeed useful traits, given that the backbone of Santa Cruz's power was the army. He was not a great landowner who had workers and peons to provide him with a basis for government. Although the Bolivian government did assign him some land, Santa Cruz never dedicated much effort to the role of landowner. He remained throughout his

[11] Lynch, *Caudillos in Spanish America 1800–1850*, p. 9.

[12] Letter from Daniel F. O'Leary to Simón Bolívar, 1828. In *Detached Recollections*, edited by R. Humphreys London: Institute of Latin American Studies, 1969. I thank Matthew Brown for pointing me to this reference.

life, even when in exile, a committed member of the military and always took pride in using his uniform and his rank of army general. Santa Cruz was not an exception, and many other leaders of this period in the Andes had very similar experiences. Some, such as Agustín Gamarra or Felipe Santiago Salaverry, were not as successful as Santa Cruz in applying the model, whereas another, Ramón Castilla, perfected it in a later period of economic bonanza in Peru. This makes it necessary to reevaluate the term *caudillo* in the Andean context.

Some of the most interesting recent research on *caudillismo* has focused on trying to understand why people followed these leaders. The work of Gootenberg opened this path of inquiry, as he stressed the importance of trade policies in the *caudillo* struggles.[13] Walker deepened this analysis for the case of the Andes, showing how *caudillos* created multi-class alliances and emphasized the importance of understanding their ideology.[14] Ariel de la Fuente took the debate in the River Plate to a further level by studying the close relationships between leaders and their followers, and how this led to the identification of the "clients" with the *caudillos*, concluding that these were not class-based movements, and caudillos were not completely autonomous political actors.[15] The work of Cristobal Aljovín has argued that Indians in Peru participated in the army from the end of the colonial period and how after independence *caudillos* eagerly sought their backing.[16] Cecilia Méndez has further demonstrated the way in which peasants were involved in the process of "state making" and did not remain "impervious to this process."[17] She asserts that peasants related better to liberals and chose to support them because the state proposed by their *caudillos* allowed them "a greater degree of political autonomy and legitimacy."[18] This

[13] Paul Gootenberg, *Between Silver and Guano. Commercial Policy and the State in Postindependence Peru*, Princeton, NJ: Princeton University Press, 1991.

[14] Charles Walker, *Smoldering Ashes, Cuzco and the Creation of Republican Peru, 1780, 1840*, Durham, NC: Duke University Press, 1999, p. 224.

[15] Ariel De La Fuente, *Children of Facundo: Caudillo and Gaucho Insurgency Suring the Argentine State Formation Process (La Rioja, 1853–1870)*, Durham, NC: Duke University Press, 2000, pp. 3, 4, 192.

[16] Cristóbal Aljovín de Losada, *Caudillos y constituciones. Perú: 1821–1845*, Lima: Fondo de Cultura Económica, 2000, pp. 191–212.

[17] Cecilia Méndez, *The Plebeian Republic: The Huanta Rebellion and the Making of the Peruvian State 1820–1850*, Durham, NC: Duke University Press, 2005, p. 13. Also see "Tradiciones liberales en los Andes: militares y campesinos en la formación del estado peruano," *EIAL* vol. 15, no. 1, 2004, pp. 35–63.

[18] Méndez, *The Plebeian Republic*, p. 218.

new scholarship makes it possible to look at *caudillos* in a different, more nuanced light. They were of course still patrons who provided their "clients" with goods and services, but they were also able political operators who managed to put together alliances among multiple classes and who were closely bound to their men in such a way that their followers developed a close identification with them.

*Caudillos* and the armed forces were at the center of Andean politics. This was how Santa Cruz and his contemporaries understood the practice of politics. These were not, however, military dictators as we picture them after the experiences of twentieth-century Latin America.[19] Santa Cruz, although he wore a military uniform, was not the same kind of leader as Augusto Pinochet. Neither was it the case that the military, as an institution, controlled government in the same way that it did during the 1970s in Argentina or Peru. In the nineteenth century, in the years after independence, the leaders of these new countries all established their legitimacy to govern based on the idea that they had fought for the nation. They were the *padres de la patria*, the "fathers of the nation," citizens who took up arms. This gave them the right to participate and lead in the political sphere. In reality the army provided these leaders with potential clients. Lynch also included Antonio López de Santa Anna among his case studies, and in his detailed biography Will Fowler concurs that this Mexican leader could be described as a *caudillo* and sees his power as originating from his position as a landowner who could count with the backing of his peons and the popular sectors in his region of Veracruz.[20] Although there are differences with the leaders of the plains, some similarities with the *caudillos* of the Andes do emerge. The most striking similarity is the origin of these leaders in the wars of independence, and their background in colonial militias that gave them a strong understanding of the importance of maintaining at least the semblance of an institution.

At the most basic level, the army provided soldiers with benefits such as uniforms, salaries, and retirement pensions. During this time, the records show a close relationship between the state, particular *caudillos*, and the members of the army. This relationship also had a negative

[19] This is an association that authors such as Hugh Hamill have repeatedly made; see *Caudillos: Dictators in Spanish America*, Norman: University of Oklahoma Press, 1992.

[20] Will Fowler, *Santa Anna of Mexico*, Lincoln: University of Nebraska Press, 2007, pp. 88–9.

effect that often led to recurrent political instability. Because the future of mid-ranking officers and even soldiers could be linked to particular leaders, they had considerable incentive to ensure that their *caudillo* would remain in power. This was an important reason why leaders were able to maintain the loyalty of their backers at the times of uprisings. If their *caudillo* was defeated by an opponent, the men who backed him could face reprisals, such as losing their pay, losing their appointments, or even being sent into exile. Unless they were co-opted by the new leader, the prospect of these reprisals gave them an incentive to support their *caudillo* in any attempt to retake office. The question of providing a political future for subalterns was also crucial. Antonio Zapata has argued that a great weakness in the Confederation designed by Santa Cruz was that it thwarted the promotion possibilities for Bolivian and Peruvian generals.[21]

Not only did *caudillos* need to maintain the support of their closest allies, but they also tried to enhance their power by appealing to support from a wide circle. In the case of Santa Cruz, this was done in public ceremonies that fêted his accomplishments. Special days, such as his birthday, were occasions for feasts that often lasted for days. The leader who had brought so much success to the country was celebrated in the public sphere. This built on and deepened the relationship between the *caudillo*, who provided material goods, and his men, who were there to back him. Santa Cruz took great care to maintain the core of his support. He paid a great deal of attention to providing soldiers with all they needed, and made every effort to ensure that the provinces that were the source of most of his backing received tangible economic gains. The difference between a successful campaign and a failed one, in a particular region, often had to do with the ability of a leader to ensure that the local economy and the local elites benefited from their connections with the *caudillo*. During the Confederation, this was the case in the provinces of Southern Peru, from which most of Santa Cruz's backing came. The people in these areas could see the difference between his intervention there and the looting and forcible conscription carried out by his enemies. The question of clothing soldiers and officers was fundamental, as it benefited not only those serving in the army, but also

---

[21] Antonio Zapata Velasco, "La Política Peruana y la Confederación Perú Boliviana" in *Guerra, región y nación: La Confederación Perú Boliviana 1836–1839*, Carlos Donoso and Jaime Rosenblitt, eds., Santiago: Universidad Andrés Bello, 2009, pp. 93–116.

those producing the uniforms. From the late colonial period, cloth production became an important industry in Cuzco, and the many tailors established in the city had the expertise needed to make uniforms at the scale required. These artisans wanted to make sure uniforms were purchased from them and not imported, and they wanted to maintain their links to other markets such as Bolivia. Santa Cruz's astute provisioning of his armies developed broad trust and support beyond the military.

To be successful, a *caudillo* needed the backing of core regions. In the long term, however, for an ambitious project such as the one put forward by Santa Cruz, it was necessary to co-opt several regions. The way in which each particular one was able to influence a *caudillo* and obtain benefits in exchange was crucial. These leaders cultivated relationships with people at all levels, not just the soldiers, but also the commercial agents, traders, artisans, and elites. In the Andes, where the soldiers and the irregular forces (the *montoneras* or guerrillas) were made up of Indians, it was crucial to have a close relationship with them. Cecilia Méndez has shown that in the case of the Indians of Huanta, the relationship of the *caudillo* extended beyond the members of the armed forces to include irregular forces such as *montoneras* who sought official recognition and tax exemptions.[22]

Successful leaders in the southern Andes had to be able to speak to their troops in their native languages. Because there are few archival records of the way in which oral communications were carried out, and because present-day experience makes it difficult to conceive of elites speaking in indigenous languages, we find it hard to believe that Quechua and Aymara were widely spoken at the time by those at the very top of the social scale. This was nevertheless the case. Santa Cruz, like most of his contemporaries who had been brought up in the Andes, spoke indigenous languages.[23] He understood very well the importance of maintaining many of the traditional rights of indigenous groups, as is clear from the legislation he implemented. It is also evident in the way in which he entered into agreements with particular Indian groups.

[22] Méndez, *The Plebeian Republic*, pp. 201, 202.
[23] Felipe Pardo y Aliaga made an issue of this, considering it a virtue in the case of Gamarra and a liability in that of Santa Cruz. He asserted that they both spoke Spanish, French, Quechua, and Aymara, although he does not make clear their level of linguistic competence. There are references to them giving speeches in Quechua, even though the written versions of these speeches do not survive. Up to the twentieth century it was common for elie children in Andean cities, including Arequipa to speak to the servants and other children in Quechua.

Patronage relationships in the Andes were different from those in the pampas, although the courtship of elites and regional power brokers was evident in both places. In contrast to the *caudillos* of the River Plate, those in the Andes saw their legitimacy linked to constitutions. In the Andes, these were considered as the basis of the right to govern. This was also different from the Mexican context, where *pronunciamientos*, the texts that accompanied the support to particular *caudillos* during civil conflict, became the basis of claims to legitimacy as well as a tool to challenge the established government.[24] Not one of the men who fought for the control of the state in this period in the Andes could imagine a government without a written charter. Indeed, most leaders also believed they had to consolidate their power through elections. Even taking into consideration all the problems that existed in the representative system at the time, these *caudillos* still thought that there should be regular elections. In their eyes, voting gave presidents and representatives the legitimacy to govern.

Elections at the time were of course deeply flawed, and it would be a simplification to consider these leaders "democratic" by the modern definition simply because of their faith in the ballot box. The idea that legitimate power was only obtained through elections and following a constitution was introduced in 1812, when the Cádiz Constitution was applied in the Andes. This experience had long-term repercussions in the thinking of both elites and popular sectors. Imaging a better constitution or a better institutional arrangement was also part of what these leaders saw as their mission in government. Constitutions were the basis of legitimacy. Constitutions, however, could be rewritten. This followed the ideas of Rousseau, who was convinced that a better constitutional arrangement could improve the societies that were being governed.[25]

Constitutions were seen as central by the *caudillos* of the Andes, even as they were firmly embedded in the institution of the army. *Caudillos* here were seldom landowners. Those who did own land did not draw their clients from their peons, but from the soldiers and officers who would benefit if they succeeded in their endeavors. Many times these

---

[24] For more on *pronunciamientos*, see the work of Will Fowler, http://arts.st-andrews. ac.uk/pronunciamientos/.

[25] Cristóbal Aljovín has developed this argument fully; *Caudillos y constituciones*, p. 22.

soldiers and officers came from the militias that, in contrast to the army, were made up of the "citizens" who were nevertheless expected to carry arms in defense of their city, province, and country. *Caudillos* used patronage and entered into relationships with Indian communities, with urban-sector groups such as artisans, and even with commercial and landed elites. This was how they gained support. In exchange they provided favorable legislation, such as tax exemptions to Indians, and higher or lower import and export tariffs depending on the needs of their clients. Providing patronage was important, but another element that could play to the advantage of a *caudillo* was to limit the excesses carried out by his troops when in a particular territory. When men were better equipped, they could be better controlled, and there was less risk that they would loot and steal when they traveled to different communities. The result was that the incoming forces were seen with much more sympathy. Key to this was the control of the state apparatus, and the use of the army to provide goods and services. Andean *caudillos* owed their support to the army, in contrast to the patronage of the River Plate *caudillos*, which originated in their large landholdings.

Successful leaders were also capable of developing a cult of personality, although most of them did not take it as far as the Argentine Juan Manuel de Rosas, who expected all the population to dress in red to honor him and to wear badges denouncing his political enemies. Laudatory articles in the press, poems, and speeches were all used to build a cult around the leader. Nevertheless, leadership was considered by the *caudillos* in the Andes as secondary in importance to a constitution. A written charter was the basis of the legitimacy to govern the nation. This was a clear difference from the Argentine case in particular, where there was such lack of interest in creating institutional bodies that would transcend the leader that the first constitution was not enacted until 1853. The attitude of the Andean *caudillos* was to a degree a result of their longer constitutional experience, but it was also a legacy of Bolívar, who thought new political entities could be created with new charters.

Santa Cruz was in that sense the greatest heir to Bolívar. He attempted to create a union where his mentor had failed. He did so using similar tools and hoping that a new constitutional arrangement would be strong enough to engender a durable union between the former viceroyalties. A strong incentive for Santa Cruz to create a federation came from the conflicts of identity that resulted from the emergence of the separate independent republics of Peru and Bolivia.

## The Difficult Issue of Identity

In the aftermath of independence, Santa Cruz had to deal with several issues regarding his identity. As the grandson of an Indian nobleman, he faced the question of indigenousness. He had to come to terms with how much of an Indian he was, or at least how much of an Indian others perceived him to be. On the other hand, there was the matter of his nationality, which only became relevant after Bolivia was created in 1825. In the late colonial period, both of these issues were quite different from how we would imagine them today and unlike what they were in the early independence period. Colonial ideas of ethnicity were fluid and allowed people to move within categories, which were not tightly bound by questions of racial origin as they came to be understood later in the nineteenth century. With the disappearance of legal differences between the Spanish and the Indian, the distinction between noble and common Indians also ceased to be considered relevant. A man like Santa Cruz could shift from being "Spanish" to being considered "Indian" by the 1830s. Although Santa Cruz very seldom made reference to his indigenous origin in his writings, other people did. Some, like the first British chargé d'affaires in Lima, considered it to be a positive thing. This diplomat believed that Santa Cruz could lead the people of the Andes because he was a direct descendant of the Inca. Others, like politician and writer Felipe Pardo y Aliaga, used Santa Cruz's Indian background to portray him as an invading barbarian intent on destroying civilized Lima. Being an Indian could be perceived as a positive or a negative thing.

It is interesting, however, that Santa Cruz was not willing to embrace or exploit his Indian identity. He instead chose to model himself on classical culture, noting that he wanted to create a Sparta in the Andes, or a new Macedonia. Whether this was because he did not think being Indian was useful, or because he did not consider himself to really be indigenous, we do not know. We do know that the colonial authorities believed him to be Spanish, and that is what his birth certificate stated. Both his parents were considered Creoles – the term used to describe the children of Spaniards in America – even if his mother was the daughter of an Indian noble.[26] She came from a wealthy background, and her

---

[26] Although in most of the texts of the period the term used to described them is "Spanish Americas" as opposed to "Spanish Europeans" they are now nearly always called Creoles, so this is the expression used in this book.

mother was also a rich Creole woman. This is significant because most of the literature on Santa Cruz in the twentieth century has described him as an Indian hero. This was an identity he did not embrace.

The question of nationality was not much simpler. At the end of the colonial period, regional identities had been formed around the administrative centers, mainly the judicial courts known as *Audiencias*. These administrative regions had a long-lasting influence in creating a sense of belonging. The judicial courts represented the king himself, so in the places that were distant from the viceregal capitals, this was where the power of monarchy rested. The importance of administrative units as the basis for the development of identity has been much debated since Benedict Anderson theorized their capacity to "create" meaning and aid in the formation of "imagined communities" that led to the development of a sense of self.[27] Although many of the reasons Anderson gave for why Creoles sought independence have been challenged, the views he developed following existing work that highlighted the central role played by Audiencias in identity formation remain central.

Borders, however, were porous, at both the judicial and viceregal levels. People from border areas were used to operating in more than one administrative space. In the southern Andes this was clear for the people of Cuzco, La Paz, and Arequipa, who were closely tied by circuits of trade and intellectual exchange. The most important cities in the Andes had been settled by the Spanish since the sixteenth century. With time, they had expanded and grown in importance and were linked to each other through a web of smaller towns and villages that crossed a vast space from the Pacific to the Atlantic oceans through many mountains and valleys. At the very center of these networks was the mining city of Potosí. All the urban centers and rural areas around it were either dedicated to producing foodstuffs to sustain Potosí, or were part of the circuit through which the silver was exported. Lima, the capital of the viceroyalty, was on the Pacific coast, and it grew because of the importance of the court and the trade monopolies that sustained it.

Until the Bourbon Reforms of the eighteenth century, this was the way the Spanish dominions in South America were organized. Things changed dramatically with the creation of the Viceroyalty of New Granada in 1717, which centered on today's Colombia. Although it

---

[27]  Benedict Anderson, *Imagined Communities: Reflections on the Origin and Spread of Nationalism*, London: Verso, [1983] 1991, p. 53.

was suspended briefly between 1724 and 1739 for financial difficulties, it succeeded in establishing a strong identity separate from the Viceroyalty of Peru. Much later, in 1776, a Viceroyalty of the Río de la Plata was set up in the south. This administrative reform of Peruvian territory coupled with increased taxation brought upheaval to the southern Andes and resulted in a large-scale Indian uprising that took control of the area between Cuzco and La Paz between 1780 and 1783. These were the Túpac Amaru and Túpaj Katari rebellions that had far-reaching consequences. In terms of identity formation, the creation of the viceroyalty of the Río de la Plata was no less revolutionary.

Provinces developed the idea that they were separate "kingdoms," with particular histories. This was very clearly the case of the two oldest and most established Viceroyalties, New Spain and Peru. In both places the new republics of Mexico and Peru were able to incorporate more than one audiencia in the new country. In Peru, this was mainly because the judicial court in Cuzco had not long existed at the time of independence. Other provinces, however, particularly Guatemala and Chile, were known as kingdoms and had a strong identity at the time of independence. The new Viceroyalties of New Granada and Río de la Plata also developed a sense of self, as well as an ambition to encompass the whole area that had been under their jurisdiction. This was, however, problematic: the areas linked to the Audiencias of Quito and Charcas already had their own identities that propelled them toward independence from the new viceroyalties in whose jurisdiction they belonged as well as from the longer established Viceroyalty of Peru.

When the Spanish monarchy found itself under siege after Napoleon's troops invaded the Peninsula in 1808 and captured the king, American regions reacted in different ways. It was at this point that the identities that had been created over a long period of time in these administrative units became central. The people from Quito and Chuquisaca, the colonial judicial courts that lay between the older Viceroyalty of Lima and the newer Viceroyalties of New Granada and Río de la Plata, were the first to assert their right to create autonomous Juntas similar to the ones that were being set up in Spain to look after the government while the king was being held in France. This struggle for autonomy and independence has been reconsidered in the historical studies produced during the past decade, and some authors believe these were not part of an anticolonial movement but part of a wider Hispanic revolution.[28] In the Andes, the first Juntas created in 1809

[28]    This is the case of Jaime Rodriguez and François Xavier Guerra.

were quickly overpowered by the Viceroy of Peru, who sent troops from Lima, Cuzco, and Arequipa to control them. The next to insist on their right to create Juntas were the newer Viceroyalties of New Granada and Río de la Plata, as well as the Captaincy Generals of Venezuela and Chile. The viceroy in Lima was successful in subduing the efforts in Chile. Troops from Peru reached the southern section of the King-dom of New Granada, which was engulfed in such internal fighting that sustaining a Junta, against external threats, was impossible. Venezuela had to fight against troops sent from the Peninsula, whereas the Junta of Buenos Aires faced conflict with the royalists in Montevideo and began a campaign to claim control over the Audiencia of Charcas, as an area that had been part of their viceroyalty.

Santa Cruz came of age during the wars against the troops sent by the Junta of Buenos Aires to take control of the Andes. He fought on the side of the king alongside men from the southern provinces of Peru – men from Arequipa, Cuzco, Puno, and La Paz. His identity was forged during war, and it was clear to him, at least at the start of the conflict, that he was a subject of the king of Spain. Because of his personal experiences to that point, he had much more in common with Peruvians than he did with Rioplatenses. For over a decade, Santa Cruz remained a royalist, and even after being taken captive in the prison outside Buenos Aires, he still endeavored to return to Lima and look for a commission with the army of the king. It was only after being captured a second time, and with few options available, that Santa Cruz changed sides.

We do not have a single surviving letter that mentions the reasons why he chose to do this, or a reference to his motivations, or his feelings of belonging – even in his later writings – so we can only speculate as to why he made this change. What we do know is that he was not alone, and that many of his contemporaries, men like him who had valiantly fought for the king for more than ten years, suddenly decided to change sides. Some, like him, did so after a military defeat; others, like his school companion and former comrade in arms Agustín Gamarra, did so as a result of more direct political calculation.

Once the issue of choosing the side of independence was resolved, the question of what nationality was open for someone like Santa Cruz became important. Although for a great majority of those fighting for separation from Spain this was not problematic, and their allegiance to a new nation was beyond question, this was not the case for all the participants. Many, like Bolívar, believed in the possibility of creating federations that would transcend the borders set up at the Audiencia level. Bolívar believed that Americans had too many things in common to have separate identities, and that they should be united. At this point, options for different national organizations were still open. During the years immediately following the wars, all those who had fought for the victorious side were given citizenship in the countries they helped liberate. It was still possible to think that a person's place of birth was not the most important issue to consider. This was the case of Santa Cruz, who although born in La Paz, felt and acted as a Peruvian, especially during the first years after independence.

Studies of the establishment of the Hispanic American republics have tended to highlight the importance and long history of the identities that shaped them. As a result, not much attention has been paid to the border areas or to the individuals who were caught in the middle and were unsure of what identity to take. This was the case for Santa Cruz, who felt most comfortable in the Southern Peruvian space that included both Cuzco and La Paz: the city of his birth, and the city where he had studied. His ambivalence was clear from the moment he joined the congress called by Sucre in Chuquisaca, in charge of deciding on the possible independence of the provinces that had been part of the Audiencia de Charcas. Unable to stop the creation of Bolivia, Santa Cruz opted for the second-best outcome: the union of the new republic with Peru. He had always supported the possibility of creating a federation with Peru, and was one of the most important backers of Bolívar's constitution that aimed to create a union between the countries he had liberated.

At this time, in the very first years of independence, it was still possible to imagine that countries could take shapes different from the ones we now know. The option for larger political entities in the form of federations was still considered desirable, and the union of Colombia, which at the time encompassed present-day Venezuela, Colombia, Ecuador, and Panamá, made many believe that unions were possible. However, once it became clear that Bolívar would be unable to create the Andean Federation he longed for, and he would not even be capable to keep Colombia together, faith in larger unions began to wane. Some leaders, such as Caracas native Juan José Flores, who became president of Ecuador, were able to neutralize the controversy over being foreign and remain in power. This avenue was not open to Santa Cruz. He faced much opposition from Peruvian leaders, who had initially considered him a compatriot, but now used his place of origin to delegitimize him. It was only when he realized that, because of an accident of birth, he would never be considered Peruvian that he came to terms with becoming president of Bolivia. Even at this point his identity was in flux, and his many letters from this period show how difficult he found it to abandon his feelings of being Peruvian. His loyalty to his adopted country was such that he even asked the Congress of Peru to allow him to become Bolivia's president but retain his Peruvian nationality. Although this was legally possible and the law had given all those who fought for independence full citizenship, his enemies were quite capable of exploiting this issue to destroy his political career in Peru.

Once it became clear that his political enemies would capitalize on presenting him as a foreigner, and that he would never be able to govern Peru, Santa Cruz dedicated all his energy to making Bolivia a strong and prosperous country. He embraced his Bolivian identity and began to observe Peruvian politics from afar. But when an opportunity arose to intervene, he did so. His strategy was to wait until the situation in Peru was so desperate and anarchic that the people, especially those from the southern provinces, clamored for his intervention. His idea of dividing Peru into two republics and federating it with Bolivia had been proposed a decade earlier during the first attempts at a union and was popular in certain areas. This support is what made the Confederation a possibility. His political ability and his skills as a *caudillo* made it a reality.

There were limits to his enterprise, and in the end his enemies proved successful in joining against him. His supporters were not so capable of rallying around, so his project did not last. By then, however, Santa Cruz had come to see himself as Bolivian. Many of his letters show that part of his interest in dividing Peru was to protect Bolivia from what he perceived as a more powerful neighbor. His letters from this period continuously reaffirm his Bolivian identity and show no signs of his previous ambivalence.

The Confederation was put forward by Santa Cruz not only because he believed this was the best possible political arrangement, but as an attempt to navigate his problematic identity. It appealed to many who like him felt bound to more than one area, to the men who had grown up at the end of the colonial period and had to come to terms with the emergence of strong national sentiments. What was interesting about Santa Cruz's proposal – and in this he followed Bolívar very closely – was that he believed that it was important for separate "national" identities to exist within the state structure of the union. In 1836 Santa Cruz wrote that Peru should disappear and be transformed into two states that would be federated with Bolivia. The three would become a "great body politic" in which each of the three would retain its individuality and independence.[29] These "nations" or "states" would form a union that would encompass these various nationalities in a larger federal identity. The inherent tensions of trying to reconcile these two ideas, on the one hand a strong sense of identity in the smaller units, and on the other a strong sense of federation, were linked to the failure of the project.

Santa Cruz invested all his political capital in the creation of a union between Peru and Bolivia. This he saw as a way to solve his own identity crisis, as well as an opportunity to organize an administrative unit that he thought was more convenient for both countries. The government of Chile, which was the Confederation's greatest enemy, agreed with this assessment and feared the union. They thought the Confederation was such a great threat that it should not be allowed to prosper. With that conviction they battled it with total resolve.

Even the destruction of the Confederation, however, did not mean the end of the possibility of uniting Peru and Bolivia. Other visions of how this union could be realized were still present, particularly from Agustín Gamarra, who was convinced that Bolivia should be annexed to Peru. In the end, none of these plans came to fruition because it was not possible for one country to invade the other and successfully take control of any of the neighboring provinces, until the war of the Pacific in the 1880s. After the defeat of the Confederation, nationalities had developed, and the sense of belonging to a particular nation prevented these projects from succeeding. Two decades after independence, a process of consolidation had begun, and the window for possible change had closed.

\* \* \* \* \* \* \*

This study of the *caudillo* of the Andes has been written combining private letters, official documents, and newspaper reports contemporary to the events. It also draws heavily on pamphlets and books written by the protagonists, as well as on the many works that have been written in the 200 years that have elapsed since the main events took place. The book is divided into six chapters. The first provides the background of the place where Santa Cruz was born and explains his social milieu.

---

[29] Letter from Andrés de Santa Cruz to Vicente Pazos Canqui, Huancayo, 13 July, 1836, in *Archivo Histórico del Mariscal Andrés de Santa Cruz*, vol. V, p. 238.

It pays particular attention to the rebellions that shook the Andes in the 1780s that had such a great impact, not only on the whole region, but particularly on his family. It describes the world in which Santa Cruz came of age and the conflicts that engulfed the area from the late eighteenth century. Chapter 1 also discusses his education and his formative experience fighting on the side of the king from a young age. The second chapter looks at Santa Cruz as the hero of independence. It examines his participation in the campaigns to liberate present-day Ecuador, Peru, and Bolivia and analyzes the impact of Simón Bolívar on Santa Cruz and on his subsequent conception of nationhood and the process of state building. The creation of Bolivia is examined in the third chapter, which traces the origin of the difficult sense of identity that began to be problematic for Santa Cruz after 1825. It also seeks to understand the complex relationship between southern Peru and northern Bolivia, as well as the consequences of having proper access to an accessible port on the Pacific.

These first three chapters study the end of the colonial period and the process of independence. The next three are focused on the creation and disintegration of the Peru-Bolivia Confederation. Chapter 4 charts the consolidation of Bolivia and Santa Cruz's subsequent intervention in Peruvian politics. It closely follows the events that led to the creation of the union, and it evaluates the importance of the army in Santa Cruz's project and how his previous experiences shaped him. This chapter also explores to what degree *caudillismo* played a role in this process. Chapter 5 seeks to understand who was behind the Confederation. It looks at why some supported it, and then explores the rationale of those who were opposed to the union. The main object of this chapter is to probe the reasons for the failure of the union, concentrating both on its internal and external enemies, as well as in the underlying weaknesses that existed within the project. The sixth chapter charts the end of the Confederation and follows Santa Cruz into exile first in Chile and later in France. These final three chapters examine the questions of identity, state and nation formation. An epilogue examines the long-term consequences of the failure of the project for the whole region. It follows events all the way to the present day in order to explain the reasons for ongoing tensions between Bolivia, Chile, and Peru, and it closes with a reassessment of *caudillismo* in the Andes.

# CHAPTER 1

# EARLY YEARS AT THE TWILIGHT

# OF THE COLONIAL PERIOD

Andrés de Santa Cruz was born at the end of the colonial period and was part of the generation that lived the transition from being subjects of the Spanish monarchy to becoming citizens in the republican era. To understand the process by which these new countries were created, it is necessary to be aware of the realities that shaped the worldview of men such as Santa Cruz. His childhood was spent in the high Andean region of La Paz and Cuzco and was deeply affected by the Indian rebellions that took place just ten years before his birth. Both his father and grandfather had been involved directly in the fight against the rebels and had suffered from their involvement in the conflict. The world he grew up in was still coming to terms with this legacy of insurrection when another external shock, the taking of the Spanish Peninsula by Napoleon, threw the region once again into disarray. It was in this context that Santa Cruz joined the army at seventeen and fought for a decade to defend the rights of the king in La Paz and later against the troops sent in from Buenos Aires. In 1809, he had his first experience of war, and he was exposed to the realities of fighting in the Andean region. It was also in this context that he grew familiar with the regional sentiment that made people from Arequipa, Cuzco, Puno, Arica, and Tacna fight so decisively to maintain their links to the Altiplano, La Paz, and Potosí.

This chapter provides a detailed background of the world into which Santa Cruz was born. It begins with the Túpac Amaru and Túpaj Katari rebellions, their long-term consequences in the region, and how they affected the family of Santa Cruz. Next it discusses his education in Cuzco and the influences he encountered there. His training in the colonial militias during the wars of the early nineteenth century is also

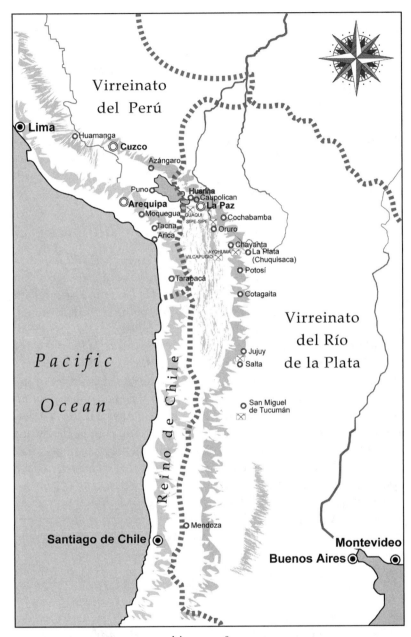

Map 1 – 1810s.

explored, as these influenced his later experience. Although Santa Cruz himself is not the protagonist of the events covered in this chapter, he was greatly influenced by them. Both his experience in the armed forces and his exposure to regionalism had a lasting influence on his political career, informing many of the actions he undertook later in life.

Santa Cruz lived during times of acute transformation and had to adapt to a rapidly changing world. He used the knowledge he acquired during the colonial period to create a new political organization under the very different conditions of the republican period. One of the issues that was going to change most dramatically was the way in which ethnicity was conceptualized.

## THE GREAT REBELLION

The world into which Andrés de Santa Cruz was born in 1792 was still recovering from the acute disruption caused by the great Andean rebellion of Túpac Amaru and Túpaj Katari. This was the largest Indian uprising in colonial times, and it shook the southern Andes between 1780 and 1783. It began in Cuzco and then spilled over to Upper Peru and what is now northern Argentina. After three years of intense fighting, tens of thousands lay dead, and land and property were devastated.[1] Its repercussions were felt throughout the ensuing decades. One of the main reasons for this unprecedented violence was the implementation of a series of changes to colonial administration known as the Bourbon Reforms, which had a deep impact in the social and political landscape of the area.[2] Not only was the Church still reeling from the expulsion of the Jesuits in 1767, but the creation of the Viceroyalty of the Río de la Plata in 1776 affected a vast territory that had to come to terms with being divided. The bureaucratic center shifted from Lima to Buenos Aires, splitting the political and economic space that surrounded and supplied the beating heart of the Andean economy: the silver mines of Potosí. The reforms hit the highland region especially hard, because political changes were compounded with increased taxation, more efficient tax collection, and the continued pressure of the

---

[1]   For an overview see Scarlett O'Phelan Godoy, *La gran rebelión en los Andes: de Túpac Amaru a Túpac Catari*. Cuzco, Peru: Centro de Estudios Regionales Andinos Bartolomé de las Casas, 1995.

[2]   For the Bourbon reforms in the Andes see John Fisher, *Bourbon Peru, 1750–1824*, Liverpool: Latin American Studies Series, 2003.

traditional colonial practices of the *reparto* that forced Indians to purchase goods at inflated prices.

Riot and revolt had been endemic throughout the 1770s, but unfair
conditions remained. This discontent made conflict especially intract-
able in Upper Peru, where it lasted longest and took on the charac-
teristics of social revolution. Here, rebels targeted rural elites and their
property. The Great Rebellion began in a small town outside Cuzco,
where local Indian leader Túpac Amaru executed the governor, charging him with harmful and tyrannical behavior. The abuses of these
provincial authorities, the *corregidores*, were widespread. They had to
purchase their posts from the crown, and as these positions had no proper
remuneration, those who held them sought to supplement their income
by graft. The rebellion began as a multiethnic coalition of discontented
Creoles, Indians, and mestizos, but most non-Indians abandoned the
cause after a church where many whites had sought refuge caught fire,
burning most of the refugees alive. And so it was the native peoples who
persisted, especially those from the towns and valleys south of Cuzco
toward Lake Titicaca and Upper Peru. Their rebellion escalated to the
point that the city of Cuzco itself lay under siege.

The ethnic question during Túpac Amaru's rebellion was quite complex. It would remain so throughout Santa Cruz's lifetime. To the modern reader, the category of *Indian* might seem homogeneous, but in the
late colonial world there were important differences between Indians.
It was because of this diversity that Indians responded in a variety of
ways first to rebellion and later to independence, influencing the political world constructed in the new republics. Túpac Amaru had initially
aimed to organize a multiethnic coalition, but not only did he fail to
maintain the support of Creoles and mestizos, he was ironically defeated
by troops among whom were many Indians. The rebel leader had actually
been in conflict with some of the most established indigenous nobles,
because he had fought over the control of the Marquisate of Oropesa,
as well as for the right to be officially acknowledged as a descendant of
the Inca.

The issue of Indian nobility was important in the colonial context, and Santa Cruz was himself of noble Indian stock. Crucial social
and economic differences existed between those Indians who were
deemed to be "common" and those who were considered noble, known
in the Andes as *kurakas* or in the Spanish system by the Caribbean
name of *caciques*. Noble Indians were important to the system, because
they tended to be in charge of tax collection and were in effect

an arm of colonial administration. Differences could also be found between Indians who lived in their towns of origin, and were therefore know as *originarios*, and those classed as *forasteros*, which meant they were not originally from the community. *Originarios* were subject to taxation and to the *mita*, which conscripted them for work in the mines of Potosí, whereas *forasteros* had no ownership of common land and were not subject to community responsibilities. In the colonial period, the category of Indian was strongly identified with the issue of taxation. Only common *originario* Indians paid a head tax that noble Indians were in charge of collecting. All other groups were exempted from all but the sales tax and other value-added taxes, linked to royal monopolies. The issue of taxation had a great effect on Indians, who made many of their political choices based on the stance of the belligerents toward taxation. There was also an important difference between those who were incorporated in the colonial system and those considered to be "savage." Recently contacted groups, the bellicose, and those who lived in frontier areas, often in the lower-lying areas closer to the Amazon basin, were seldom seen as forming part of colonial society.

During times of conflict, differences between Indians were further complicated as regional realities came into play, and some Indians sought to profit from the infighting. Many followed the lead of their caciques, but others took sides because of the effective gains they obtained when successful. Others changed sides depending on how the conflict progressed. The Great Rebellion provides a good example of these divisions in that Indians defeated other Indians. Túpac Amaru was seen by the other indigenous nobles as a mestizo outsider who threatened their positions. The uprising has been described as between rural and urban groups, because the highland herders fought against the farmers from the valleys.[3] The reaction of the noble Indians in favor of the crown was far from surprising, because they sought to maintain the prerogatives they had enjoyed during more than two centuries of collaboration. The case of Mateo Pumacagua, one of the most important loyalist Indian nobles, shows how Indians chose sides to further their interests. He was the *kuraka* of a town just outside of Cuzco and had the support of many tribute-paying Indians with whom he fought for the crown. His success against Túpac Amaru was handsomely rewarded

---

[3]  David Garret, *Shadows of Empire: The Indian Nobility of Cusco, 1750–1825*, Cambridge: Cambridge University Press, 2005, pp. 204–7.

with an appointment to the rank of brigadier, the highest level in the militia.

This rebellion, however, was not limited to Cuzco. Even before it began, Tomás Katari, the governor of the mining town of Challanta, had already deposed illegitimate caciques and was governing virtually on his own in the name of the king. He maintained that he was loyal to the colonial administration, but after his death in January 1781, those who succeeded him turned to Túpac Amaru for support.[4] In February, expecting success in Cuzco, Creoles and Indians rose against Peninsular Spaniards in the mining town of Oruro. Creoles donned indigenous clothing, but the initial goodwill to work together was short-lived. After Indian demands for the abolition of tribute and redistribution of lands were rejected, both sides became polarized. Intraethnic unity was also difficult to maintain in Cuzco, and by the time of Túpac Amaru's death in April 1781, the rebellion was less of an alliance and had become much more focused on indigenous needs. Túpac Amaru had claimed to be the new Inca and received tribute payment from communities as far south as Upper Peru. The insurrection, however, did not end after he was tried, found guilty, and quartered (each of his limbs was tied to a horse that was led in a different direction). The uprising became even more entrenched, initially around Lake Titicaca and later in the Altiplano: La Paz, the city where Santa Cruz would be born, was besieged twice between March and October 1781.

It was at this point that the conflict became most radical and violent as ethnic antagonism took central stage. The leader of the coalition in La Paz was Julian Apasa, an illiterate Aymara trader from the highlands who spoke no Spanish and who, during the conflict, took the name of Túpaj Katari. This *forastero* paid homage to the leaders of the movement of Challanta and Cuzco by taking their names in the hope of inheriting their political mantle. The three leaders had been traders and travelers who had all been disadvantaged by the Bourbon Reforms. Apasa, however, did not own a large train of mules dedicated to the long-distance transport of goods in the area spanning from modern northern Argentina to southern and central Peru, as did his Cuzco counterpart. Nor could he claim noble origin because, being a *forastero*, even his links to his own community were tenuous. He was nevertheless able to bring together

---

[4]    For the uprisings in present-day Bolivia and particularly Indigenous politics see Sinclair Thompson, *We Alone Will Rule: Native Andean Politics in the Age of Insurgency*, Madison: University of Wisconsin Press, 2002, pp. 165, 166.

a coalition of Aymara and Quechua Indians from throughout Upper Peru, and although he had initially advocated an alliance with mestizos and Creoles, after the failure of collaboration in Cuzco and Oruro, his movement became radicalized along ethnic lines. Many communities were galvanized into further action with the death of Tomás Katari, after which they declared that they were happy to die killing.[5]

Much has been written about the Great Rebellion and whether it was a precursor to the wars of independence. It is important to remember that even as Túpac Amaru began his movement claiming to defend the king and good government, as the rebellion became ever more radicalized, there was talk of returning to the status quo before the conquest with an Inca taking control of an Andean throne. As Scarlett O'Phelan has shown, the radius of action of the rebellion covered the areas linked to Potosí, in Upper and Lower southern Peru.[6] The Great Rebellion was nevertheless at its most ferocious in Upper Peru, particularly in La Paz and the southern Altiplano, where communities thought it possible to govern themselves.

The rebellion was defeated militarily in 1783 when all its leaders were captured. This was achieved by the troops who were drafted from the Viceroyalties of Peru and the Río de la Plata. It was in this context that the father of Andrés de Santa Cruz, Joseph de Santa Cruz y Villavicencio, arrived in La Paz to defend the crown against the uprising. He was a Creole militia officer born in Huamanga, who had studied in Cuzco and joined the militias in Azangaro. He had then left southern Peru and had been transferred to Buenos Aires, a move that demonstrated how even in the late Bourbon period the borders between the viceroyalties were quite porous, and men such as Joseph de Santa Cruz moved fluidly from one jurisdiction to the next.

Not only was Santa Cruz's father directly involved with fighting against Túpaj Katari in La Paz, but his maternal grandfather had much to lose in this conflict. Matías Calaumana had been the governing cacique of the community of Huarina at the edge of Lake Titicaca since

[5] For more on the radicalism of Túpaj Katari and his followers see Thompson, *We Alone Will Rule*, pp. 211–15.
[6] Scarlett O'Phelan Godoy, "Santa Cruz y Gamarra: El Proyecto de la Confederación y el Control Político del Sur Andino." In *Guerra, región y nación. La Confederación Perú Boliviana 1836–1839*. Santiago de Chile: Gobierno de Chile, Universidad Andrés Bello y Centro de Investigaciones Diego Barros Arana, 2009 Carlos Donoso y Jaime Rosenblitt eds., pp. 17–38, p. 19.

he had gained formal recognition from the viceroy in Lima in 1742.[7] His family had ruled over one of the sections of the community since the sixteenth century, and from the 1730s onward, it had all been brought under the command of his father. After the rebellion, an old and infirm Calaumana was not allowed to return to his cacicazgo, because crown officials feared he would antagonize the Indians. So even though he had supported the crown during the uprising and had the military title of *Maestre de Campo*, his hereditary right was passed on to a community Indian who had initially sided with the rebels. The rebels had appointed this Indian as town magistrate. He was nevertheless quick to change sides, just as the tide was turning, and was appointed cacique as a reward for his support to the counterinsurgency forces. The backing of the Indians made him an ideal candidate, albeit as an interim. It was clear that in the rarified climate that prevailed after the rebellion, control over the community was more important than the inherited right to govern. Calaumana did not survive this arrangement long, and his Creole widow agreed that the Indian interim could govern and collect tribute until her eight-year-old daughter came of age. María Justa Salazar challenged this agreement in 1783 and asked to be granted control of the post as the tutor of the sole heir to the cacicazgo. Although she was not successful in retaking total control, she took charge temporarily in 1789. Afterward, several other "Spanish" notables from the town stepped in as interim caciques.

In Huarina and elsewhere, after the Great Rebellion it became increasingly common to have Creoles and mestizos taking over caci-cazgos that had previously been hereditary indigenous positions.[8] Long before the rebellion, many Creoles and mestizos had married into cacique lines. It was not unusual for people like Matías Calaumana to marry Creoles; similarly, Túpac Amaru and his wife were not purely Indian. After the rebellion, many hereditary caciques lost their positions of power, not only because they had been implicated in the uprisings, but also because they were seen by the Spanish authorities to have lost legitimacy. Although some cacicazgos were awarded to Indians, in most

---

[7]  Thompson provides a detailed genealogy of the Calaumanas as well as a richly documented case study of the life of Santa Cruz's grandfather in *We Alone Will Rule*, pp. 27, 31, 56, 64–6, 82–3, 87, 232–3, 234, 235, 290, 291, 300, 317, 341.

[8]  For more on this process see David Cahill, *From Rebellion to Independence in the Andes: Soundings from Southern Peru, 1750–1830*, Amsterdam: Askant, 2002.

cases the position was given to people classified as "Spanish." This category is nevertheless a difficult one to define. In the southern Andes,
"Spanish" identified not only those born in the Spanish Peninsula, but
also those born in the Americas, and in some cases, all those who were
not identified as Indians, which could even include mestizos and blacks.
More often than not, those born in the Peninsula, when they were
not pejoratively described as *chapetones* or *godos*, were referred to as
"from the kingdoms of Spain" or with some reference to their region of
birth: Galicia, Catalonia, Andalusia, or Biscayne. In the context of the
Bourbon policy of privileging those born in the Peninsula, these were
important distinctions to make.

Identity, and the way it was viewed and lived by various groups,
became even more crucial after the triumph of crown forces that resulted in backlash against Indian symbols of power. The wearing of
European clothes was enforced, and literary works such as those by mestizo author Garcilaso de la Vega, who wrote about Inca times, were
banned. The reaction against the caciques and their prerogatives was
strong, even though most had actually remained loyal and fought to
defend the colonial order. As a result, the institution of the cacicazgo
began its inexorable decline. The aftermath of the rebellion was also an
opportunity to institute reforms that had been previously discussed
and outlined, and that were now enforced in a climate of antagonism and distrust. Some of the reforms advocated by the rebels, such
as the abolition of the forced purchase of products and the establishment of a judiciary court in Cuzco, were implemented. French-inspired
Intendancies were also rolled out with the hope that they would improve
administration and curb the abuse by mid-ranking authorities. This did
not mean that these changes were effective. In most cases the situation
remained not too different from before the rebellion. Even as the office
of *corregidor* was replaced with that of the subdelegate, abuse remained
much the same because once again these officials were not provided with
a decent salary. Although the *reparto* was abolished, populations felt the
increased levels of taxation. The burden was especially onerous in areas
such as La Paz, which, with the largest Indian population anywhere in
the Andes, continued to pay large amounts of money in the form of
tribute, ranking the city third in economic importance after Lima and
Cuzco.[9]

---

[9] For more details on this see Thompson, *We Alone Will Rule*, p. 247.

## Santa Cruz's Early Years

Andrés de Santa Cruz was born a decade after the Great Rebellion, and the severe instability of that upheaval had left an important mark in the region where he spent his youth. In 1786 his father was awarded a post as inspector of the rents accrued by the tobacco produced in the province of Caupolicán in the low-lying areas north of La Paz. It was then that Joseph de Santa Cruz met his future wife Juana Bacilia Calaumana, the daughter of the late *cacique* of Huarina. Even if her mother had failed to reclaim her father's cacicazgo, it was clear she had a comfortable position, as her dowry of 65,442 pesos testified.[10] Much has been made of the fact that she was of Indian descent, and indeed one of the major accusations raised against Santa Cruz in the 1830s by the elites from Lima was that he was an Indian. In the 1820s the first representative of the British crown had commented that being "descended from the Inca" would be beneficial to his task of leading the newly created Andean republic. It is important, however, to consider that Santa Cruz was always part of the local elite. In the late colonial context, being an Indian noble meant not only that his family did not need to pay tribute, but indeed that they were in charge of collecting it from the "common" Indians.

When Andrés de Santa Cruz was baptized in December 1792, he was recorded as being "Spanish."[11] This says little about his ethnicity as we would understand it today, but in the latter part of the colonial period it was clear that it meant that he came from a well-respected, elite family. At the time there was no contradiction with the fact that on his mother's side his heritage included an Indian grandfather. His father was a relative newcomer to La Paz, but he came from an established Creole family in Huamanga. He worked for the colonial state and held the position of *Maestre de Campo* as a high-ranking member of the militia, adding to his prestige. After his marriage to Juana Bacilia he could have litigated to try to regain control over the cacicazgo of Huarina, but he never did, even though his son was in theory the legitimate heir to that post.[12]

---

[10]  Phillip Parkerson, *Andrés de Santa Cruz y la Confederación Perú-Boliviana, 1835–1839*, La Paz: Editorial Juventud, 1984, p. 21.

[11]  Some documents give 1785 as his date of birth, but this is highly unlikely given that he was baptized in 1792.

[12]  Thompson, *We Alone Will Rule*, p. 341.

Santa Cruz was the second child born and the eldest son. His education began in the local Franciscan monastery, after which he followed
his father's footsteps and continued his studies in Cuzco. He studied at
San Bernardo, a school initially founded by the Jesuits for noble boys but
that after their expulsion was administered by the regular clergy.[13] This
was standard preparation for a member of the local elite, and the fact
that he studied at the University of Cuzco instead of Chuquisaca shows
not only that his father retained contacts there, but that there were still
important connections between Lower and Upper Peru (even though
the former now belonged to the Viceroyalty of the Río de la Plata). During his years in Cuzco, the men who later were at the forefront of the
independence movement in Buenos Aires all studied at Chuquisaca,
often described as the Oxford of America. There, the philosophical
theories of Suárez that had been prohibited in the Peninsula were still
taught to all the lawyers in training.[14]

Instead of sharing a school bench in Chuquisaca with the future
leaders of the uprising against the crown, in Cuzco Santa Cruz met
a man with whom he would compete for prominence throughout his
political career: Agustín Gamarra. Born in Cuzco in 1788,[15] Gamarra
was a member of a clan of notaries who had been part of the social
fabric of the city for at least two centuries.[16] Like Santa Cruz, he was of
mestizo origin. Although it is impossible to ascertain his exact ethnic
descent, it is clear that his family was not part of the local elite, but
was instead firmly embedded in the middle sectors of society dedicated
to the colonial bureaucracy. It was therefore no surprise that he studied
in the School of San Buenaventura, which, established by the Jesuits
in the seventeenth century, was incorporated in the University of San
Antonio Abad in Cuzco after their expulsion. Not much is known about
the reform of education in Cuzco. Certainly the amount of detail is not
comparable to what is known about these changes in the universities

---

[13] For more details see O'Phelan, "Santa Cruz y Gamarra," p. 24.

[14] Francisco Suárez (1548–1617) was a Jesuit theologian who argued that God had
given people the ability to make laws and that therefore the state was a human
and not divine creation. The king governed because of a tacit pact with the
people; if that pact was broken, people had the right to rebel.

[15] The year of his birth is contested and 1785 is often given, although this would
make him much older than Santa Cruz.

[16] For more on this see Kathryn Burns and Margaret Najarro, "Parentesco, Escritura
y Poder: Los Gamarra y la escritura pública en el Cuzco," in *Revista del Archivo
Regional del Cuzco*, No. 16, 2004, pp. 118–19.

and seminaries of Lima, Arequipa, and Chuquisaca. It is clear, however, that some influence of the Enlightenment had made its mark there as well.

The first years of the nineteenth century saw a tense calm in the ancient Inca capital where Santa Cruz was a student. The official policy undertaken by the first Intendant, who had been in Cuzco during the Túpac Amaru rebellion, was to attack the prerogatives of both Indian and Creole nobles. He persecuted the Creole bishop of Cuzco, accusing him of having supported the rebels even though he had excommunicated all those who participated in the uprising. The Intendant successfully banished the bishop from the city and managed to raise the level of Indian taxation. From 1786 to 1812, income from tax quadrupled in comparison with the mid-1700s, and most was spent on military expenses.[17] In spite of the rising fiscal pressure, elites in Cuzco felt vindicated when the long-awaited *audiencia* was finally established in 1788 with a large jurisdiction over areas in the viceroyalties of Peru and the Río de la Plata. Optimism was short-lived, because the newly organized judicial court was completely controlled by appointees sent from the Peninsula.

A strong regionalist sentiment could be found in Cuzco; colonial administrators identified it and wanted to ensure that it was harnessed to benefit the crown. The Intendant of Cuzco considered the inhabitants of his jurisdiction to be more important to the crown than those of Lima or Buenos Aires. Whereas the Intendant of Potosí believed that Cuzco should replace Lima as the capital of a viceroyalty that would unite Peru and Upper Peru. This plan was backed by a Peninsular member of the Cuzco ecclesiastical hierarchy who in 1801 advocated a plan to create a Viceroyalty in the southern Andes. Interestingly, he did so because he believed it would help economic development and act as a buffer in an area inhabited by what he described as "unfaithful Indians."[18] All these regionalist plans came to bear when in 1805 two Creoles, miner José Gabriel Aguilar and lawyer Manuel José de Ubalde, attempted to convince the president of Cuzco to crown an Inca.[19]

Like Santa Cruz, most of those involved in this plot were described as "Spaniards" in official documents, but have been referred to as Creoles

[17] Garret, *Shadows of Empire*, p. 213.
[18] For details of these proposals see John Fisher, "Royalism, Regionalism and Rebellion in Colonial Peru," *Hispanic American Historical Review*, vol. 59, no. 2, 1979, p. 239.
[19] Both Garret (p. 243) and Fisher (p. 240) present details of the uprising.

by historians, in spite of the fact that many of their leaders claimed to be descended from the Incas. The plot did not escalate further than to the stage of a conspiracy, and its leaders were hanged in the main plaza in Cuzco after they were denounced. As a thirteen-year-old schoolboy, Santa Cruz witnessed these events in which Indian nobility was invoked as a basis for legitimacy to govern, and yet during his long military and political career he never made direct reference himself to his noble Inca lineage, even if it was often remarked on by others.

The conspiracy of 1805 did not amount to much in terms of action, but it did show a willingness to imagine a political option that included complete separation from the Peninsula. In this context the events in Europe had important repercussions that convinced many that the crown was unable to govern America. After the defeat of Spain in the battle of Trafalgar, the British controlled the seas. As an ally of France, Spain was considered an enemy whose possessions could be legitimately targeted. In June 1806, British troops disembarked south of Buenos Aires and captured the city. An expedition sent from Montevideo supported by urban militias ousted the invaders after just over a month of occupation. The municipal government made a French-born officer governor of the city and subsequently Viceroy after the man in charge fled during the invasion. A second attempt by the British was rebuffed in mid-1807 by the newly reorganized militias. As a reaction to the invasions, and to aid the capital of the viceroyalty, the cities of La Paz and Potosí sent 100,000 pesos each, while Cochabamba and La Plata each sent 50,000 pesos.[20] This was an important way of expressing loyalty to the center of colonial administration. Sermons were pronounced in Chuquisaca and La Paz thanking God for being on their side.

Tensions throughout the southern Andes continued to simmer even though things had remained peaceful on the surface between the end of the eighteenth century and the beginning of the nineteenth. In 1808 these tensions exploded as a reaction to events that took place in the Peninsula. The ascendancy of Napoleon in Europe had important consequences in the Americas. Not only were the French North American territories sold to the United States in 1803, but a year later Haiti became independent in the aftermath of a slave revolt. Events in mainland Spain were to prove even more fateful. After historically having been allied to the French, Bourbon King Charles IV found himself

[20] Jose Luis Roca, *1809: La revolución en la Audiencia de Charcas en Chuquisaca y en La Paz*, La Paz: Plural, 1998, p. 68.

surrounded by increasingly unfriendly forces. He had allowed Bona-parte's men into his territory to fight the Portuguese, who were allied with the British. Spanish troops mutinied against the government in the city of Aranjuez in March 1808, and the king was forced to abdicate in favor of his son, who ascended the throne as Ferdinand VII. Two months later, in the city of Bayonne, Charles IV abdicated again, this time in favor of Napoleon, whose troops now controlled the country. The people of Madrid reacted angrily, and a mob took over the city. After intense fighting, the Napoleonic forces were able to impose their will. This was the start of a protracted war, because many refused to accept French control.

While the Bourbons remained in captivity under Napoleon, the king of Portugal fled to Brazil aboard British ships and established a new seat of imperial power in Rio de Janeiro. This was an important difference with profound implications for the divergent histories of the two empires. Whereas Brazil did not suffer from instability during the Napoleonic wars, metropolitan control in Spanish America began to unravel. In the Peninsula, Juntas were established in the name of the King, claiming that in his absence sovereignty reverted to the people; in the Americas the reaction varied. The sister of captive King Fernando was married to the King of Portugal and was therefore in Brazil. One option was for her to take direct control over the dominions of the King of Spain (her brother). This was a particularly polemical issue in the Río de la Plata where the conflict between the Bourbon and the Braganza dynasties had been played out with particular viciousness.

The other option was to establish Juntas among lines similar to those in the Peninsula. This did not happen in Lima, where a decisive viceroy had ample local support, but in other viceregal capitals conflict between Peninsular and Creole elites resulted in the deposition of the officially appointed viceroy, and later in the creation of Juntas. A first attempt to set up these "caretaker" governments was seen in the provincial capitals of Chuquisaca, Quito, and La Paz, where short-lived Juntas were organized in 1809. Chuquisaca and Quito were the seats of *Audiencias*, which were subordinated to the viceregal capital but had direct links to the crown, and were more than just judicial entities because they represented the king. Both Quito and Chuquisaca had been initially under the control of Lima, and having been made subordinate to Buenos Aires and Bogotá during the Bourbon Reforms, both felt they had lost out with this arrangement. Chuquisaca led the charge on May 25 when the *Audiencia* called for the establishment of a Junta using as legal precedents the example of the Peninsula, and the entire body of Spanish colonial law and the depositions of the viceroys in Buenos Aires and Mexico City.

Two important issues were in play at the time this Junta was created. On the one hand, it was a direct reaction against the pretensions of the Infanta, who wanted to take control over her brother's domains from Brazil. She had used the offices of José Manuel de Goyeneche, the special envoy from the Junta in Seville to America, to send letters to the *Audiencia* presenting her claims. On the other hand, this was an excellent opportunity for the people of Chuquisaca to get rid of the unpopular president of the Intendancy. Troops were sent from neighboring Potosí to quell the attempt to create a Junta. They were dissuaded from attacking by the militias that were swiftly organized in Chuquisaca. Because this was all done in the name of Ferdinand VII, Buenos Aires grudgingly accepted the situation.

Calm was restored, albeit temporarily, when on 16 July 1809 a much more violent uprising erupted in La Paz. This time, although once again the absent king was invoked, a Junta was created, and independence from the jurisdiction of Buenos Aires was called for. This was an immediate reaction to the increased taxation of Upper Peru, imposed from Buenos Aires to cover the shortfall resulting from not charging tariffs to trade with Brazil, because Portugal was a neutral power.[21] Taking advantage of the festivities of the patron of the city the Virgin of Carmen, Pedro Domingo Murillo, a mestizo trainee lawyer, took control of the militia barracks while the municipal officers of the *cabildo* deposed the Intendant and the bishop. Murillo was then appointed president of the Junta that took the name of Tuitiva, because it claimed to be a caretaker entity looking after the interests of the King. Much more ambitious than the one set up in Chuquisaca, this Junta issued a proclamation calling for the organization of a new system of government. Because at least five versions of the proclamation survive and they vary in quite substantial ways, Bolivian historians differ quite starkly in their interpretations of this document.[22] What all agree is that those who drafted it sought to improve the situation in the area of La Paz and redress policies imposed by Madrid. To do so, the Junta aimed to

---

[21] For more on the issue of taxation and these Juntas see Roca, *1809: La revolución en la Audiencia de Charcas*, p. 67.

[22] For details of this debate see Roca, *1809: La revolución en la Audiencia de Charcas*, who reproduces all five and analyzes the differences; see pp. 95–107.

construct a multiethnic alliance: noble Indians were called on to repres-
ent their people, and deputies were to be sent to each town to explain to
Indians, in their own language, what the Junta was trying to achieve.[23]
The sales tax, the *alcabala*, was abolished just as it had been in 1781, but
Indian tribute was not.

Immediate action was taken against the Junta from the viceroyalty of
Peru. The very man who had been sent by the Junta of Seville to explain
the situation to the American subjects, José Manuel de Goyeneche y
Barreda, was sent from the Intendancy of Cuzco to quell the movement
in La Paz. Born in Arequipa in 1776, Goyeneche was the son of a
miner and landowner. His father was a native of Navarre who held
the title of Captain of the Militia and had been Mayor of Arequipa.
His mother was a Creole heiress and daughter of a *Mariscal de Campo*,
whose family owned much property in Arequipa.[24] In 1788, Goyeneche
traveled to Spain to be educated, and seven years later, at the age of
nineteen, he graduated as a doctor in Seville. At this point he embraced
a military career and was named captain of the Grenadier Regiment
after a payment of 10,000 pesos. He defended Cádiz from Nelson's
bombardment in 1797 and against the British attack in 1800. Two years
later he was knighted in the Order of Santiago and was sent around
Europe to learn military strategy. After presenting his report in 1805, he
was made a colonel. In June 1808, he was entrusted by the government
resident in Seville with the mission to communicate the events that
had occurred in the metropolis to the Viceroyalties of Río de la Plata
and Peru.

Once in Cuzco, Goyeneche was appointed interim Intendant because
the incumbent died while Goyeneche was in the city. Having heard the
latest developments in La Paz, Goyeneche swiftly organized the militia.
He took advantage of the military machinery that had stood ready in
Cuzco since Túpac Amaru's rebellion, and marched on Lake Titicaca.
Goyeneche put together the army that is widely acknowledged to have
sustained the royalists until 1824 and was the basis for the armed forces
inherited by the Republic of Peru. He recruited officers like himself,
who were part of the local elite, had joined the militia as children, and
had completed their military training in the Peninsula. The Viceroy

[23] Roca, *1809: La revolución en la Audiencia de Charcas*, pp. 83, 84.
[24] For a hagiographical account of his life and deeds see Luis Herreros de Tejada, *El
Teniente General D. José Manuel de Goyeneche primer conde de Guaqui*, Barcelona:
Oliva de Villanueva, 1923, p. 43.

ordered 200 men to be sent from Cuzco, Puno, and Arequipa. Alarmed by events, the staunchly royalist Arequipeños agreed to send 1,500 men paid by voluntary subscription.[25] It was at this point that seventeen-year-old Andrés de Santa Cruz joined the militias and began his military career.

## THE START OF A MILITARY CAREER

One of Santa Cruz's biographers, Alfonso Crespo, maintains that Santa Cruz had fled school in 1809 protesting an undeserved punishment. Although there are no documents to prove this, it is an established fact that he abandoned his studies and traveled to the province of Apolobamba, in the mountainous area as between La Paz and Lake Titicaca, where his father was the subdelegate. Under his father's command, he joined the militia on the first of August, just a fortnight after the Junta was established in La Paz.[26] Joseph de Santa Cruz did not approve of the Junta Tuitiva and he, along with several other subdelegates, paid the tribute they had collected to the authorities of the Intendancy of Puno. This area had been reclaimed by the Viceroyalty of Peru and was under the control of Goyeneche, who organized his army on the edge of the lake.

Goyeneche was an expert in military strategy, and coming from a wealthy family in Arequipa, he had the means to put together an army to fight against the uprising in La Paz that showed he came from a prominent background. He called the most distinguished members of the elite from Cuzco who, like him, had been trained overseas. Because of their social standing and positions in the militia, they were able to bring their own troops. From Arequipa he called on his cousins Domingo and Juan Pío Tristán y Moscoso, both of whom had also been trained in the Peninsula. Pío had spent time in the Altiplano as a child when his own father fought against Túpaj Katari. He was fluent in Aymara. Of the men of highest rank in Goyeneche's army, the only one who was Peninsular-born was Colonel Juan Ramírez. He had arrived in Peru to fight Túpac Amaru in 1784 and had stayed after his defeat, making

---

[25] For a classical account of these campaigns see Fernando Díaz Venteo, *Las Campañas Militares del Virrey Abascal*, Seville: Escuela de Estudios Hispanoamericanos, 1948, p. 68.

[26] For full details of his military career see Julio Diaz Arguedas, "Trayectoria Militar de Santa Cruz, Mariscal del Tiempo Heroico" in *La Vida y Obra del Mariscal Andrés Santa Cruz*, La Paz: Biblioteca Paceña, 1976, p. 115.

a career as a military officer. Viceroy Fernando de Abascal, who had been seeking a better position for him than the Intendancy he held in the Central Andes, appointed Ramírez second in command of the expedition.

On 25 October, Goyeneche attacked La Paz. Because most of the rebel troops organized as militias disbanded, the city fell without much difficulty. Goyeneche found Cuzco much quieter when he returned, but the calm lasted only until a Junta was organized in Buenos Aires in May 1810. The Viceroyalty of the Río de la Plata had seen repeated strife since the British invasions, and a new viceroy had been appointed in August 1809. Having been sent from the Peninsula, he was not very popular. When news of the dire situation in the mainland arrived in mid-May 1810, he immediately came under suspicion. After a prolonged siege in Cádiz, the reigning Junta dissolved into a five-person Council of Regency. News of this led to immediate reaction in Buenos Aires, and an open session of the municipal council was called. During this meeting, at the instance of a Creole lawyer trained at the University of Chuquisaca, Juan José Castelli, it was agreed that a Junta would be established to reign in the name of King Ferdinand VII until he was able to retake control of his crown.

The May revolution immediately set out to assert control over all the provinces of the viceroyalty, and the provinces were invited to send deputies to Congress. This included Upper Peru, which after Goyeneche's incursion had returned to the jurisdiction of Lima. Castelli therefore returned to the area he knew well in order to recoup it for Buenos Aires. He succeeded in the Battle of Suipacha in November 1810, and with uprisings erupting in Cochabamba and Oruro he soon controlled most of the provinces in Upper Peru. Domingo Tristán, Goyeneche's cousin who had been left as Intendant of La Paz, gave his tacit support to the rebels, while Ramírez marched from Potosí to Oruro with 1,500 men. The Cochabambinos defeated the Royalists' advance troops, and La Paz, under Tristán, sided with the Buenos Aires Junta. Meanwhile, Goyeneche stood with 4,000 men at the Desaguadero River, the natural border between Lower and Upper Peru.

It is not clear whether Andrés de Santa Cruz joined Goyeneche's forces in 1809 or 1810. What is known is that by the time the Porteños had reached La Paz, he was under the command of the Arequipeño officer with the rank of *alférez*. This was the most junior position available to start a career in order to become an officer, but was already higher than those who entered the service as plain soldiers or even cadets. There is no doubt that Santa Cruz attained this rank because of his father's connections.

Goyeneche organized the royalist counteroffensive. He gathered his troops at the edge of the lake and trained them according to the latest European military strategy, organizing battalions, each with a commander, a major, an aide, and three officers for every hundred men. He encouraged Indians to join his forces by exempting them from tribute. Most of his men came from Cuzco, Puno, and Arequipa, although 600 soldiers of African descent were sent from Lima. This was the context in which Santa Cruz received his first training, combining the traditional Spanish and European military traditions brought by Goyeneche with the realities of fighting in the Andes, where most soldiers were indigenous.

Porteños retained control of all the upper provinces for just over six months, and during this time they introduced radical legislation that appealed to the ideas of liberty espoused by Castelli. Indians thought about their situation in very different terms than Creoles. These changes, as seen through the lens of their local realities, were often framed in terms of disputes over the control of cacicazgos and had taxation as one of their central preoccupations. By April 1810, Indians in Cochabamba were wondering how their tribute payment was being spent and whether the king was still absent. Indians were amenable to Castelli's arguments because they did not trust the authorities with this money and felt that their "pact" with the king, of tribute in exchange for protection, was not being respected. But they were not against tribute per se. Scholars have shown that there was a disconnect between Castelli's idea of civic liberty and equality, and the indigenous discourse against domination and exploitation. Indians argued against the illegitimate use of tribute and the unfair exactions by civil, religious, and ethnic authorities.[27]

In February 1811, Castelli called for the election of Indian authorities to represent their people in the congress that was to meet at the Río de la Plata. Although these elections never took place, they show how Castelli thought about the incorporation of Indians into the nascent political framework. This debate climaxed in May when he completely

---

[27] María Luisa Soux, "Los discursos de Castelli y la sublevación indígena de 1810–1811" in *La Republica Peregrina: Hombres de armas y letras en América del Sur 1800–1884* Carmen McEvoy and Ana María Stuven eds. Lima: IEP, IFEA, 2007, p. 237.

abolished the payment of tribute. He did so at a public ceremony held in the ancient pre-Inca ruins of Tiawanaku at the edge of Lake Titicaca to celebrate the first anniversary of the Junta in Buenos Aires. After the event, he had official *bandos* published in Spanish, Quechua, and Aymara that were to be fixed on public spaces in Chuquisaca, Potosí, Cochabamba, and La Paz. He abolished tribute because he considered it to be inequitable, since only Indians had to pay it. Indians, on the other hand, saw tribute as a pact with the monarch and were not against it on principle, but did want to ensure it was properly spent.

The Junta of Buenos Aires and its representatives in Upper Peru were not the only ones using elections to obtain legitimacy. By 1810 all of the Spanish dominions had been engulfed in electoral fever. The last decree of the Supreme Central Junta that had been set up outside Cádiz had called for the election of deputies to General Courts. In September the elected members met for the first time. Of 104 deputies, 26 represented the Indies, and most of these were already resident in the Peninsula. This introduction of new elements to the debate made the political climate vary markedly after news of the establishment of the Cortes in Cádiz reached the Andes. Based on this news, Castelli negotiated an armistice in mid-May 1811. Goyeneche chose not to respect the agreement and engaged his forces in battle on the shores of Lake Titicaca outside the town of Guaqui on 20 June 1811.

Before their defeat, the Porteños had been convinced that they could advance to Lima, because they established a web of supporters and were sending written propaganda all over Peru. In Tacna this came to bear as a local Creole read out proclamations in his home while the son of a local Indian cacique took control of the barracks. This happened the same day as the battle of Guaqui. The troops the rebels in Tacna were expecting never arrived to give them support, because they were already fleeing to the Río de la Plata. Without this backing, the uprising failed. The royalists defeated their enemy, but did not immediately pursue them. Before entering any rebel cities, Goyeneche requested that they declare for the crown. This was in large part because most municipal governments had sided with the Porteños. The first city to swear its allegiance was La Paz, still under the command of Domingo Tristán. The only city not to surrender was Cochabamba, where the battle of Sipe Sipe was fought in August 1811. This was the second battle in which Santa Cruz was involved, and once again it gave him the opportunity to observe the academy-trained Creole officials fight with Indian troops against an irregularly organized enemy.

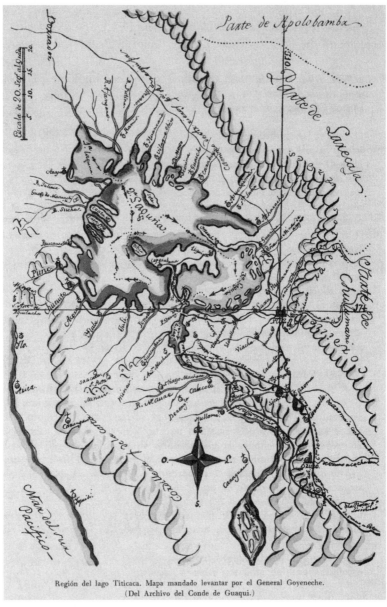

Región del lago Titicaca. Mapa mandado levantar por el General Goyeneche.
(Del Archivo del Conde de Guaqui.)

Figure 1. Map of the area surrounding Lake Titicaca made for General José Manuel de Goyeneche between 1809 and 1813, in the Archive of the Count of Guaqui, taken from Luis Herreros de Tejada, *El Teniente General D. José Manuel de Goyeneche primer conde de Guaqui*, Barcelona: Oliva de Villanueva, copy from the Beinecke Rare Book and Manuscript Library, Yale University.

While the army moved eastward, an Indian uprising took control of La Paz. Cuzqueño caciques Mateo Pumacagua and José Domingo Choquehuanca, who had proven their loyalty fighting Túpac Amaru, were sent to combat it. Viceroy Abascal noted in his memoirs that the former brought 3,000 men and the latter 1,200, and together they easily put the rebellion down. Many strategic decisions were taken based on the Indian participation in these conflicts: Goyeneche, for instance, refrained from attacking until harvest time, because he was aware that indigenous troops in the areas around Cochabamba would desert.[28] Once control was regained, a headquarters was set up in Potosí while Pío Tristán advanced with 1,000 men to the Río de la Plata. He did so with great ease through the Altiplano to the valleys of present-day northern Argentina, which is populated to this day by Quechua-speaking Indians. He encountered no opposition, and as he reached the wide-open lower valleys, he had to beg for reinforcements. He was now in a vulnerable position with no way to protect his rearguard.

Goyeneche asked Lima for help, but because an expedition to Chile was being prepared, none was sent. Deep into the Palatine territory, Tristán was trapped in Tucumán. There he sustained a heavy defeat that has been described as the bloodiest confrontation of the campaigns, with more than 150 dead and 462 prisoners and disappeared. In spite of this, Tristán was able to retreat to Salta, where he signed a capitulation in February 1813 encircled by the forces of his old school companion Manuel Belgrano. To save his life and the lives of his troops, not only did they all swear that they would never again fight against the United Provinces of the Río de la Plata, but Tristán also agreed to release all prisoners being held in Peru. He wrote a note in French to his cousin who was in the headquarters in Potosí, noting that the enemy would reach the city shortly and that he should flee. Goyeneche abandoned his position. The viceroy considered his retreat, as well as Tristán's defeat, clear signs of incompetence and disobedience and relieved them of command in a war council held in Lima. With their reputations in tatters, Tristán retired to Arequipa and Goyeneche to Madrid, where he was to be rehabilitated and later made Count of Guaqui in honor of his 1811 triumph.

By the time Goyeneche had stepped down, the situation in the Peninsula and in the colonies had patently changed. The Courts in Cádiz abolished Indian tribute in March 1811, but in Arequipa, Cuzco, and

<hr />

[28] Díaz Venteo, *Las Campañas Militares*, p. 162.

Upper Peru many chose to continue paying the now (so-called) voluntary contribution. In contrast, Indians in the North of Peru thanked the courts for the abolition.[29] There was no defense of or desire to continue with the practice of the *mita*. This was the rotation duty to work in the mines, finally abolished toward the end of that year. On many occasions, however, community members who were still forced to work in the mines appealed to crown officials to halt this abuse, using the new decrees to support their cases. Moreover, it has been argued that in some areas the voluntary contribution was tied to the right to have access to land, and that as a result many questioned to what extent this was actually an improvement. Reactions among Indians to the abolition of tribute varied; those who were least incorporated into the market welcomed abolition because they now did not have to pay the other types of tax that were linked to the market.[30]

Indians became legally equal to all other Spaniards when the *Constitución Política de la Monarquía Española* of 1812 was completed. Known as "La Pepa," the female nickname given to those called Joseph, it was sworn on the day of that saint. This innovative document brought to life many of the ideals of the group of reformers who had become known as liberals during the constitutional debates. The equality of all subjects of the Spanish monarchy was one of their greatest achievements, as the constitution dismantled the system of government that had hitherto maintained a legal divide between the Indian and the non-Indian. Another of the great liberal victories was the creation of municipal councils in every town of more than 1,000 inhabitants. In theory many prerogatives were to be devolved to these councils, and as a result the annual elections for those officials were hotly contested. Because only those in domestic service were barred from voting, and literacy requirements were to be implemented in several years' time, there were many areas in which Indian voters were more numerous than the non-Indians. There had been much experience of Indian voting during the earlier period, but this had been to elect their own representatives in councils that had jurisdiction only over other Indians. With the disappearance of the division between the "Spanish" and the "Indian," it

---

[29] Scarlett O'Phelan Godoy, "Ciudadanía y etnicidad en las Cortes de Cádiz" in *Revista Elecciones*, vol. 1, no. 1, 2002, p. 177.

[30] Nuria Sala i Vila, *Y Se Armo el Tole Tole: Tributo Indigena y Movimientos Sociales en El Virreinato del Perú, 1784–1814*, Ayacucho: Instituto de Estudios Regionales José María Arguedas, 1996, and several articles in Boletín Americanista of the University of Barcelona.

became possible to have Indians in charge of government. This became a source of much contention, and reactions varied in every particular case.

Elections took place with dizzying frequency, and in Southern Peru they were invariably contested, pitting Europeans, Creoles, mestizos, and Indians against each other in some cases and joining them into surprising coalitions in others. This made for an explosive situation in 1813, when the capitulation of Salta was signed. Arequipa, Cuzco, and Puno, the three areas that had provided most of the men for the expeditions in Upper Peru, witnessed the most electoral turmoil. Men who returned to their homes after the capitulation were deeply discontented, and this new political climate was ripe for further confrontation. Joaquín de la Pezuela, a native of Santander, was sent from Lima to lead the army. He was an academy-trained military specialist in artillery who had arrived in Peru in 1805 to reform the arsenal. In 1813 he was appointed brigadier and was sent to Upper Peru as general in chief of the army. He noted in his diary that during his trip south, he had met several officers and soldiers who, in spite of having capitulated at Salta, were eager to return to service. He recognized their ranks and organized a special battalion with them that went on to obtain several key victories. Santa Cruz was among those who were incorporated into this battalion.

## Fighting for the Crown: Success and Defeat

Pezuela was a keen observer of the army in the Andes. He left vivid descriptions of how Indians made up the majority of the troops and how the language most widely spoken in the camps was not Spanish, which was used only by some officers and some of the troops from Arequipa and Lima. He was also one of the first to describe the way in which women were involved in army life as they traveled with their men during the campaigns, providing them with sustenance throughout. In his diary, Pezuela noted how surprised he was by the fact that most of the men did not eat from a general provision, but that each had a woman who cooked and provided him with food and sexual favors. He explained that it was impossible to eradicate them from the camps, because men fled if the women were not allowed to follow. He found the soldiers in tatters with no clothes, shoes, or money. Pezuela brought together all the troops in the headquarters he established in Oruro. There he reorganized the army using all his technical knowledge, ensuring that his men had training in military tactics and, because he was an artillery expert, that they could make the best use of firepower.

Because the enemy controlled Potosí, Pezuela moved his men to the valley of Vilcapuquio. A month later Porteños, Indian guerrillas, and Cochabambinos advanced toward the royalists, who defeated them in the battles of Vilcapuquio and Ayohuma in September and November 1813. Superior organization and artillery skills gave the royalists the upper hand, although Pezuela did remark in his account of the battle that the enemy had been formidable, because both the Indians and mounted gauchos shared in their determination to win. He duly noted that the royalists' great success had been achieved because of the enemy's lack of leadership. Santa Cruz participated in both of the battles and earned a distinguished record. After the first battle he was made lieutenant, and in the second he was recommended for honor. Thus he was awarded a public symbol of recognition ordered by Pezuela, a badge embroidered in gold thread to commemorate victory. It had a bleeding blue cap – the same design used during the French Revolution – that represented the Buenos Aires government being pierced by bayonets and a motto reading "Lavó la afrenta (washed the affront) of Salta and Tucumán in the plains of Vilcapuquio, 1st October 1813." Nevertheless, in spite of this great success, the royalists still faced open revolt in many provinces, and in some places, particularly in the low-lying areas close to the Amazon basin, they were unable to regain control and so-called republiquetas were established. From these bases, guerrilla-style campaigns continued until final independence was achieved in 1825.

The victorious army in which Santa Cruz fought failed to bring an end to instability in Cuzco. There the new political context promoted by the 1812 Constitution encouraged much confrontation between the Creoles and peninsulares. Eight months after the military victories in Upper Peru, a full-blown rebellion erupted on 2 August 1814. Conflict had been brewing for much longer, and some believe trouble had in fact begun a year earlier during the Constitutional Council elections.[31] The rivalry between the royal court, dominated by Europeans, and the municipal power, the Cabildo, in the hands of the Americans, intensified when it became clear the former would not allow the latter to implement the

---

[31]   Luis Miguel Glave, "Antecedentes y naturaleza de la revolucion del Cuzco en 1814 y el primer proceso electoral" in La Independencia en el Perú: De los Borbones a Bolívar, edited by Scarlett O'Phelan Godoy, Lima: Pontificia Universidad Católica del Perú, 2001, pp. 77–97.

reforms included in the 1812 charter. It is remembered as the rebellion of Pumacagua, though the elderly cacique only joined once it was a *fait accompli*; most studies highlight the conflict between urban factions in the city of Cuzco. Nevertheless there was an important Indian element to the uprising, particularly in the rural highlands south of Cuzco.[32]

As in most other cases, the highland rebellion combined a reaction against tax increases that were perceived to be unjust and excessive, with a reaction to the continued political instability linked to the lack of legitimacy of local representatives, which included caciques. Pumacagua had been eager to support the crown to defend his rights against Túpac Amaru and had been happy to fight against a Junta that in 1809 talked about the abolition of cacicazgos. By 1814 the cacique of Chincheros was temporarily made *Intendente*, but his appointment to the presidency of the Audiencia was rejected by the peninsulares. His disillusionment was further compounded by the Cortes's attack on hereditary offices.[33] Once underway, the revolt became increasingly radicalized. What had begun as a defense of constitutional rights and the absent king became a movement that sought an independent Peruvian empire with an Inca at its head and Cuzco as its capital, thus demonstrating the strength of regional sentiment found in Cuzco.

Lasting for just over six months, at the brief height of its success, the Pumacagua movement controlled Huamanga, Puno, La Paz, and Arequipa. The revolt included members of the lower middle class who resented the cost of the war in Upper Peru and were frustrated by high taxation, widespread corruption, and the failure to implement the promised constitutional reforms. They were joined by veterans returning from the campaigns in Cuzco and Puno (where the whole garrison defected), and by Indians who resented the assault on their traditional rights, especially the encroachment by Creoles and mestizos on the cacicazgos. This uprising put the whole royalist army of the Andes at risk. Forces from the United Provinces of the River Plate had only just been ousted. From the advance guard near Salta, General Ramírez marched with reinforcements to fight in the increasingly vicious campaign. In September 1814, the barracks in La Paz were accidentally set alight and Santa Cruz's father was killed. Santa Cruz was not able to avenge his death and was

---

[32]  David Cahill and Scarlett O'Phelan, "Forging Their Own History: Indian Insurgency in the Southern Peruvian Sierra, 1815," *Bulletin of Latin American Research*, vol. II, no. 2, 1992, pp. 125–67.

[33]  Cahill and O'Phelan, "Forging Their Own History," p. 139.

sent to Jujuy instead. By early November, Ramírez had retaken La Paz, a month later Puno and Arequipa, and in March 1815, Cuzco.

With the rearguard now under his complete control, it was possible once again for Pezuela to focus his fight against the Porteños. After six months of preparation, victory was forthcoming. First Ramírez defeated the rebels at the battles of Venta outside Oruro, and then Pezuela outmaneuvered the enemy in the outskirts of the perennially rebellious city of Cochabamba. The battle of Viluma sealed the fate of the armies of the United Provinces of the River Plate. As in the two previous encounters, European military tactics and modern artillery defeated indigenous guerrillas and mounted gauchos. Even though this was to be the last Porteño attempt to take this area, the royalists were unable to advance further south and a status quo that lasted for the rest of the war was established: the main cities in the highlands remained under the control of the crown, and the low-lying valleys in the hands of the *republiquetas*. Conflict continued throughout the period but was much less intense, with royalists sometimes taking valleys, advancing to Salta and Tucumán at times, but never being able to consolidate their hold over these regions.

For his success, Santa Cruz was made captain and was presented with a red badge with two hands holding a crown that read: "To the valiant defenders of Ferdinand VII, In Viluma 29 November 1815." At this point the tide started to turn, when Napoleon was defeated in Europe and the king was returned to the throne. His first action was to abolish the constitution and reestablish his reign as an absolute monarch. The end of the war in Europe at last made it possible, after nearly seven years, for new troops and officers to be sent from the Peninsula. All those who, like Viceroy Abascal and General Pezuela, had received the charter and its liberal innovations with reservations now celebrated the return of the old legitimate government. Although there was a strong reaction against Creoles, who had mostly taken the side of the constitutional government, influential ones who had continued to support the crown in difficult moments – such as Pío Tristan – were still appointed to important posts. Tristán had organized troops defending Arequipa from Pumacagua and had been lucky to escape with his life. As a reward he was made President of the Audiencia of Cuzco in 1815.

Santa Cruz continued to fight in Upper Peru in the ever more entrenched guerrilla warfare. He distinguished himself in two battles in the area of Cinti (which lies between Potosí and Tarija) at the beginning of 1816. A year later he was promoted to the rank of lieutenant colonel with command of forty horsemen and twenty-five infantrymen stationed just outside the town of Tarija. In April 1817, he was captured and sent to prison 200 kilometers south of the city of Buenos Aires. After nearly two years of confinement, he managed to escape and flee to Rio de Janeiro. He presented himself to the Spanish representative and traveled back to Peru by way of Havana and Panamá, finally arriving in Lima in January 1820.

When he arrived at the viceregal capital, he found the port of Callao under a blockade by the forces fighting for independence. In 1816, Pezuela had taken over the post of viceroy. Having commanded the royalist troops in the southern Andes for more than six years, his experience in the theater of war, as well as his knowledge of the terrain in this part of the country, was unsurpassed. Pezuela felt so close to the army he had raised and with which he had been victorious that in his official portrait as viceroy he was depicted with the two badges of honor he shared with Santa Cruz, Vilcapuquio and Viluma. The new viceroy found an economy in ruins and did not have a good working relationship with the members of the merchant guild, the *consulado*, who were now providing most of the funds to support the government. After their complete defeat in Upper Peru, the Porteños, now under the military command of José de San Martín, attempted to reach Peru with a different strategy. They supported independence efforts in Chile and, after their success there in 1818, they established a maritime blockade over the Pacific. Pezuela had hoped that the expedition being prepared in the Peninsula would come to his aid, but when news of the uprising of the garrison in Cádiz was received in Lima in May 1820, it became clear that this would not happen. The return to power of the liberals, adamant on bringing back the 1812 Constitution, weakened Pezuela's position even as he was able to delay the proclamation of the Charter until 4 September 1820, just six days before San Martín disembarked in Pisco.

With the arrival of the enemy, the situation in Peru became even more complex. Because of the renewal of the constitutional regime in the Peninsula, San Martín opted for negotiations, but he did send Juan Antonio Álvarez de Arenales, a veteran of the campaigns of Upper Peru, to the Central Andes with 600 men to encourage the creation of raiding parties, *montoneras*. Arenales had been born in the Peninsula, but had chosen the side of independence as early as 1809 in La Paz and had fought in all the major battles of Upper Peru and Chile. The centerpiece of San Martín's policy in Peru was to promote desertion, and this was highly successful. Hundreds of officers stationed on the coast, as well as the Numancia Battalion, from New Granada, changed sides in early December.

Mass desertion really began to bear fruit toward the end of 1820. By that point it had become even more clear not only that the opportunities to develop a military career for those who had been born in America were increasingly limited, but that those fighting for independence actually had a good chance of winning. It was simple to conclude that joining early would increase the chances of sharing in the spoils. General José La Serna, a veteran of the Napoleonic wars, had replaced Pezuela as the head of the army in Upper Peru. He disagreed with the viceroy on how the American-born should be treated. Pezuela considered it dangerous to antagonize Creoles and lose their support, whereas La Serna did not trust them. As soon as he had reached Upper Peru, La Serna disbanded two experienced military regiments from Cuzco, including the one that had defeated Pumacagua, allegedly to allow for the promotion of his Peninsular subalterns. Among the displaced was Agustín Gamarra, Santa Cruz's erstwhile school companion who had followed a similar path of military advancement. Gamarra was not taken prisoner by the patriots, but after 1814 his superiors became suspicious of him because he befriended captured Porteños and gave lenient sentences to those accused of treason. He was kept under close watch, and in 1820, after two years collecting taxes in Puno, he was charged with being in contact with San Martín and with planning the desertion of important battalions in Cuzco and Arequipa. His punishment was to be sent to Lima to join the viceroy's guard. In a private interview, Gamarra confided to Pezuela that he was grateful for the treatment he had received and asked to be allowed back to Puno, where he offered to recruit 700 men. That same night, after having assured the viceroy of his feelings toward the king and his cause, Gamarra left the capital under cover of darkness and joined San Martín.

Santa Cruz's experience was different. In his first surviving published letter, written in Chorrillos, the coastal suburb of Lima, in January 1820, he asked the viceroy to clear his name and honor. He provided all the details of the last commission he held before he was taken prisoner: training the troops under his command. Santa Cruz wanted full recognition for this job, which did not appear in the official documentation held in the capital, as well as his salary, including the portion he had not been able to claim because he was imprisoned. Appealing personally to the man he had fought and triumphed with, he asked Pezuela to provide what La Serna, his commanding officer at the time, had not. Interestingly, he signed the document using his father's full last name, Santa Cruz y Villavicencio, not mentioning his mother's patronymic of Calahumana.[34] Soon after he was reincorporated into the army, he spent most of the year south of the capital, and finally in November his squadron left the capital in the direction of the central sierra to fight Arenales.

Arenales's campaign in the central Andes had been very successful, and as the volumes of published documents show, support for independence was immediate. The cities of Huancayo, Jauja, and Tarma had all declared their separation from the crown in November 1820, and on December 6 the rich silver-producing town of Cerro de Pasco was taken by Arenales. There was a public ceremony the next day to swear allegiance to a new patria, where three royalist flags and five banners, two cannons, several French-style muskets known as fusils, and drums were exhibited as trophies.

Santa Cruz, who was one of the 26 officers captured with 320 royalists, decided to change sides and forever bid farewell to the white flag with a red cross at its center for which he had fought for more than a decade. With him was a man from Tarapacá who would be one of his closest collaborators and eventually his enemy, Lieutenant Antonio Gutiérrez de la Fuente. Although Santa Cruz never made his reasons for this change explicit, it is possible to speculate that having been made prisoner for a second time, he had no real option if he wanted to continue his military career. The move brought him immediate fruits. By January 1821, San Martín had commissioned Santa Cruz to fight under Arenales in the central Andes with the same rank he had held in the Spanish army.

The formative experiences that made Santa Cruz who he was at the time of independence were all informed by acute political disruption and recurrent violent conflict. His childhood was marked by the aftermath of the Túpac Amaru rebellion, and his youth was shaped by his experiences in the army of the Andes. Although he had not trained in a formal military academy, his apprenticeship was at the hands of men who had trained more formally in the Peninsula. Santa Cruz had not been part of a militia that rarely met and only wore uniforms for parades. Instead, he had learned about war during intense conflicts and saw battle frequently

---

[34]  The letter appears in Andrés de Santa Cruz Schuhkrafft, *Archivo Histórico del Mariscal Andrés de Santa-Cruz*, La Paz: Universidad Mayor de San Andrés, 1976, vol. I, 1820–1828, pp. 27–8.

during the years he fought in Upper Peru. He had even been a prisoner of war and had experienced defeat as well as victory. This background would continue to be relevant throughout his career, as he remained a man of uniform, a member of the army corporation who sought to modernize the newly created countries he ruled by making the armed forces more efficient. The question whether this made him a *caudillo* or not was not directly relevant to him, as he considered himself to be part of an institution that had its origins deep in the army of Upper Peru with which he trained between 1809 and 1819.

# CHAPTER 2

# Great Marshall of Zepita

## HERO OF INDEPENDENCE

Santa Cruz abandoned the royalists and became an important member of the forces that fought for independence. These were heterogeneous, comprising men from places as diverse as the provinces of Buenos Aires, Chile, and northern and central Peru. Among those fighting were many slaves, from both the River Plate and coastal Peru. They had been granted freedom in exchange for joining the army. This chapter explores the new experiences of warfare Santa Cruz gained. These were quite different from what he had seen in the Andes and became even more diverse when he came into contact with the men from northern South America. In the campaign to liberate Quito, he met many who became long-lasting friends and allies. His previous experience of war under the banner of the king stood him in good stead, and in the context of war, he progressed rapidly through the ranks.

During this second act in his military career, he came in contact with Simón Bolívar, the most prominent South American liberator. An extremely charismatic and successful hero and political thinker, Bolívar exerted a lasting influence on Santa Cruz: he became a "bolivarian," one of the Liberator's closest associates, who, long after his death, endeavored to keep his legacy alive. Under the guidance of Bolívar, Santa Cruz had the opportunity to fight for independence and was responsible for training troops and commanding them successfully in battle. Like his previous experience in Upper Peru, this was formative and influential during his later career. It was also at this juncture that Santa Cruz began to directly participate in Peruvian politics.

This chapter examines the instrumental part played by Santa Cruz in the first attempt by the military to make their candidate president. It also delves into the seldom-remembered campaigns that sought the

Map 2 – 1820s.

independence of southern Peru and the Upper Provinces in 1823, with Peruvian troops. Had these attempts been successful, the history of Peru, and what was soon to become Bolivia, would have been very different. Defeat, however, made it imperative for Peru to have more outside support to achieve independence. In this moment of the birth of nations, Santa Cruz had to come to terms with his identity. He felt Peruvian, but had been born in La Paz. In the first years after independence, this was not a problem. He was close to the most prominent men in Peruvian politics and participated in all the most important events in the creation of the Republic that followed the declaration of independence in Lima in 1821. Santa Cruz not only thought of himself as a citizen of Peru, but believed he had a right to participate directly in its government.

## THE NORTHERN ANDEAN THEATER

The process of independence in Peru involved many actors, and Santa Cruz had direct contact with all of them. When Santa Cruz joined the cause, San Martín had been appointed Protector of the independent northern provinces of Peru. Lima had only been taken when the royalists abandoned the city, creating a new viceregal capital in Cuzco. Bolívar's army was advancing on to Quito, and the port city of Guayaquil had declared its independence. With the royalists holding on to pockets in the Andes, San Martín and Bolívar reached an agreement under which Peruvians would aid Colombians to liberate the north, and in exchange Colombians would travel south to finish off the last vestiges of Spanish power in the continent by defeating Viceroy La Serna. Santa Cruz was put in charge of the Peruvian troops to fight under Sucre's command, where he distinguished himself.

After gaining all his experience of war in the southern Andes under the command of royalist generals trained in the Peninsula, Santa Cruz now moved to a very different territory. When he changed sides in early December 1820, he was stationed in the central Andes under the command of Juan Antonio Álvarez de Arenales. This general, although born and raised in Castile, had long fought for independence. He pion-eered the use of guerrilla forces in the valleys of Upper Peru, gaining a great deal of experience of unconventional warfare. After fighting on the opposite side for a decade, Santa Cruz now had the opportunity to use the tactics he had learned. These combined gaining the support of the local population and training local militias. The first chance Santa Cruz had to put this into practice came in late December when he was in Huánuco, an important town in the Andean foothills that overlook the Amazon basin, when its inhabitants declared independence.

In the three months since the arrival of San Martín's forces from Chile, they had gained control of the central Andes. They had the coast under a complete blockade and had gained the backing of an important number of people, including Creole elites and members of the army such as Santa Cruz. San Martín had not been personally involved in the successful campaign in the Andes. His aim was to take the capital, so he oversaw the campaign from the coast near Lima.

Like many of the Creoles who fought in the conflict, José de San Martín had done most of his training in the Peninsula, joining the army at the tender age of eleven. He was a veteran of the Napoleonic wars and had not arrived in Buenos Aires until 1812, after he became involved with several of the Masonic lodges set up to promote independence. His success in the River Plate against the royalists in 1813 cemented his position, allowing him to pursue a different strategy to attack the Viceroyalty of Peru. Instead of trying to cross the Andes through Upper Peru, like all his predecessors, he concentrated his forces further south and aimed to cross through Chile. He organized his army in the province of Cuyo, where a large number of Chilean émigrés were preparing their campaign. Among those who had already attempted to liberate their province, but had been rebuffed by an expedition sent from Lima, was Bernardo O'Higgins, whom San Martín had met in London. After a punishing march across the Andes, San Martín's campaign was successful, and by 1818, Chile had been liberated. This experience taught San Martín that the best possible strategy was to gain support from the local population and thus make his enemies' position untenable. San Martín pursued this strategy once he reached Peru. Not all of those fighting for independence agreed with this approach, and some accused the general of putting possible victory in jeopardy because of his lack of action and desire for negotiation.

San Martín's policy, however, was vindicated after a string of desertions and victories over the royalists. Then, on 28 December 1820, without any violence, the whole north of Peru declared for independence. On 6 January, the notables of the city of Trujillo, in the recently elected constitutional municipal authority, met and swore to defend the *patria* until the last drop of blood. The royalist Intendant José Bernardo de Tagle, Marquis of Torre Tagle, was in charge of the seamless transition from the colonial to the independent administrations. He ensured that all the army and militia members also changed sides. Torre Tagle had been employed by the crown for most of his life, having had many important posts in the military. The scion of a wealthy Creole family, he had joined the militia at an early age, and in 1803 he had been made General Commissioner for War and Navy. He had been a deputy to the Cortes in Cádiz, and on his return in 1813 he retained his previous post and was made Minister of the Royal Court of Artillery and Sergeant Mayor in the militia. In 1817, he was appointed Intendant for La Paz, but thanks to his connections he was reassigned to Trujillo. The northern coast of Peru had historic trading ties centered on Peruvian sugar and Chilean wheat, which sustained most of the elites in the region. Torre Tagle epitomized this closeness between Chilean and Peruvian elites, because he was married to the widow of O'Higgins's cousin. As a token of his friendship, he had sent the Chilean liberator the copy of the family tree that the late Viceroy Ambrose O'Higgins, Bernardo's father, had had prepared and that Torre Tagle's wife had inherited from her previous husband.[1] Elites from Lima, Trujillo, and Chile were connected in myriad ways, just as they were with the elites in the port of Guayaquil. Returned to the control of the viceroyalty of Peru in 1803, Guayaquil opted for independence in October 1820. Residents of Trujillo, the largest Intendancy in Peru, came to see that changing sides was in their best interest as well, when they were faced with a growing independence movement and Bolívar's advance toward present-day Ecuador.

The loss of the north dealt a severe blow to the royalists. Divisions among them had surfaced with the arrival of the veterans of the Napoleonic wars and became more acute as the royalist commander José de la Serna refused to continue serving in Upper Peru. Stationed in the capital and awaiting instructions, La Serna had the complete support of most officers in the army. It was rumored that he headed a large and important Masonic lodge and that he represented the radical currents of Spanish liberalism then in control of the Peninsula during the so-called *Trienio Liberal*. He forced the viceroy to accept a military Junta in charge of making all military decisions. Public opinion considered inaction to be the overture to a capitulation to San Martín, because a propaganda war was waged in the press that, under the auspices of the 1812 Constitution, was once again free. On 29 January, with more

[1] See Scarlett O'Phelan, "Sucre en el Perú: Entre Riva Agüero y Torre Tagle" in *La Independencia en el Perú: De los Borbones a Bolívar*, edited by Scarlett O'Phelan Godoy, Lima: Pontificia Universidad Católica del Perú, 2001, p. 399.

than 7,000 men stationed at the barracks of Aznapuquio just outside Lima, a mutiny forced Pezuela to resign his post as viceroy. This was the first time since the conquistadors that a crown-appointed official had been ousted in Peru. Many historians have seen this as a prelude to the political preeminence the army was to have in the independent period. The letter to the viceroy, not signed by La Serna himself, but by four of his subalterns, argued that too many errors of judgment had led the royalist cause to suffer. The gravest one was once again to have trusted Creoles in positions of power. It stated in no uncertain terms that Pezuela was to relinquish his post as viceroy and leave it to La Serna. Pezuela complied, if only to prevent further trouble for the cause, and retired to his weekend villa in Magdalena, a small town in the outskirts of the capital. He had in fact already tried to leave his post, but the king had refused to accept his resignation. Unable because of the blockade to obtain a passport that would allow him to abandon Lima, the erstwhile viceroy and decorated hero of many dangerous campaigns was forced to escape under cover of night in a canoe.

In spite of all the bellicose rhetoric, La Serna's first action as viceroy was to resume talks with San Martín. They were restarted under the auspices of a commissioner especially sent by the liberal government. In May 1821, a truce was signed and the guerrillas in the central Andes were ordered to stop all attacks. It was initially agreed that a Bourbon prince would be crowned in Peru, but the entire process was frustrated because the royalist military commanders wanted the express consent of the king and proposed that La Serna and San Martín travel to the Peninsula to receive it. San Martín, however, had made it his only condition that the agreement be accepted by the royalists in America.[2] La Serna later claimed that he had only entered into negotiations to improve his position, but after months of talks, when hostilities broke out again, the royalists left the capital. Considering their position indefensible, they retreated to the Andes, where they maintained a strong core of support. Once Lima was abandoned, San Martín was invited by the municipal council and entered triumphantly to declare independence on 28 July 1821. The colonial ceremonies of royal proclamations that had been adapted for the enacting of the Cádiz Constitution were used as a blueprint for the celebrations. This is the day Peruvians celebrate

---

[2]   José de San Martín, "Respuestas a las preguntas del general Miller en carta del 9 abril de 1827 (borrador)" in *San Martín su correspondencia (1823–1850)*, Editorial América: Madrid, 1919, p. 131.

as Independence Day, even though at this point the royalists still held more than half the country. This is similar to the United States and Mexico, where the day that is commemorated as that of independence was at the very start of the conflict, when the outcome was not clear.

San Martín was swiftly installed as Protector of Peru and controlled the north and the capital, while the royalists still held all the south and Upper Peru with an iron fist. Lima had been evacuated because it was evident to La Serna that without control of the sea, it could not be defended. The royalists were also aware that, because the majority of their troops were indigenous, they held a clear advantage in the highlands. They had the support of the elites of Cuzco and Arequipa in southern Peru as well as of the cities of La Paz, Oruro, and Potosí in Upper Peru, which all provided funds that made it possible to continue financing their government. The new viceregal capital of Cuzco felt vindicated as it finally had become the capital of an empire.

In terms of recruitment of troops, the highland afforded them much better opportunities, because royalist attempts to recruit slaves had been fruitless. In contrast, San Martín's camp had been extremely successful in adding slaves to the ranks, not only because freedom had been promised to those who served, but because the Protector had decreed that all the children born to slaves would be free. Moreover, recruitment on the coast was difficult, and the royalists could not count on the local militias, as mass desertion in the north and central Andes had made more than evident. The royalist forces concentrated in the central Andes, and the 4,300 men under Arenales, including Santa Cruz, abandoned the area and marched to Lima in late July.

The fortresses in the port city of Callao remained in royalist hands under the command of José de la Mar y Cortázar, a native of Cuenca. In spite of being a Creole from an important clan from Guayaquil, La Mar had spent most of his life in the Peninsula and had fought in the Napoleonic wars. Like La Serna, he had been decorated after the brutal siege of Zaragoza in 1809, and both were members of the Order of Saint Hermenegildo. The king had appointed La Mar inspector of the troops in the Viceroyalty of Peru and Governor of Callao. Arriving in 1817, La Mar was made field marshal within two years and general by 1820. With no real support and isolated in the fortress, La Mar surrendered and joined San Martín in September 1821. Just like Santa Cruz, he was allowed to leave with military honors and was accepted with his same rank in the new army. The text of the capitulation also shows that the few men who preferred to return to the royalists were permitted to do so.[3] La Mar was sent to Guayaquil to promote the cause of independence through the press in Cauca, as in the north now only Quito remained in the hands of the royalists.

The campaign to liberate the northern section of South America had been long and intense. It had begun as early as 1806 when Francisco de Miranda had attempted to disembark off the coast of Venezuela with the support of French troops and the British Navy. This native of Venezuela had already fought for the independence of the United States and in the French Revolution. He worked tirelessly in his attempts to promote the independence of the Spanish colonies and, in spite of failing in his invasion, he was successful in inspiring others. Among those he moved into action were San Martín and O'Higgins, but most importantly another Venezuelan who became the preeminent liberator: Simón Bolívar.

The only son of an extremely wealthy landowning family from Caracas, Bolívar quickly became the most famous man fighting for independence. He was often referred to as the Washington of the south. Both Lafayette and the heirs of Washington called him that.[4] He had had a privileged upbringing, studying French philosophy with a private tutor and traveling extensively through Europe. As a witness to the coronation of Napoleon in Paris in 1804, he was no doubt inspired by Napoleon's imperial designs and grandiose schemes. Bolívar combined a masterly ability for organization and military planning with an acute intelligence and prolific passion for writing political tracts. His unwavering charisma was often described by those who knew him. For example, the first British representative in Peru was so taken by Bolívar that he allowed him to read and correct the official dispatches before sending them to London.[5]

Bolívar participated in all the campaigns for independence in Venezuela and was instrumental in the creation of a republic established in Caracas in 1811. The First Republic in Venezuela, stemming from the local Junta set up a year previously, did not last long, although it was an important first attempt toward political freedom. By 1813 a "war to death" was declared by Bolívar, in which anyone captured who

3   Capitulación del Callao, 21 septiembre 1821, Letter from Thomas Guido to San Martín in Juan Pedro Paz-Soldan, *Cartas Históricas del Perú*, Lima: Imprenta Gil, 1920, p. 35.
4   The letters published by O'Leary include missives from the French general and the son of George Washington, among others.
5   The National Archives, FO61/7 1826.

was considered "Spanish" would be killed, although those Spaniards who voluntarily changed sides would be spared. After a long and arduous campaign that included periods of exile (first in Haiti and later in Jamaica), Bolívar finally managed to start turning the tide in 1818. He chose to fight first for the liberation of New Granada, after his repeated defeats in Venezuela. The battles of Boyacá, in the outskirts of Bogota in 1819, and of Carabobo in central Venezuela in mid-1821 ensured the independence of northern South America. General Antonio José de Sucre figured prominently during this campaign and emerged as the most able of Bolívar's lieutenants. Born in a provincial town in Venezuela, he came from a prominent Creole family with a long military tradition. He had joined Miranda at fifteen and had participated in all the campaigns for the independence of what came to be known as Gran Colombia, the union of the present states of Venezuela, Colombia, Ecuador, and Panamá.

After success in the north, Sucre traveled to Guayaquil to aid in the attempts to liberate the highland area of present-day Ecuador. Local forces had already failed, and it was not possible for Sucre to recapture Cuenca or to even approach Quito throughout 1821. Unable to obtain victory on his own, he advanced on to the highlands to await the troops San Martín had promised Bolívar for this campaign. Santa Cruz headed the expedition of 1,500 men being sent from Peru. He did so because Arenales, an older and more experienced commander, had refused to serve under Sucre, who was much younger. Santa Cruz had had a very successful campaign under Arenales. He was promoted to colonel, and after leading an action against a royalist uprising in the town of Otuzco, he was awarded the Order of the Sun in July 1821, a decoration that San Martín had created based on Spanish models. The Order of the Sun would also include those who excelled in the art of war, and would thus link nobility with military, continuing the traditions of the Bourbon era. San Martín's objective was to maintain some form of social distinction in order to win the support of the Lima nobility, who had been slow to accept the idea of independence. The Protector had also wanted to install a constitutional monarchy in Peru and had sent representatives to Europe in search of a suitable prince. A Patriotic Society was established in Lima by his main secretary to debate the best form of government for the new nation. The debates clearly showed that there was not much appetite for a monarchy and that many feared San Martín wanted to install himself as king. As a result, elections were called for a constituent assembly.

It was in this context that Santa Cruz began to prepare his troops to march north in order to aid Bolívar. The letters Santa Cruz wrote to Arenales, now in charge of the province of Trujillo with the title of president, show how important the forces sent from Peru were in the campaign on Quito. In a letter written from Piura in December 1821, Santa Cruz stated that they could commit 1,300 men for the campaign and asked for 20,000 pesos to finance clothes, ammunition, and the repair of rifles. At this point in his career, at the age of twenty-nine and having spent more than a decade in the army, he was finally in charge of training troops and preparing a campaign. Santa Cruz reached Cuenca at the end of February 1822. He was prepared at that point to give the command of the Peruvian army to La Mar, the higher ranking officer, but La Mar never arrived. Santa Cruz thus remained in charge of the men who came from the provinces of the River Plate, Chile, and northern Peru. He joined Sucre and fought under his command. Sucre's 1,700 men included veterans from the campaigns in Colombia, new recruits from the area, and the Albion battalion that was made up of British, Irish, and French volunteers. A first engagement took place in Riobamba in April, and Santa Cruz reported in his official description of the action that, in spite of the heavy rain, the enemy had been properly beaten and pushed back toward Quito.

A month later, on 24 May 1822, Sucre began the ascent of Pinchincha, the volcano that overlooks the city of Quito. His men and the Albion battalion led the way, but because they were affected by altitude sickness, the Peruvian battalions of Trujillo and Cazadores del Paya, under the direction of Santa Cruz, took over the advance guard. After a rainy night, the battle was fought mostly by the infantry, because the steepness of the mountain slopes rendered the horses useless. In his official report, Sucre mentioned Santa Cruz's important participation at the beginning of the engagement. Several hours later, the nearly 3,000 men under his command succeeded in defeating the royalists, who numbered just over 2,000. A capitulation was signed allowing all those who wanted to return to the Peninsula to do so with full military honors. Many of those who decided to stay joined the Colombian or Peruvian armed forces. Because the capitulation included even the troops who were defending the city of Pasto, where Bolívar was stationed, no more battles were required to free the whole of Northern South America from Spain.

After this success only southern Peru and the Audiencia of Charcas remained under the iron fist of La Serna and his army of veterans from the Napoleonic Wars. During his time in charge of the Protectorate, San Martín had not engaged the royalists directly in battle, leaving most of the action to Arenales, while negotiating first with Pezuela and later with La Serna. The only battle fought in Peru after Arenales's triumph in Cerro de Pasco had ended in disaster in April 1822 in the outskirts of Ica. Domingo Tristán and Agustín Gamarra – both veterans of the campaigns in Upper Peru who had changed sides in late 1820 – showed that they had no capacity to defeat the royalists who still held sway over most of the Andean region. Independence in the rest of the continent could not be secured until the royalists were completely defeated, so Bolívar and San Martín met in Guayaquil to discuss a joint strategy. There are no accounts of what actually happened at this meeting on 26 July 1822, and much speculation has shrouded the conference. But thereafter, San Martín abandoned Peru for good, and Bolívar sent military aid to Peru first under General Paz del Castillo and later under Sucre.

## The First Peruvian Governments

The first year of independence was difficult for Peru. Only part of its territory was free, with war raging in both the north and south, while the debate in Lima was whether the country should become a monarchy or a republic. San Martín was a tired man who did not engage in a single battle during his time in Peru and who mostly remained in the weekend villa that former Viceroy Pezuela had built in the town of Magdalena. Unable to complete the liberation of Peru, he sought help from Bolívar and left the country in the hands of Congress. Peru proved not only difficult to liberate, but also hard to govern. Its first independent governments were weak and ineffective and controlled only the northern part of the country. Under constant threat from the royalists, who managed to regain control of the city twice, ephemeral regimes came and went. Chaos and confusion reigned, and independent Peru had at times more than one president claiming to be in power legitimately.

San Martín had called for elections to Congress before traveling to meet Bolívar. He knew his position was precarious, and his health had suffered greatly. His policy of confiscating property owned by Spaniards had resulted in as much opposition as his attempts to install a constitutional monarchy. During his absence, his main secretary was ousted by the people of Lima, and it was evident that San

Martín had overstayed his welcome. In September 1822, after the newly elected Congress was installed, he bid farewell to Peru forever. He traveled first to Buenos Aires, but after some months it became clear he did not have much political space there, either. He ultimately abandoned America and lived for the rest of his life in Europe, supported in his old age by a pension provided by the Peruvian government.[6] San Martín is remembered mostly for his strategic genius and his lack of personal ambition, because he stepped aside to let Bolívar take command. During his time in Peru, the Protector had been exhausted and no longer wished to continue the fight. He faced many conflicts, as even the area that was independent was overrun by infighting between factions that made governing difficult. San Martín had looked for possible rapprochement with the royalists, because he shared an ideological disposition with the Spanish liberals who controlled the government in the Peninsula between 1820 and 1823. On a more basic level, San Martín was very far away from his sources of power and, given the difficult political situation in the Provinces of the River Plate, he could not count on any kind of support from there. In contrast, Bolívar was triumphant after a successful campaign, and even as he faced some opposition and factionalism, he had the backing of his main lieutenants in Caracas and Bogotá, who continued to provide him with troops and funds.

Santa Cruz had not come into much contact with San Martín, because he had served directly under Arenales and then traveled north to fight with Sucre, with whom he became close. On the other hand, Bolívar, whom Santa Cruz met shortly after the battle of Pichincha in June 1822, exerted a great influence over him. Santa Cruz was completely taken by the charismatic leader, who was legendary among his lieutenants, with whom he loved to discuss his ideas and plans for the newly independent nations. The proposal of a federal state of Colombia, to unify Venezuela, New Granada, and what eventually became Ecuador, was to have lasting effects on Santa Cruz's thinking. Bolívar decorated him with three medals for his important services in battle and gave him the rank of general in the army of Colombia. Santa Cruz then returned to Peru, first to Piura in September and finally to Lima in December. The independent northern part of the country was governed by the Constitutional Congress that had been elected under the auspices of San Martín. The representatives to this assembly had been chosen

---

[6]   He died in Boulonge-sur-Mer France in 1850, after having spent time there, in Brussels and London.

in direct elections with nearly universal male suffrage. Even though it was only possible for these to be carried out in the liberated provinces, representatives for those areas that were still under the control of the royalists were also elected from the residents of these provinces living in the capital.

Congress installed a triumvirate to administer the executive, aiming to achieve a balance of power. It was headed by La Mar, the discreet military officer who had abandoned the royalists in September 1821 and had sought the independence of Quito through the press. It had two other members. Felipe Antonio Alvarado was a merchant from Salta, whose brother was a prominent General who had support among the troops that had come from the River Plate and Chile. Manuel Salazar y Baquijano was a member of the nobility of Lima who, despite the banning of the use of titles, was still referred to as the Count of the Vista Florida. Bolívar considered La Mar to be not only the best soldier, but the best civilian. But he also commented that a government controlled by Congress would be unable to really provide solutions in the complex context of war.[7]

All commentators agreed nevertheless that the real power in the Junta was a cleric from Arequipa named Francisco Xavier de Luna Pizarro, who was not actually a member. He had trained as a lawyer in Cuzco and had traveled to the Peninsula in 1809 as the secretary of the bishop under whom he had studied. There he witnessed the Napoleonic invasion and was in Cádiz during all the constitutional period, returning to Peru only in 1812 once the charter had been enacted. As one of the men with most experience in constitutional matters by 1822, he dominated the political scene as the president of Congress.

The economic situation faced by this first independent government was dire, though in spite of this, much effort was still made to dispatch an expedition to the southern ports. These were known as the *Intermedios* or middle ports because they lay between Callao and Valparaiso. They were considered to be the royalists' weakest flank. The idea was to disembark in Tacna and move inland to Upper Peru and join the rebel forces there. The expedition, led by Rudencino Alvarado, the brother of one of the members of the triumvirate, disembarked near Moquegua in January 1823. The strategy involved opening two fronts, one advancing from the south and the other, under the command of Santa Cruz, charging

---

[7]  Quoted by Jorge Basadre, *Historia de la Republica del Perú*, Lima; editorial Huascaran, 1961, vol. I, p. 18.

to the central sierra from the capital while the royalists were distracted in the south. By January, Santa Cruz had reached Huancayo, but he was unable to continue because of lack of resources. The Colombian General Paz del Castillo, who was supposed to provide support to this expedition, abandoned Callao with all his troops, claiming that his men were not being paid. The situation was indeed difficult, in part because of the way in which Guayaquil had been incorporated into Colombia. La Mar, who had been born in that port and who had many connections in Cuenca, was considered the head of a party that was opposed to the annexation of that region to Colombia and who thought it should be part of Peru or become an independent country. Some believe that this friction caused Paz del Castillo not to support the expedition to the central Andes.

Santa Cruz, who was part of the expedition and who had advanced to Huancayo, considered the triumvirate, and La Mar in particular, responsible for its failure. In a document presented to Congress in January 1823,[8] he and Arenales argued in favor of advancing to the sierra to at least to improve their economic situation by taking control of the mineral-producing town of Cerro de Pasco. This was an area both men knew well, and they felt confident that they could take it back. After their experience in the central sierra, they knew they could count on the local population that had given them so much support; in some valleys in the Central Andes, *montoneras* continued to exert complete control until the end of the war. Congress, however, did not take heed, and the troops remained outside the capital when the news of the total destruction of the expedition to the south was received in February.

The only man who remained fighting in the south was the British soldier William Miller. This veteran of the Napoleonic wars and the Anglo-American war of 1812 had arrived in South America by way of Buenos Aires and joined San Martín in Chile in 1817. He had trained the marines who had supported the blockade of 1819 by teaching them how to specialize in dangerous missions. Miller had been in charge of organizing the first Peruvian battalion, taking it to the campaign of the middle ports. As the only commander not to flee, he continued to fight the royalists on the desert coast of Arequipa and Ica for months. He later went on to become one of Santa Cruz's closest allies. In contrast

---

[8]  *Archivo Histórico del Mariscal Andrés de Santa Cruz*, Andrés de Santa Cruz Schuhkrafft, La Paz: Universidad Mayor de San Andrés, 1976, vol. I, pp. 56–61.

to the loyalty he displayed by Miller, another of the commanders of the expedition, Agustín Gamarra, returned to the capital, where he soon joined the rest of the disenchanted military who began to plot openly against Congress. On 26 February 1823, Santa Cruz was the first signatory of a statement that was strongly reminiscent of the one the men backing La Serna had been presented to oust Pezuela. It made clear that if Congress did not designate José de la Riva Agüero as president, all these men would stop backing the government.

Limeño nobleman José de la Riva Agüero y Sánchez Boquete was born in Lima in 1783. He was the son of a knight of the royal order of Charles III, director general of the royal tobacco monopoly of Mexico City, and superintendent of the mint in Lima.[9] His father was from Murcia in Spain and his mother the daughter of a rich Limeña heiress, who had inherited the title of Marchioness of Montealegre through her mother. Riva Agüero had joined the militia while still a child, and at the age of thirteen he was an *alférez* in the company of the nobility of Lima, where the viceroy himself was the Colonel. In 1805 he was made a knight in the Order of Charles III, but in 1809 he abandoned a military career and took employment in the mint. He remained in the militia and in 1811 was named lieutenant in the 2nd Company of the distinguished volunteers of the *Concordia Española* under the command of his uncle the Marquis of Montealegre. He was implicated in most of the conspiracies against the crown, and in 1818 and 1820, he wrote pamphlets promoting independence. The most notorious was the one known as the "28 Causes," which circulated widely in Lima. As a result he spent most of the second half of 1819 in prison. Riva Agüero sought to contact San Martín and presented him with a plan for how to operate in Peru. News of the plan was intercepted; although Riva Agüero was tried, he once again avoided a harsh sentence because of his connections. Riva Agüero was credited with helping men escape into the guerrilla-controlled central Andes. Once the capital was liberated, he supported San Martín and was appointed president of the department of Lima, as the colonial post of intendant was now called. He opposed the policies of confiscation of Spanish property put forward during the protectorate and was instrumental in deposing the minister who had been left in charge when the Protector went to Guayaquil.

---

[9] A whole tome of the *CDIP* is dedicated to Riva Agüero, "Archivo Riva Agüero", vol. XVI.

Given the rank of Great Marshall, Riva Agüero was made president after the army mutinied in February 1823. He at first refused the rank, reminding Congress he had only ever been a colonel of militias, but the military were adamant that as president he should have the highest position in the army.[10] Much more successful than the Junta that preceded him, he was able to organize a government using the money that had just arrived as loans from London. He rebuilt the navy, was respected by the main army officers, and was able to pay them once again. Peruvian militias were created in the capital following the Spanish model of citizen participation, and a squadron of hussars was also trained and kitted out. To further increase his fighting capacity, Riva Agüero renegotiated with Bolívar the agreement reached with San Martín to send Colombian troops and received a contingent of 4,000 men under the command of Sucre. He then contacted the viceroy and offered him a truce so that peace negotiations could commence, threatening otherwise to declare a "war to the death."

After the viceroy halted negotiations, Riva Agüero did exactly as the triumvirate had done before him and attempted to attack the royalists by sea, putting together the second campaign of *Intermedios* with 5,000 men. Santa Cruz, who was appointed general in chief of the Peruvian army in March 1823, was in charge of the expedition. A month later he wrote to his close friend Antonio Gutiérrez de la Fuente that it was crucial to provide all the support possible to the president, in spite of the differences they might have, because the most important task was to maintain harmony and order. It was imperative to back the authorities, even if they did not always act with the greatest ability. Riva Agüero considered that, given the situation in which they were preparing to fight, some sacrifices were needed to sustain what he called public opinion.[11] In his speech to Congress, just before his departure in May, he promised to spill his own blood to defeat the enemy. As he set sail, he begged Bolívar to come to Peru and "save it."

## THE CAMPAIGN OF ZEPITA

Santa Cruz sailed south for more than a month to the port of Arica, planning to advance directly on to La Paz. He was in charge of over

---

[10]  On this see Basadre, *Historia de la Republica*, p. 32.
[11]  Letter to Gutiérrez de la Fuente, 2 April 1823 in *Archivo* Andrés de Santa Cruz Schuhkrafft, *Archivo Histórico del Mariscal Andrés de Santa-Cruz*, La Paz: Universidad Mayor de San Andrés, 1976, vol. I, pp. 67, 68.

5,000 men and expected the Colombian forces who remained in Lima
under General Sucre to march to the central Andes. He wrote to Paz
del Castillo that he knew Sucre was not very eager to come, but that he
trusted that in the hour of need Sucre would give him the cooperation
he required.[12] Tacna and Moquegua were taken immediately without
much difficulty. But as soon as they were under his command, Santa
Cruz noted that they were unable to support the campaign, because the
royalists had destroyed and taken everything of use. In his next letters he
complained bitterly to the ministers in Lima and to the president that
he was not being given enough resources to continue the fight and that
he feared for its success. Nevertheless he moved on toward Arequipa,
where there were a very small number of royalist soldiers.

Santa Cruz was well aware that this campaign was of utmost importance, because it was the only opportunity available for independence
to be obtained by Peruvians themselves. He wrote to Riva Agüero
that "this was the only way to save the country and to make ourselves
Peruvian."[13] This echoed the language he had used in the proclamation
that had called for the appointment of Riva Agüero as president only
six months earlier. Sending such a large contingent of troops left Lima
vulnerable, and in June 1823 the capital was retaken while the government and the newly arrived Colombian forces sought refuge in Callao.
As soon as the royalist forces took the capital, in June 1823, Riva Agüero
wrote a letter stating his hope that this would benefit Santa Cruz. He
saw the entrance to Lima with more than 7,000 veterans as providing
a unique opportunity for the campaign in the south to progress. Aware
of the difficulties that he faced and the lack of support he had from the
rest of the allies, the president wrote to Santa Cruz that he should take
advantage of the situation, as he thought that Peru had no friends and
that this was their only chance for an independence they really could
take credit for and control.[14]

In spite of this nationalistic rhetoric, Riva Agüero relinquished all
military authority and asked Congress to give Sucre total control of the
armed forces. Forced to accept this command, Sucre wrote to Bolívar
that the army was divided along national lines. Sucre believed that

[12] Letter to Paz del Castillo, 24 May 1823 in *Archivo Histórico del Mariscal Santa
Cruz*, pp. 74, 75.
[13] Letter to Riva Agüero, 22 June 1823 in *Archivo Histórico del Mariscal Santa Cruz*,
p. 82.
[14] Letter from Riva Agüero to Santa Cruz, 19 June 1823, in Mariano Felipe Paz
Soldán, *Historia del Perú Independiente, Segundo periodo 1822–1827*, Le Havre:
Lemane, 1870, p. 145.

the various armed forces stationed in the city were not working for a common goal, and there were divergent opinions regarding the conduct of the war. Sucre was of the opinion that only Bolívar would be able to bring together all of these conflicting views, unify the army, and take it to victory. The campaign in which Santa Cruz was engaged in the south suffered from this division, and Sucre argued that it only had a chance of success if Santa Cruz followed his instructions scrupulously. He noted that there was limited support from Chileans as well as from Porteños. Many believed that Santa Cruz's real aim was to free Upper and Southern Peru to create an independent country. The Porteños were against the establishment of such a state because they claimed these provinces as their own and had fought for them bitterly for more than a decade. Chileans, on the other hand, argued that this new state would become their economic rival, because the expedition was partly financed by some commercial houses that were to be granted exclusive trade contracts.[15] This is an interesting angle that has not received much attention, because Santa Cruz's expedition has normally been portrayed as a failure, with no consideration being given to the larger geopolitical conflicts among those who were fighting for independence.

Not even Bolívar harbored illusions that the campaign undertaken by Santa Cruz would be successful. He replied to Sucre just days after receiving his letter, saying that this would be the third act of a tragedy. This was only a week after having approved of the plan publicly and having written to Riva Agüero giving him his backing. Bolívar believed that no matter how good the instructions to Santa Cruz were, the presence of Gamarra as chief of staff, just as in the two previous occasions when those fighting for independence were defeated, was a liability. He also stated in his letter that even if Santa Cruz triumphed – which he thought very unlikely – the royalists would still not be finished, but simply weakened. Bolívar considered that it would only be worthwhile for him to embark on a similar campaign once the terrain had been thoroughly reconnoitered.[16] In spite of his private pessimism, Bolívar was adamant that Sucre should travel south to provide the support that

[15] Letter from Sucre to Bolívar, Lima 10 May 1823, *Cartas de Sucre al Libertador (1820–1826)* edited by Daniel Florence O'Leary, Madrid: Editorial América, 1919, p. 45.

[16] Letter of Bolívar to Sucre, 18 May 1823 in, Paz Soldán, *Historia del Perú*, pp. 79, 80.

had been promised to the expedition. It was agreed that Sucre's forces would leave the capital forty days after the date originally planned, but because of the occupation of the capital and the disarray in which this had left public administration, Sucre was delayed until late July 1823.

The occupation of Lima lasted for only a month, but once again the royalists proved that they could take the city at will. Reports state that up to 10,000 fled, although many stayed and left the city only after the royalists abandoned it. The situation in Callao was one of total confusion. Riva Agüero's lack of military experience was evident when he gave up all his military power to Sucre. Congress agreed to relocate the center of government to the city of Trujillo, where they would not be under such a threat. Congress also decreed that Riva Agüero would only be president in the areas not affected by war and that Bolívar would be given supreme authority as soon as he arrived in Peruvian territory. Sucre signed an agreement with Riva Agüero that he would take care of the army in the north and advance from the central Andes to fight the royalists while Santa Cruz would do so from the south.[17] Instead of doing this, and still considering himself in charge of the executive power, Riva Agüero traveled to Trujillo. Some members of Congress went with him, whereas others stayed in Lima. Sucre, now in charge of the capital, designated the Marquis of Torre Tagle to temporarily organize government in Lima. Meanwhile, in Trujillo, Riva Agüero quarreled with some Congress members and expelled them to Lima. At this point, two rival independent governments existed in Peru. Torre Tagle headed the one in the capital with support of part of the Congress, and Riva Agüero the one in Trujillo with the rest of the representatives.

Along with two governments claiming to be in charge of the independent section of Peru, there was a large contingent of armed men in the far southern provinces. These men took advantage of the fact that the royalists had totally abandoned their rearguard to concentrate all their manpower in an effort to take over the capital. This allowed Santa Cruz to travel through to Moquegua and on to La Paz with little trouble. He divided his troops and the rest of the men went with Gamarra through Arica on to Oruro. Both cities were quickly abandoned by the small royalist garrisons and did not oppose the incoming forces when they were at the peak of their strength. Instead they waited until the troops who had been engaged farther north returned to the southern

[17] All the details of this treaty can be found in Paz Soldán, *Historia del Perú*, pp. 101, 102.

Andes. Sucre did not want to travel south and feared that he would be
unable to provide any real help to Santa Cruz; he was convinced that
his former comrade in arms and fellow hero of the battle of Pichincha
resented his presence and did not really want his help, wanting glory
only for himself.

From Arequipa, Sucre wrote to Bolívar that Santa Cruz was full of
himself and talked only of working as a team, making no reference
to fighting under Sucre's command. To this, Sucre wrote to Bolívar,
he could never agree, preferring if pressed to abandon the campaign
instead. He was worried, however, about the Colombian troops he had
with him. Sucre thought that he ought to leave them with Santa Cruz,
but did not want to do so because he felt very closely bound to them. He
also commented on the difficulties of fighting a war in this terrain, which
was mostly desert on the coast, making it impossible for beasts and men
to survive. The highlands, he noted, were littered with punishing passes
at extreme altitude. Sucre was in awe of the ability of the royalists to
recruit and maintain an army under these conditions as well as of the
amount of money they were able to obtain from Arequipa, Cuzco, La
Paz, Oruro, and Potosí. All except the last contributed 30,000 pesos,
and the mining city provided 50,000. This, Sucre remarked, was outside
the regular contributions and he believed that if the independentists
managed to take control over some of these provinces, the royalists
would not be able to survive.[18]

At the end of August, Santa Cruz finally had the opportunity
he had been waiting for and committed his forces to battle. At the
edge of Lake Titicaca, very near the spot where, twelve years earlier,
he had fought in his first armed encounter, he triumphed at the battle
of Zepita. In the official report, he described how his 1,300 men were
able to defeat the same number of royalists. The battle lasted for most
of the 25th of August, and the taking of royalist stragglers ended only
at nightfall. Santa Cruz described how his subalterns fought valiantly,
and it is interesting to note that among those whom he mentioned were
many who later became close collaborators, including Federico Brand-
sen, Blas Cerdeña, and Manuel de Mendiburu. Now an older man who
had presided over a victory, Santa Cruz showed how much his experience under Goyeneche and Pezuela had influenced him. Not only did
he seek combat in an area he knew well, having grown up close to the

---

[18] Letter from Sucre to Bolívar, Arequipa, 7 September 1823, *Cartas de Sucre al
Libertador*, pp. 112–116.

lake and having fought in Guaqui in 1811, but he also designed medals for those who had participated in the battle that were very similar to the ones he himself had been given after the victories of Vilcapuquio and Ayohuma in 1813 and 1815. The inscription for the simple medals he designed, in the shape of a pentagon with two laurel leaves, read: "In the cradle of tyrants I carved their sepulcher."[19]

Nevertheless, this was not to be the beginning of a winning streak for Santa Cruz. Instead he found himself in an increasingly precarious situation in Upper Peru. By September he was in Oruro, but the royalist troops were still holding on to Potosí and advancing from southern Peru on to the lake, ready to surround him. Santa Cruz was unable to push to the territories controlled by the United Provinces of the Río de la Plata, or even join the "republiquetas" who remained on the eastern Andean piedmont. This meant that with no support forthcoming from Sucre, who was stationed in Arequipa, his situation became ever more difficult. The royalists waited and did not engage him in battle when he was at his strongest, but when he was at his weakest. Santa Cruz wrote to Sucre detailing that he had not expected the viceroy to be so hot on his heels and that even with the support of Cochabamba and the guerrilla forces in the lower valleys, they had no real hope of triumph unless they received immediate support, either from the troops who were being promised from Chile or from Sucre himself. By October the whole adventure in Upper Peru was over: Santa Cruz and Gamarra had been forced to flee back down to Moquegua.

Santa Cruz had indeed been desperately unlucky. As soon as he arrived back in Arica with the remnants of his troops, the men who had so eagerly been expected from Chile finally arrived. Seeing how dire the situation was, some were immediately embarked for Lima, but the majority returned to Valparaiso. Sucre, with whom Santa Cruz met briefly in Moquegua, was also traveling north as now the royalists had over 7000 men in the valleys between Arequipa and the coast. Indeed it had not only been a question of bad timing as with the Chilean support, but also of bad faith. As his letters to Bolívar show, Sucre had never really been keen on providing support to someone else's campaign. So he dithered and delayed his departure first from Lima and later from Arequipa. The division among Peruvians also took a high toll, because having two independent governments did not work to Santa Cruz's

---

[19] The official reports of the battle appear in *Archivo Histórico del Mariscal Santa Cruz*, pp. 94–100.

advantage. As Riva Agüero had relocated to Trujillo, instead of setting off with an expedition on to the Central Andes, the Peruvians were unable to distract the royalists' rearguard. In October, Santa Cruz wrote to Bolívar from Arica, delighted with the news of his arrival in Peru and of the decree issued by the Congress in Lima giving him absolute powers as dictator. Santa Cruz made it clear that if Bolívar had not been given such prerogatives, his coming to Peru would have been in vain.[20] A week later, a War Council met in Arica. Its members were Sucre, Porteño General Alvarado – the man defeated in the first campaign of the *Intermedios* – Chilean General Pinto, and Santa Cruz. They decided that because the Chilean troops on whom they had pinned most of their hopes had left, and because the royalists had regrouped and gained much strength, the only course of action still open to them was to return north to reorganize the army under the leadership of Bolívar. With this, hopes of a "Peruvian" victory were dashed, and all energy was dedicated to working as a real alliance and extricating the royalists from Peru.

## Bolívar in Peru

When Bolívar arrived in Lima at the end of 1823, the political situation was extremely complex. There were two independent governments, with Riva Agüero heading the one in Trujillo. He had traveled north in late June with some members of Congress, but as soon as he had some army backing, Riva Agüero dissolved the legislature and appointed a ten-man Senate instead. In August, when news of these events arrived in Lima, Torre Tagle was sworn in as president; his first action was to call for Congress to meet again. So the representatives who had remained in the capital – some of whom had stayed in Lima during the royalist occupation – together with the members of parliament who had been forcefully returned to the capital from Trujillo, reconvened. The established legislative power appointed Torre Tagle as president. Meanwhile, in the north, Riva Agüero dedicated all his energy to putting together an army. Only a month after these events, on the first of September, Bolívar arrived in Lima and was given a hero's welcome, because he was considered to be the only man capable of saving Peru.

In spite of being invited by Congress to take over the presidency, Bolívar refused, saying that his only interest was to defeat the enemies

---

[20] Letter from Santa Cruz to Bolívar, Arica 10 October 1823, in *Archivo Histórico del Mariscal Santa Cruz*, p. 113.

of independence and that as such he would be no more than a servant to the law. He declared that he was delighted with the fact that Congress had reconvened and elected a new president, and he emphasized that he would devote all his energy to the military campaign. Congress invited him again, and ten days after his arrival he was invested dictator. Torre Tagle remained nominally as president, but in reality he no longer had any control of affairs outside the department of Lima. In the banquet given in his honor, the newly appointed dictator raised his glass and toasted first the genius of San Martín, then the generosity of O'Higgins for sending troops to Peru, and finally Congress and the president whom they had appointed. In his second toast, he wished for the union of the flags of La Plata, Colombia, and Castile. He hoped to achieve victory soon and settle a peace agreement with Spain. Bolívar closed his speech by saying that he hoped never to see a throne established in America, noting how both Napoleon and Iturbide had failed in establishing empires. This was an important statement of faith, because Bolívar wanted to make sure everyone understood that although he admired and respected the work of San Martín, he had no appetite or desire to establish an empire or a monarchy.[21]

Desperate to stay in power, Riva Agüero hoped that he could persuade Bolívar to acknowledge him as the legitimate president. Riva Agüero believed he had the right to remain in his position because he had been the first to call on Bolívar's support. The president in Trujillo considered Santa Cruz and his army of 5,000 faithful men stationed in Upper Peru as the guarantee of his hold on power. Trying to buy valuable time, he had written to Santa Cruz in August, instructing him to enter into negotiations with the viceroy, hoping to establish a ceasefire. As soon as Bolívar arrived, Riva Agüero wrote to him, reminding him that the army in the south recognized his government in Trujillo as the legitimate authority. Riva Agüero's calculations proved fruitless, once the independent Peruvian forces in the Altiplano had been defeated. La Serna wrote on 23 October pointing out that Riva Agüero had no real ability to negotiate because his forces had been thoroughly destroyed, but that La Serna would be eager to accept his return to the royalist fold because he, too, recognized that a peace agreement should be reached.[22]

[21] All the details of his speech are in Paz Soldán, *Historia del Perú*, pp. 165, 166.
[22] Paz Soldan, *Historia del Perú*, p. 181.

Riva Agüero sent several emissaries to try to communicate his plans to Santa Cruz and to convince him to travel north to sustain Riva Agüero's presidency. One of the men he sent south in a secret mission south was Luís José de Orbegoso. In the context of having the country divided between north and south, Orbegoso played an important role that he was to repeat little more than a decade later. In spite of being summoned to the north by Riva Agüero, Santa Cruz chose to remain faithful to Bolívar and swore allegiance to President Torre Tagle with all the troops under his command in Arica at the end of October. He agreed with Sucre to remain on the southern coast to distract the royalist forces for as long as possible. Santa Cruz was prepared to undertake another incursion into the Altiplano if the situation changed and the Chilean troops arrived, because this was still considered to be a good strategy if it was backed by the right amount of force. To this effect, Santa Cruz resumed communications with the leader of the independent guerrillas in Upper Peru and dedicated all his efforts to reorganizing the troops under his command in Arica. While traveling from Quilca further south, commanders of two of the ships transporting 1,500 of his men, seeing that they had no chance, changed their course and deserted his command, leaving him only with 300 armed men.[23] Circumstances varied markedly, as the royalists had more than 8,000 men stationed in Arequipa ready to attack. This was compounded by the fact that the government in Buenos Aires negotiated an armistice with the royalists. A ceasefire was agreed to, and each side was to respect their borders as they stood. This meant that the whole of Upper Peru and Southern Peru were to remain under the control of the crown, and that it was useless to try to take over the far south with the hope of uniting with the freed provinces, because these would no longer provide support to their cause.

Under these circumstances, the 2,000 Chileans troops who had arrived in Arica swiftly set sail once again to regroup with the rest of their forces who were stationed further north. With few options available, Santa Cruz took to sea in late November, holding a precarious position. A month later, when his ship had reached the northern port of Huanchaco, he wrote to the minister of war that he had been unable to stop the desertion of the two boats transporting his men, but that he had been in no way involved in any conspiracy and that he had never

[23] Letter to Rudencino Alvarado, 21 November 1823, in *Archivo Histórico del Mariscal Santa Cruz*, p. 126.

taken any sides in the conflicts that engulfed the young republic. To his friend Colombian General Tomas Heres, Santa Cruz explained that given his predicament, he had chosen not to stop in Lima, where his enemies would have taken every opportunity to destroy him. Instead he decided to travel north in the hope of being able to mediate with Riva Agüero.

Once Santa Cruz arrived, he found that the situation had changed completely because Riva Agüero, who attempted to negotiate with La Serna and with Bolívar at the same time, had been deposed. In September, the commissioners sent from Lima had given a choice to the army in the north to return to the fold of the Torre Tagle government and had offered Riva Agüero the chance to return to Lima as a private citizen or to travel to Colombia. Both his men and Riva Agüero refused. He proposed instead to resign the presidency, even promising not to be candidate again if the Congress and government in Lima were also barred from running. Bolívar rejected this possibility outright: even though it might have offered a solution because the legislature was not the most representative of bodies, it was the body that had invested him as dictator. If it disappeared, he would no longer have legitimate authority. Antonio Gutiérrez de la Fuente, the man with whom Santa Cruz had abandoned the royalists after the defeat of Cerro de Pasco three years earlier, was now commissioned to present a counteroffer. Instead he agreed with Bolívar to accept Torre Tagle, but to have Riva Agüero be the head of the army or to travel to Europe to a diplomatic mission. On discovering that discussions with the royalists were still ongoing, on 25 November La Fuente took Riva Agüero prisoner and, rejecting Torre Tagle's calls to have him executed, sent him into exile instead.[24]

On his return to Northern Peru, Santa Cruz was ready to explain his actions and decisions to Bolívar himself. But when he disembarked, the Dictator had already abandoned the port of Huanchaco. Santa Cruz complained to Heres that he was being treated as an enemy and requested a passport to leave the country.[25] Sucre argued in his favor, writing to Bolívar that Santa Cruz had followed his instructions in the south to the letter. As had been agreed, he had traveled first to Pisco, but

---

[24]  All these events were described to Paz Soldán by La Fuente, who provided him with all his letters from this period; see *Historia del Perú*, pp. 200–4.

[25]  Letter to Tomas Heres, Huanchaco 21 December 1823, in *Archivo Histórico del Mariscal Santa Cruz*, p. 128.

because Sucre had not been there, Santa Cruz had left his 300 men and continued north. The Colombian general remarked that Santa Cruz was no fool and who knew that fighting for Riva Agüero was a lost cause.[26] Sucre incorporated the men into his own regiments and continued the fight against the guerrilla leader Ninavilca, who had declared in favor of the Trujillo government. On the last day of 1823, Santa Cruz wrote to La Fuente saying that he was leaving the country whose happiness was more important than his own, and that all his sacrifices had been in vain. He hoped that destiny would bring freedom and that La Fuente would be a witness of all the glories deserved by their homeland. A fortnight later he was given a passport to travel to Piura so that he could regain his very badly affected health.

By the end of 1823, it was clear that the only way to succeed against the royalists was to organize the army so that it could campaign in the highlands. To this end, Bolívar left the capital and took to the northern Andes where the army that Riva Agüero had put together was headquartered. In December, the Dictator wrote to Torre Tagle (whom he still referred to as president) that he was training 2,500 Peruvians and 4,000 Colombians while he awaited a further 3,000 from Panamá and Chile. He remarked in his letter that he had to teach them how to jump between the rocks like the highland creatures and to resist altitude sickness. Bolívar trained his troops, and Santa Cruz recovered his health in Piura. Meanwhile, in Lima, the first Peruvian Constitution was enacted at the end of November 1823. The result of many months of debate in difficult circumstances, it was an important development in Peru – even though it was never actually implemented because it was suspended until the end of the military campaign.

To be able to better prepare for the campaign and in light of the agreements already signed with the government of Buenos Aires, Bolívar asked Torre Tagle to make contact with La Serna and to ask for a six-month ceasefire. The aim was to construct a treaty that accepted the independence of the northern part of Peru. Torre Tagle had already commenced negotiations with royalist officer José de Canterac, but on a different basis, agreeing to Bolívar's departure. The royalist general, who was stationed at Huancayo, was close to the capital, and the situation of the independent government there was extremely precarious because nearly all the troops had been evacuated to the north. The only men who

---

[26] Letter from Sucre to Bolívar, Yungay 19 December 1823, *Cartas de Sucre al Libertador*, pp. 138, 139.

remained guarding the capital were the last remnants of the contingent that had arrived with San Martín in 1820. They were sent to Callao to guard the castles. Completely demoralized, unpaid for the past four months, the men mutinied in February 1824. What had begun as a strategy to obtain their back pay and be sent back home, rather than further north, ended in the loss of the whole garrison to the royalists. Unable to trust the independent government because there were rumors that they would be embarked only to be sent to the north, the mutineers followed the advice of some of the royalist prisoners they were looking after and turned the fortress over to them. Bolívar sent a communication to Lima asking Congress to depose Torre Tagle, who in turn decided to join the royalists, who by March had regained control of the capital.

Once he heard the news, Santa Cruz immediately wrote to Bolívar offering his help and assuring him that his health had improved sufficiently to allow him to take any position that was available.[27] In spite of his difficult circumstances and of his own very severe bout of tuberculosis, the Dictator never had any doubts that he was more than capable of winning. Colombian General Mosquera visited Bolívar in the small town of Pativilca. After seeing Bolívar so diminished, close to death and in such disadvantageous circumstances, Mosquera asked Bolívar what he was going to do. Bolívar responded, "To triumph." The Venezuelan liberator, in spite of his health and facing logistical difficulties, planned to continue raising a strong cavalry in Trujillo and to work on acclimatizing his men to the altitude. He was convinced that if attacked on the coast, his horsemen would win, and if he was given enough time to grow strong, he could develop the ability to attack in the highlands. The country was divided exactly through the center, with the Andean city of Huancayo serving as headquarters of the northern royalist garrison, with Lima also under royalist control.

It was at this point that things changed again because of circumstances beyond the control of anyone in America. The Spanish constitutional government in the Peninsula was brought down by the Holy Alliance, and Ferdinand VII returned to power. This in turn resulted in the division of the royalists in America. In March 1824, Pedro Antonio de Olañeta, a Spaniard who had lived most of his life in Upper Peru, and many considered a Creole, was the highest-ranking officer in the

---

[27] Letter from Santa Cruz to Bolívar, Piura, 8 March 1824, in *Archivo Histórico del Mariscal Santa Cruz*, p. 134.

southernmost tip of the royalist-controlled area.[28] He had fought in the campaigns in favor of the king since 1810, and after news of the abolition of the constitution arrived from Buenos Aires, he abandoned Oruro and marched further south to Tupiza, declaring himself loyal to the king and not the constitution. La Serna saw this as insubordination and sent 4,000 men to seize him. Because the circumstances had changed so greatly, the viceroy was forced to abolish the constitution as well and to argue that all his support for that regime had been pretense. Olañeta claimed not to believe him and continued his stance against the viceroy, and a campaign between the two royalist factions was duly begun. It was this division that gave Bolívar, Sucre, and Santa Cruz the opportunity to strike a fatal blow to the power of those loyal to the crown.

In April, as soon as news of these events had traveled north, Bolívar decided to take action and ordered all his troops to move to the valleys in the central Andes. By this time, Santa Cruz had already been reincorporated into the army and was busy organizing the campaign with Sucre, La Mar, and Miller. In mid-May, the march south from Cajamarca began, and by the end of the month they had reached Huaraz, where they joined Bolívar. By August, all was in place in Cerro de Pasco to fight against the royalists. The same city where Santa Cruz had changed sides only four years earlier would again be the backdrop of the confrontation between two great armies that by this point had grown to 1,000 mounted and nearly 8,000 on foot on the side of independence, and 1,300 mounted and nearly 3,000 on foot for the royalists. On 6 August, as General Canterac was trying to maneuver and avoid battle, he was surprised in the flat, high-altitude expanses at the edge of Lake Junín, at 4,100 meters above sea level. The battle was fought exclusively with cavalry, and in the forty-five minutes it lasted, not a single shot was fired. All the fighting was done with sword and lance. Santa Cruz had a prominent position in this battle as the main chief of staff, and as such he presented the report of events.[29]

Santa Cruz followed the fleeing royalist troops and was appointed head of the advance guard. Thus he reached Huamanga, the city where

---

[28] Information on his birth place is scant, but points out that he arrived at a young age to Jujuy. Because he was a trader he was nicknamed "the contrabandist."

[29] "Batalla de Junín parte pasado por el General Santa Cruz, Jefe de Estado Mayor, General Ejercito Unido Libertador, Los Reyes," 7 August 1824, in *Archivo Histórico del Mariscal Santa Cruz*, pp. 139, 140.

his father had been born. He remained there from August to November and was made governor of the province. There he worked to provide provisions to the advancing army. This particular area of the South Central Andes at the level of the river Pampas has served as an unofficial boundary between northern and southern Peru since the latter days of the colonial period. This point was the furthest north reached by Túpac Amaru and his men during the Great Rebellion, as well as by the uprising of Angulo and Pumacagua. It was where the final battle between those fighting for the crown and those seeking independence took place. Sucre and the majority of his men continued farther south, and Santa Cruz traveled back to the Mantaro river valley just north to ensure that arms and foodstuffs were continuously sent to sustain the campaign.

The situation La Serna faced was quite difficult. After the defeat of Canterac at Junín, he had to recall the regiments he had sent to deal with Olañeta. With the rainy season approaching and 3,000 more men expected from Colombia, La Serna needed to act quickly. His first reaction was to try to trap Sucre and his men in the south, separating them from their provisions. To this effect he marched and countermarched around the narrow valleys circling first Cuzco and later Ayacucho. When he saw that his enemy did not react and on the contrary remained in position, he was forced into action. La Serna engaged in battle on 9 December 1824. A large number of his troops, made up of recent recruits who were mainly indigenous, fled at the first opportunity.

Santa Cruz was not the only one absent from this major battle that marked the end of colonial domination of Peru. Bolívar was now on his way to Lima, so the troops organized by country of origin were under Sucre's command. José de La Mar, who had only abandoned the royalists in late 1821 when he surrendered the fortress in Callao, was the highest ranking officer among the Peruvians, and Gamarra was strategically appointed, at the last minute, as chief of staff. The position of the United Armies was well chosen in the Quinua esplanade, because the more numerous royalists had to descend a hill to the battleground. The United Armies won largely because indigenous troops refused to follow their leaders down the treacherous descent where they were exposed to enemy fire, fleeing instead en masse.[30] When the royalist army capitulated, 751 officers returned to Spain and 1,512 went back to their home provinces of Lima, Arequipa, Huamanga, Cochabamba,

---

[30] For accounts of the battle see ibid., and John Miller, *Memoirs of General Miller in the service of the Republic of Peru*, London: Longman, 1828, Vol. 2.

La Paz, Potosí, and Salta, among others; the rest of the royalist troops returned to their provinces in the southern Andes.[31]

In Cuzco, Pío Tristán, the highest ranking royalist officer, was briefly appointed viceroy, but with assurances from Sucre that all those who capitulated would be incorporated into the new state, and threats that those who did not would be executed, he soon relinquished command. All the corporations of the city swore allegiance to the new state.[32] After the capitulation, the cabildo of Arequipa took the side of the crown and the government in Lima surrendered, although some retreated to Callao, refusing to accept defeat. It was not until the end of 1826 that the last diehard royalists gave up, having sustained a high death toll. Torre Tagle died in the besieged fortress of Callao; one of the first to declare for independence, he ended his life resisting it and accused of treason.

Independence in Peru was a long and protracted affair, where regionalism played a pivotal role. The way in which the former viceroyalty had been divided between a northern and coastal section that had most of its commercial and social links with Chile, and a southern and Andean area with most interests in the lands on the other side of Lake Titicaca, had deep repercussions during the years of conflict. The northern coast and Lima declared for independence as soon as they felt they had enough support from the forces arrived from Chile; the south, with its new viceregal capital in Cuzco, became the new center of power for men who supported the idea of maintaining their links to the government in the Spanish peninsula. Elite Limeños such as Torre Tagle and Riva Agüero tried to lead the process of independence, but found it impossible to galvanize enough support for their cause. They established rival independent governments, but soon realized that the Colombian contingent and Bolívar in particular, did not consider them to be real interlocutors. In their effort to maintain control both, at some point, negotiated with the royalist forces. As a result, their political careers ended in disgrace. In contrast, men from the south, such as Santa Cruz and Gamarra, who knew much of the art of war in the Andes, having trained in the armies of Upper Peru that fought against the forces sent

---

[31] For complete lists see "Relación de los generales, jefes y oficiales del ejército español tomados por el Ejército Unido Libertador en consecuencia de la batalla y capitulación de Ayacucho, con expresión de los que se van para Europa y los que se quedan en el país," *CDIP*, Vol. 6, No. 9, 1974, pp. 241–252.

[32] Fisher, "The Royalist Regime in the Viceroyalty of Peru, 1820–1824', *Journal of Latin American Studies*, Vol. 32, No. 1, 2000, 55–84," p. 82.

from Buenos Aires, and who had subsequently changed sides, became the most important military and political players in the newly independent Peru. They attempted to obtain freedom without help from outside forces. But unable to do this, and aware of their weakness, they fought under the command of Bolívar and Sucre. Both Santa Cruz and Gamarra emerged after independence particularly strengthened as new administrations were being organized. The military campaign continued on to Upper Peru, which remained to be liberated.

# CHAPTER 3

# THE CREATION OF BOLIVIA

With the defeat of the royalist forces in Peru, the wars of independence in continental Spanish America were nearly over. Only the Upper Peruvian provinces remained in the hands of men who continued to recognize the king in Spain as the legitimate authority. The area that, as early as 1809, declared it did not want to be under the control of Buenos Aires or Lima and had sought to establish autonomous Juntas in Chuquisaca and La Paz was still in 1825 asserting its desire to be independent from the two former viceregal capitals. Although both were the centers of new independent republics, the provinces of the Audiencia of Charcas still wanted to remain separate from them. One way to achieve this was to maintain their links to the peninsula.

This chapter begins by looking at the process by which Bolivia came into being and the role Colombians, who were outsiders, played in finding a solution. The situation was so complicated that even they had different views on whether to create a new republic or not. Sucre and Bolívar did not agree on how to decide the future of these territories. There were two main principles used to settle this issue. Sucre favored "free determination of the people" – giving local populations the right to choose – whereas Bolívar was inclined toward *uti possidetis*, the principle under which viceregal boundaries were to be respected. Bolívar, whose ultimate aim was to create a federation between the countries he liberated, was worried that the final decision would influence the continental balance of power. Sucre, in contrast, was adamant that local people had to be given the right to decide. From the inception of Bolivia, Bolívar thought it ought to be federated with Peru, and if possible with Colombia as well. Bolívar wrote a constitution in the hope that it would bind together all the countries he had liberated. But he was not successful in

*Andrés de Santa Cruz, Manuel Ugalde (1835), óleo colección A. Santa Cruz, La Paz.*

Figure 2. Formal portrait of Andrés de Santa Cruz by Manuel Ugalde (1835), reprinted with permission of Carlos Mesa Gisbert, in his reprinted *Santa Cruz: El Condor Indio*, by Alfonso Crespo, La Paz: Presidencia de la Republica, 2005.

having it implemented, in large part because each of the new republics was busy creating its own identity.

Bolivian independence was greeted with elation by the elites of Chuquisaca and with some reservation by the people of La Paz, who still had close ties to southern Peru. The question of access to the best port, as well as the final location for the capital, confounded the new republic from its inception. Both these issues remain contentious today. Bolivia was from the start a collection of provinces, each with a clear identity. This could be seen, on the one hand, in the traditional enmity between La Paz and Chuquisaca, but it was also evident in the growing importance of Cochabamba and Oruro. This chapter also looks at the question of the best port for Bolivia. Arica, the one with the best possible access to the Pacific Ocean, was part of Peru and firmly embedded in the province of Arequipa; it was not viable to incorporate it into Bolivia. Bolivians had to develop a port in the southern desert instead. This led some Bolivians to believe that a federation with Peru would be better than to remain isolated from the coast. Santa Cruz was among them. He considered himself a citizen of both countries and was forced at this point to come to terms with becoming Bolivian.

## INDEPENDENCE OF THE AUDIENCIA OF CHARCAS

After nearly fifteen years of fighting, the provinces in Charcas were utterly exhausted. The elites in the main cities remained adamant, however, that they did not want to be under the jurisdiction of either Lima or Buenos Aires. This was clear to Sucre as soon as he came in contact with the people of these provinces. The process by which they eventually became the Republic of Bolívar, the Bolivia we know today, was not simple. The royalists who still controlled the Audiencia had to be defeated, and only then it was possible for a congress to be called into session and decide on the future political organization. Many – Santa Cruz among them – thought that it would be better to be part of a federation with Peru. Others, like Bolívar, considered that the traditional viceregal boundaries should be respected and Buenos Aires should maintain its jurisdiction over the area. This latter position did not last very long, because the fragile union in the provinces of the south was unable to assert any kind of control, and the elites in Charcas showed little interest, with the exception of the people in the border province of Tarija. The option of a federation, however, remained open.

The capitulation of the royalist forces in Ayacucho brought an official end to the war of independence. All the southern provinces of Peru
that had supported the viceroyalty until the bitter end now accepted
the terms of surrender. Nevertheless, much remained to be done. Sucre
dispatched trusted officers to take over the command of Arequipa, Puno,
and Tacna. To prepare the city that had been the capital of the viceroyalty for three years, Gamarra was sent to his native Cuzco; the rest
of the army was to follow. From Ayacucho, Sucre repeatedly wrote to
Bolívar. He asked for clear instructions on what to do with the Upper
Provinces, because it was evident they would soon become a bone of
contention. The territory of the Audiencia of Charcas remained under
the command of Pedro Antonio de Olañeta, an avowed royalist many
considered a Creole. He had rebelled against La Serna, claiming that
the viceroy was not loyal to the king, but rather to the constitutional
regime. Olañeta's uprising against the viceroy divided the royalists to
such a degree that independence became feasible. It was not difficult to
foresee that complicated political wrangling would follow. Sucre did not
want to be embroiled in these negotiations, so he claimed to be tired,
asking instead for permission to return to Colombia. Permission was not
forthcoming, however, and so Sucre continued toward Cuzco. There
he pleaded to have Santa Cruz relocated to Huamanga, so Santa Cruz
could lead the fight against the Indians from Huanta, the only people
in Peru still resisting independence. He also wanted to have Santa Cruz
closer in case a local was needed to negotiate with Olañeta.

Bolívar ordered Santa Cruz to advance to Huamanga, and Sucre continued south. Once Sucre reached the Desaguadero River, the natural
border between Lower and Upper Peru, he consulted Bolívar concerning
the state of the provinces.[1] The potential explosiveness of the situation
was starkly evident to him, because his forces were made up of generals from Buenos Aires and Peruvian mid-ranking officers. The troops
were an array of men from various places. Both Peru and the United
Provinces, the state that succeeded the Viceroyalty of the Río de la
Plata, claimed to have a right to Upper Peru. To prevent potential conflict, Sucre proposed that only Colombian troops should continue south,
but this was not considered acceptable. Before he could continue, he
needed to deal with Olañeta.

[1] Letter from Sucre to Bolívar, Abancay, 25 December 1824, *Cartas de Sucre al*
*Libertador* (1820–1826), edited by Daniel Florence O'Leary, Madrid: Editorial
América, 1919, p. 277.

Sucre wrote to Olañeta in the friendliest of terms from Cuzco, explaining that the capitulation drawn after the battle of Ayacucho had not mentioned Olañeta's name because the forces fighting for independence considered him to be one of them. The Colombian general thanked Olañeta for his brave action, noting that it had made their success possible. He stated that, because the war was over, a commissioner was being sent to finalize treaties.[2] Unsure of Olañeta's response, Sucre wrote to José Miguel Lanza, one of the guerrilla leaders who had been fighting for the independence of Upper Peru for more than fifteen years. Sucre thanked Lanza for his hard work and appointed him governor and commander-in-chief of La Paz. Sucre also told him he had a force of 10,000 men on the Peruvian side of the lake awaiting Olañeta's next move.

Sucre had been right to be wary of Olañeta. As Sucre had been forewarned by La Serna and Canterac at Ayacucho, the Upper Peruvian general was difficult to work with, prone to contradictions and changes of heart. To complicate matters further, his nephew Casimiro Olañeta, who acted as his secretary, was working undercover for the cause of independence. In their correspondence it was not easy to ascertain whether Casimiro was speaking for himself or for his uncle.[3] In late December, Olañeta had written to Bolívar, thanking him for his generosity and assuring him that he would soon show him his gratitude. A fortnight later, he signed a proposed armistice that aimed to suspend hostilities for four months. This limited each army to its respective side of the river, but Olañeta did not accept independence. While negotiations were still ongoing, Sucre intercepted letters in which Olañeta asked officers who had capitulated in Ayacucho and had returned home not to accept defeat and to continue fighting for the king. These letters claimed that troops were being sent from the peninsula and that the provinces of Upper Peru still had not given up the fight. At the end of January, Olañeta, who used his title of Viceroy of the Río de la Plata, invaded Puno. Sucre responded with an angry letter declaring war on the man who claimed to be the king's last defender in America.

[2]   Letter from Sucre to Pedro Antonio de Olañeta, Cuzco, 1 January 1825, *Bolívar y el Arte Militar*, edited by Vicente Lecuna, New York: Colonial Press, 1955, pp. 398–9.

[3]   In December 1824, Casimiro Olañeta wrote to Bolívar explaining his actions; see *Documentos referentes a la creación de Bolivia*, edited by Vicente Lecuna, Caracas: Litografía el Comercio, 1924, pp. 8, 9.

Olañeta found that his situation was increasingly fragile once the people of Cochabamba declared in favor of independence. Sucre advanced with all his force toward the border and crossed the Desaguadero in early February 1825. Casimiro Olañeta deserted his uncle and met with Sucre in La Paz. There the young Olañeta declared in no uncertain terms than a union of the Upper Provinces with Buenos Aires was impossible. Joining Peru, however, was still seen as a viable option, especially if the capital of the country were to be moved south to Cuzco.[4] Sucre repeatedly said, in his correspondence with Bolívar, that he did not want to govern Upper Peru; he pleaded to be allowed to return to Colombia. Bolívar did not permit it, exhorting Sucre to be more ambitious. Bolívar said that, as glory was to be their ultimate recompense, Sucre must stay and focus on stability and governance.

Sucre remained, and as soon as he was in control of La Paz, in February 1825, he called for elections. The elected congress would have the power to decide the future of the provinces. This was an important turning point, and many consider this the first step in the creation of the modern state of Bolivia. For the first time, local representatives were granted the freedom to choose their future. The weak government in Buenos Aires was facing such turmoil at the time that it was unable to oppose the meeting of a congress. This body would decide whether to join the United Provinces of the River Plate, to become part of Peru, or remain independent. The issue was not straightforward, and Colombian leaders wanted to approach it with utmost care. There was no agreement on how these territories, over which so much blood had been spilled, should be governed. Bolívar explained the situation to the president of Colombia. He wrote that, on the basis of *uti possidetis*, Upper Peru belonged to the River Plate. De facto, however, it remained under the control of Spain, because Olañeta was still faithful to the king. The will of the people, on the other hand, was to be independent. Peru also had to be considered in the negotiations, because the Peruvian government wanted to have the provinces back.[5]

Bolívar, who was still in Lima, resigned his position as dictator and called the 1823 Peruvian Congress back into session. He wanted to improve his support so he would have a mandate to decide the political future of the countries he had recently liberated. Santa Cruz, who

4  Letter from Sucre to Bolívar, Ilave, 5 February 1825, p. 304.
5  Letter from Bolívar to Francisco de Paula Santander, Lima, 18 February 1825, *Documentos referentes a la creación de Bolivia*, p. 101.

believed that the Venezuelan hero was the only hope for peace, pleaded with Bolívar not to abandon power. Santa Cruz did not want him to recall Congress, because he did not trust the men who had abandoned Riva Agüero, to back Torre Tagle. In spite of these fears, Bolívar's gamble paid off, and after his confirmation as dictator, he was given more troops and official permission to enter Upper Peru. A decree was drawn up stipulating that the support he was given was conditional: a final resolution on the borders and possible independence of Upper Peru would be decided only after a treaty had been agreed to with the government of Buenos Aires. Bolívar pointed out, after asking Santa Cruz to travel to La Paz, that if it had been up to him, he would never have allowed troops to cross the Desaguadero. Bolívar claimed that this was because he thought the United Provinces had a right to the Upper Provinces. He had allowed troops to cross because, as a Colombian, he could not be seen as taking a position that might damage Peru, respectful as he was of viceregal borders.[6]

Bolívar wrote a strong letter to Sucre, disapproving of his call for a congress in Upper Peru and invoking *uti possidetis.* Bolívar noted that the cases of Guatemala and Chile, where new countries had been created, had been very different. In contrast to Charcas or Quito, their governments had long been effectively independent from New Spain and Peru. Bolívar believed that it was problematic to give a congress the ability to decide the future of Charcas, because it would create a precedent for such a provision to be made for Quito. Bolívar had incorporated Quito into Colombia even though the province had ambitions to be independent. This was contested by Peru and Colombia, so Bolívar did not welcome the possibility of a Charcas example to be followed.[7]

Distressed, Sucre reminded his mentor he had repeatedly asked for instructions and pointed out that Bolívar had previously said that a congress should be called. Sucre also noted that provinces such as Salta, Córdoba, Tucumán, and La Rioja had their own independent and sovereign governments. Accordingly, there was no reason why a province with 50,000 people should not have its own provisional assembly until a government was established in Buenos Aires. Sucre pointed out that

---

[6]  Letter from Bolívar to Santa Cruz, Lima, 11 March 1825, in *Bolívar y Santa Cruz Epistolario*, edited by Armando Rojas, Caracas: Venezuelan Government, 1975, p. 45.

[7]  Letter from Bolívar to Sucre, Lima, 21 February, 1825, in *Documentos referentes a la creación de Bolivia*, pp. 105–8.

the municipal governments already represented the sovereignty of their jurisdictions within a federal system and that calling the assembly prevented more complex problems.[8]

The issue of the creation of an independent government in the provinces of his birth had important long-term consequences for Santa Cruz. As the correspondence between Bolívar and Sucre crisscrossed the Andes, Santa Cruz was en route to the Altiplano. Sucre trusted his administrative abilities. The Colombian general knew, however, that not everyone regarded Santa Cruz with such sympathy, because many considered him to be too embroiled in Peruvian affairs. This was seen as problematic because, after nearly two decades of war, Upper Peru had splintered into a multitude of factions. Each of the main cities believed it had particular rights, and each had its own interests to defend – interests that were often in conflict. The decision whether to be incorporated into Peru, to join the United Provinces of the River Plate, or to become independent was not a straightforward one. These provinces had been part of the Peruvian viceroyalty for nearly all of the colonial period. They had been under the jurisdiction of the Viceroyalty of the Río de la Plata for only thirty-four years. The first independent Juntas in the Americas were created in Chuquisaca and La Paz in 1809. One of the main reasons why they were set up was to defend their right to be independent from the government of Buenos Aires. War complicated issues further, as forces from southern Peru intervened. With support from some elites in Upper Peru, these forces fought against the agents of the first independent governments created in the River Plate.

Juan Antonio Álvarez de Arenales, the Castilian who had raised the local militia in La Paz in 1809 and who had fought with irregular contingents in the Andes until 1818, when he followed San Martín to Chile and Peru, was by 1825 the governor of Salta. Now, in coordination with Sucre, he marched north to pressure Olañeta. In March, he wrote to the people of Upper Peru, whom he addressed as Peruvians, to encourage them to fight for their freedom. He reassured them that he would support their cause even if they chose to opt out of the union with the United Provinces of the South (which he represented). He wrote that having fought alongside them for so many years and under such difficult circumstances, he considered them to be brothers.

---

[8]  Letter from Sucre to Bolívar, Potosí, 4 April 1825, in *Cartas de Sucre al Libertador*, pp. 327–9.

With all this debate raging, Sucre continued his campaign against the retreating Olañeta. In early April, abandoned by most of his men, Olañeta was killed by his own men in a scuffle. As soon as Arenales heard the news, he addressed a proclamation to the population of Upper Peru congratulating them on their victory and calling for an assembly to meet and decide on the future of their provinces. He assured them, once again, that their desires would be respected, noting nevertheless that he hoped the Peruvian army would not be involved.[9] He wrote to Sucre congratulating him not only for his military triumphs, but for having called an assembly in Upper Peru. Arenales was convinced this was the only way to find a peaceful and lasting solution to the thorny issue. Sucre used this letter from the governor of Salta to justify his own conduct to the Peruvian Congress. He repeatedly told its representatives, and Bolívar, that he would leave Upper Peru as soon as the assembly was installed.

Santa Cruz arrived in the Altiplano in April. He had been elected representative for La Paz but was unsure whether to accept this responsibility. Santa Cruz worried about the impact it would have on his political career in Peru, so he consulted Bolívar. Santa Cruz explained in his official letter to the Liberator's secretary that he was a citizen of Peru thanks to his destiny and the generosity of its government. He sought advice on whether to accept the position, because he did not want to lose his hard-earned right to participate in Peruvian politics.[10] Sucre wanted Santa Cruz to take charge of the government of La Paz, but Santa Cruz refused. Sucre complained to Bolívar, describing him as a spurious man who complimented Peruvians by denigrating his own people and Santa Cruz referred to the land of his birth as "the Upper Provinces."

Not wanting to give up a political career in Peru, Santa Cruz found himself in a difficult situation. It was far from clear, however, what kind of impact the situation in Upper Peru would eventually have on his plans. After having rejected the post of prefect of La Paz, he finally relented and accepted the position of representative to the assembly. In a letter to his close friend and companion in arms Antonio Gutiérrez

---

[9] Both proclamations in *Documentos referentes a la creación de Bolivia*, pp. 141–2 and 146–7.

[10] Letter from Santa Cruz to the Secretary of the Liberator, La Plata, 4 June 1825, in *Archivo Histórico del Mariscal Andrés de Santa Cruz*, Andrés de Santa Cruz Schuhkrafft, La Paz: Universidad Mayor de San Andrés, 1976, vol. I, p. 166.

de la Fuente, now prefect of Arequipa, Santa Cruz confided that he had accepted temporarily until the arrival of Bolívar because of the insistence of the representatives.[11] It was clear that Santa Cruz did not want to abandon Peruvian politics and that at this point he felt much more bound to them than to those of the country that was emerging to the south. While the Liberator was being fêted in Cuzco, presented with a golden crown encrusted with precious stones by the very people who had backed the viceregal government until the bitter end, the assembly in Upper Peru worked hard to resolve the issue of their own government. Every day, it became clearer that they wanted independence.

Toward the end of July, Santa Cruz wrote to La Fuente that he feared independence would be declared. He compared the euphoria he saw in Chuquisaca to what they had seen in Lima in 1821. Santa Cruz described locals' sentiments as liberal and extreme with nearly all being taken by the same feverish desire for liberty. He noted that a minority, some of the most inspired representatives, had voted for their incorporation into Peru. He assured La Fuente that no one desired a union with Buenos Aires and that he would follow the general opinion for independence as, given the circumstances, it was not possible to take any other position, at least until Bolívar arrived. Santa Cruz considered this very difficult and felt very tired; he hoped to be given a commission to Europe.[12]

The work in the assembly began in July. After a whole month of debate, on 6 August 1825, autonomy from Peru and the United Provinces was declared. Five days later, it was agreed that in gratitude to the man who had been in charge of their final liberation, Upper Peruvians would inhabit a state called the Republic of Bolívar. Bolívar was recognized as the father of the nation and given a large golden medal encrusted with diamonds with an inscription stating, "The Republic of Bolívar grateful to the hero whose name it bears." Toward the end of August, the Liberator finally arrived in La Paz. Santa Cruz welcomed him and told him that the assembly sought his protection, counsel, and even guidance for the laws that were to govern what Santa Cruz described as a "new Sparta." To Sucre, Santa Cruz confided that he had had to work hard to ensure that representatives subscribed to the document

[11] Letter from Santa Cruz to La Fuente, La Plata, 12 July 1825, in *Archivo Histórico del Mariscal Andrés de Santa Cruz*, p. 168.
[12] Letter from Santa Cruz to La Fuente, La Plata, 27 July 1825, in *Archivo Histórico del Mariscal Andrés de Santa Cruz*, p. 171.

that granted the Liberator the right to produce their constitution; four had still refused.[13]

In October 1825, Bolívar finally arrived in Potosí, where he was celebrated for nearly two months. William Miller, the prefect, described how the Liberator entered the city under enormous triumphal arches that covered the access roads for kilometers. As he passed through the arches, groups of forty Indians greeted him by doing what Miller described as "ballet steps," dressed in their high plumed headgear and medals engraved with images of Bolívar. He was then taken to the Cathedral, where he was bathed in holy water and a Te Deum was sung.[14] Filled with emotion, the Liberator wrote to the president of Venezuela about the responsibility he would forever feel for the land he had fathered.

With Bolívar in Potosí, Congress was dissolved and a new Constituent Assembly was called to decide on the constitution. Representatives were dispatched to Peru, Colombia, and the United Provinces of the River Plate to seek formal approval of the republic's independence. The issue of federalism dogged the newly created state from its inception. Indeed, the republic had been declared by the "free representatives of the free people of La Paz, Potosí, Cochabamba, Oruro, Chuquisaca and Santa Cruz."[15] The six provinces were represented, and each sought to maintain a certain degree of autonomy from the others. To prevent competition among the cities, it was decided that the capital would be a new city, to be called Sucre. Chuquisaca was temporarily designated as the capital and eventually took this name. The issue of where the capital should be located continued to be problematic throughout the country's history and still remains contentious today. This was a symptom of the difficulties these provinces had in deciding how they should be represented, and the power each of them should hold in the union.

Nationality at this point was fluid, and both Peru and Bolivia gave citizenship to all those who had fought in the campaigns of Junín and Ayacucho. Santa Cruz could therefore claim to be a citizen of both. As a representative from La Paz, he was, during the debates over independence, from the party closest to Peru. His political proximity to Lima

[13] Letter to Bolívar and to Sucre, La Plata, 20 August 1825, in *Archivo Histórico del Mariscal Andrés de Santa Cruz*, p. 174.

[14] John Miller, *Memoirs of William Miller in the Service of Peru*, London, Longman, 1828, vol. II, p. 30.

[15] *Documentos referentes a la creación de Bolivia*, p. 303.

made his position in Bolivia difficult: Santa Cruz did not want to see Peru and Bolivia go their separate ways, so he supported the proposed union of the countries liberated by Bolívar.

Bolívar set out to create what he considered the best possible constitution for the countries he felt he had fathered. He wanted it to unite them all in a federation and was convinced that his new charter would finally bring stability to the new republics. Bolívar took over the day-to-day running of the state of Bolivia, sending nearly 3,000 men back to Colombia and reorganizing the army and taxation. Recognition of the newly created state by its neighbors was soon forthcoming, in no small part because in Peru, Bolívar still controlled politics from a distance. In the United Provinces, the threat of Brazil was a more pressing issue at the moment when it was difficult to establish a stable government.

Bolívar, Sucre, and Santa Cruz worked together on the electoral legislation for the Constituent Assembly, because representatives would be elected in January and meet in April 1826. Ten representatives were to be elected for La Paz, nine for Cochabamba, eight for Potosí, five for Chuquisaca, five for the lowland province of Santa Cruz, and two from Oruro. Elections were indirect, and apart from the prerequisite of having Bolivian nationality, there were no restrictions on who could participate.[16] With the assembly in place, Bolívar dedicated all his energy to the creation of what he described as a "very strong constitution," perfectly suited for the country. He declared that it would not violate the separation of powers and would reject slavery and all privileges. Citizenship, however, was to be restricted to the rich and those who could read and write. To include more voters, he would pass laws to eventually develop education. In December 1825, tribute was abolished. Just days later, Bolívar returned to Peru, where a new congress had been elected.[17]

Sucre was left in charge of the presidency of Bolivia, and Santa Cruz, who had recently been appointed Great Marshall, was to administer the province of La Paz. As the most populous province, it presented challenges to which he was particularly well placed to respond. These included restless troops who had not been properly paid and the violent reaction among Indians against the imposition of the direct contribution that replaced tribute. The law mandated that all men between the ages of eighteen and sixty were liable to pay this tax. A new list had to be

[16] *Documentos referentes a la creación de Bolivia*, pp. 422–6.
[17] *Documentos referentes a la creación de Bolivia*, p. 498.

created by parish priests and governors by updating all information on population. Another tax would be paid on property, and a new register was to be produced. Santa Cruz noted that Indians instantly distrusted the measurement of their land and that they were not amenable to their flocks being surveyed, mainly because of the way in which the process was being carried out. To prevent further problems, Santa Cruz suspended the physical inspections and decided that work should continue on the basis of approximate figures only.

## A First Attempt to Create a Federation

The possibilities of a federation had been debated from the inception of Bolivia, and many were convinced this was the best way forward for the country. There were problems with this option, however, and as the process advanced, the difficulties grew ever harder to surpass. A border between what became the independent republics of Peru and Bolivia had existed since colonial times. The exact limits varied widely, but coincided roughly with Lake Titicaca. This was the homeland of the Aymara people, who were not interested in administrative boundaries and lived on both sides of the border. The people in the area remained close even after independence, just as they had done during the nearly thirty years they had been part of different viceroyalties. People from the southern provinces of Peru had fought to bring the provinces of Upper Peru back to their jurisdiction from as early as 1809, when the first Juntas had been established. The United Provinces of the River Plate had also attempted to recoup the territory. Although they were able to take control temporarily, they never managed to assert permanent control. After Sucre defeated Olañeta, the assembly declared for the establishment of a new state. But for this to come to fruition, recognition was needed from the United Provinces and from Peru. The United Provinces, engulfed in its own difficulties in establishing a central state and on the verge of war with Brazil, did not hesitate to accept the independence of the new republic. There was, nevertheless, some debate over the future of the southernmost province of Tarija, which eventually became part of Bolivia. Peru did not accept Bolivian independence as easily, and a discussion of a possible union between the two states began.

When Bolívar returned to Lima in February 1826, the newly established Congress discussed the possibility of establishing a "Bolivian Federation" that would encompass Peru and Bolivia, under the rule of Bolívar as president for life. Santa Cruz wholeheartedly backed this project and thought that Colombia should be included to create a larger federation.[18] Bolívar also thought it possible and wrote about it in a private letter to the vice president of Colombia. He confided that many had approached him with the idea of declaring Peru, just as the provinces of Upper Peru had done, a "Bolivian Republic." Bolívar wrote that he thought this was nothing more than a strategy to try to keep him as constitutional president, because he had already declared that he was not able to accept such a post. He pointed out that the federation would not be very constricting, but that many feared the costs the union would entail, because the Peruvian government was saddled with debt.[19]

In another private letter, Bolívar openly developed his ideas for a federation that would include Colombia. At this point, he thought the best solution to prevent all the countries he had liberated from descending into chaos and anarchy would be to join them in a federation. The Bolivian Constitution, which Bolívar mentioned in this very letter, was to be the basis of the union. He saw it as "the arch of salvation that would rescue the new republics from the shipwreck that threatened them from all quarters."[20] Recently received news from Colombia of division, lack of funds, and infighting worried him. Convinced that this would also happen in Peru, Bolívar believed that a strong constitution and a federation would safeguard the edifice he had created. He aimed for a federation of three free republics. He thought the union should be closer than the one in the United States and have a lifelong president, whose role was the centerpiece of his draft for the Bolivian Constitution.

The government of each of the federal states would be in the hands of the vice president. Two congressional chambers would legislate at the state level on all things relative to religion, justice, and civil and economic administration – in short, everything except for foreign relations and war. States would be divided into departments, and each department would send a deputy to a three-chamber federal congress. This assembly, the vice presidents, and the secretaries of state would govern the republic, while the president would spend a year in each of the departments. The capital would be at the most central point, and

[18] Letter from Santa Cruz to Sucre, La Paz, 28 April 1826, in *Archivo Histórico del Mariscal Andrés de Santa Cruz*, p. 193.

[19] Letter from Bolívar to Santander, Magdalena, 21 February 1826, in *Documentos referentes a la creación de Bolivia*, vol. II, p. 48.

[20] Manuel Felipe Paz Soldan transcribes the letter in detail but does not provide any idea of to whom it was directed, or when exactly it was written; see *Historia del Perú independiente*, vol. II, p. 84.

Colombia would be divided into three states: Venezuela, Cundinamarca, and Quito. The federation would have a newly chosen name, and there would be one flag, one army, and one nation. Bolívar was adamant that this plan would be instituted immediately in Peru and Bolivia and that Colombia could be included later. He envisioned a new great state of southern Peru, with Arequipa as its capital, which would be created to be similar to the ones created in Colombia.

The option of a federation was eagerly discussed in the Peruvian Congress, but as Sucre reported it had no support in Bolivia. Sucre noted that the plan would not be approved by the Bolivian Congress if it was officially presented by the Peruvian legislature. Sucre also asked Bolívar to banish the thought of Sucre becoming president of the proposed federation, assuring Bolívar he intended to retire as soon as possible from public life.[21] Indeed, only five days later, Sucre renounced his post to the newly convened Congress, asking for a new president who was wholly Bolivian. Peruvians viewed him with distrust because he was a foreigner, suspected of not wanting a union between Peru and Bolivia.

An issue that was closely related to the possible union, or indeed to the ultimate separation, of Peru and Bolivia was that of the port that was best suited for Bolivia. On independence, Bolivia had been given as its main sea outlet a port that had not yet been developed. It was initially given the name of La Mar, in honor of the General from Cuenca, but later became known as Cobija. Traditionally all trade from the Altiplano had gone through Arica. Indeed, the economies of the southern part of Peru and the northern part of Bolivia were tightly intertwined. As a result, both areas were adamant that the best possible solution to the question of the port was to integrate the two territories into the same republic. Sucre sent Colonel O'Connor to inspect the southern sections of Bolivia and to study the feasibility and cost of building roads from Potosí to Cobija through the Atacama Desert. One of the most arid places on earth, surrounded by vast salt plains and dried lakes, the desert offered only limited and expensive possibilities for communications. So, after receiving O'Connor's report, Sucre wrote to Bolívar pleading to have Arica ceded to Bolivia.[22] Sucre received the news of the rejection from the Peruvian representatives in January.

---

[21] Letter from Sucre to Bolívar, Chuquisaca, 20 May 1826, in *Documentos referentes a la creación de Bolivia*, vol. II, p. 142.

[22] Letter from Sucre to Bolívar, Chuquisaca, 27 January 1826, in *Cartas de Sucre al Libertador*, p. 390.

He angrily wrote to Santa Cruz this would make the discussions of a
federation with Peru more difficult, because access to the port would
now be considered their only interest in the union.

In spite of all his protestations, Sucre was unable to reject the presidency. He accepted on the condition that he would remain in power only
until Bolívar returned. This, however, was not to be, because matters in
Colombia required the Liberator's personal attention. Forced to leave
Peru because of the insurrection of Paez in Venezuela, Bolívar called
on his trusted Paceño lieutenant to come to his aid and cover for him
in Lima. Santa Cruz, who was then prefect of La Paz and Chuquisaca,
returned to Peru to take over the presidency of the governing council. He traveled through Arequipa, where he met his old comrade in
arms, Antonio Gutiérrez de la Fuente. They had both served under the
orders of Pezuela and La Serna and had abandoned the royalist cause in
1820 after they were made prisoners of Arenales in Cerro de Pasco. Just
five years later they held important posts that they could never have
dreamed of attaining under the previous regime.

The first letter Santa Cruz wrote from Lima, in early July 1826, was to
La Fuente. In it he confided that he had only accepted the presidency of
the council at Bolívar's insistence. He feared that he would not be able
to fulfill his mandate, emphasizing he would work tirelessly to maintain
order.[23] The first thing Santa Cruz was called to do, as he traveled
through Ayacucho, was to put down a royalist rebellion by the so-called
Iquichanos, with whom he had already dealt a couple of years previously.
A group of Indians and mestizos in the north of Ayacucho raised the
banner of the king and called for some of their privileges to be restored.
In early August, they capitulated to Santa Cruz.

Following Bolívar's instructions, Santa Cruz had sent a diplomatic
representative to Bolivia with the task of negotiating the creation of
the federation. Instructions to have the Bolivian Constitution sworn in
were sent to the prefects of the departments of southern Peru. The text
had been reprinted, with some modifications for Peru, although Santa
Cruz believed it needed to receive the backing of the electoral colleges
to legitimize it. The idea was to have Bolívar proclaimed president
in the two republics. Having the same constitution approved, and a
diplomatic agreement for the federation, would give them a head start
while matters were settled in Colombia. Sucre worked toward the same

---

[23] Letter from Santa Cruz to La Fuente, Lima, 3 July 1826, in *Archivo Histórico del
Mariscal Andrés de Santa Cruz*, p. 197.

aim in Bolivia but made a crucial modification to the voting provision. He considered that the president would have much more legitimacy if he was elected by the people instead of by Congress. In a letter to Bolívar, Sucre asked for his opinion on whether Santa Cruz would be the best vice-presidential candidate, as Santa Cruz would be called to replace Sucre when he abandoned Bolivia for good. Sucre implied in his question that Santa Cruz was not necessarily highly regarded by the people of Bolivia.[24] In spite of his doubts, Sucre did choose Santa Cruz for the post when he was elected president in October. Sucre assured Santa Cruz that he would not remain in Bolivia after 1828, and, as he had no intention of remaining in power, Santa Cruz would be his successor in case Bolívar did not return.

The debate on the constitution continued both in Peru and in Bolivia, while the diplomatic mission sent from Peru arrived in Bolivia to discuss the possibility of the federation. It was headed by a prominent lawyer from Quito, who arrived in Chuquisaca in October 1826. Sucre wrote to Santa Cruz that he was convinced that the bill uniting the countries would pass. When the time came for Congress to discuss the federation in December, however, it was accepted only on the condition that important changes be made on the issue of the election of deputies to the federal congress. To Bolívar, Sucre confided that the federation brought much work. He made it clear that the federation was approved only in exchange for the ports of Arica and Tarapaca and the city of Tacna. This brought outrage in Peru. Exchanging these valuable port cities for the islands on Lake Titicaca and some of the provinces north of La Paz and east of Cuzco was considered completely unacceptable, showing that there was little faith in the federation's long-term success, and that each state was more interested in the gains they were likely to extract from the agreements than in reaching one that was workable.

As grand as Bolívar's dreams for a great federation of the Andes were, this was probably not his greatest act of hubris. There was no real appetite for this project. In Bolivia, it had been accepted with the caveats that it would only last during the life of the Liberator and would only come into effect if Colombia also subscribed to it. This was, in fact, killing the plan before it was even born. Even more ambitious than the federation, and more linked to Bolívar's ultimate downfall from grace, not only in Peru but also in Bolivia, was the constitution he wrote

---

[24] Letter from Sucre to Bolívar, Chuquisaca, 12 July 1826, in *Documentos referentes a la creación de Bolivia*, vol. II, p. 212.

in 1826. This charter, sometimes known as the Bolivian or Life-long Constitution, was denounced by his enemies, headed by cleric Francisco Xavier de Luna Pizarro, as little more than a covert monarchy. The constitution had in fact several elements that made it both innovative and problematic. Bolívar created a fourth power at the same level as the executive, the legislative, and the judicial: the Electoral Power. It was to be made up of electors chosen for four years by the citizens, one for each hundred. Citizenship was granted only to those who could read and write, had an independent income, and paid taxes. Bolívar considered, however, that to be a citizen, it was more important to have qualities and abilities; wealth was not necessary. The legislative branch had three chambers: the Tribunes, the Senators, and the Censors, each with 24 members. They were to meet once a year to legislate and would control the government. The president was to hold his post until death and could choose his own successor. He had a large scope of action because he could not be held accountable.

Bolívar wrote the constitution while in Bolivia, at a time when he was being celebrated as the greatest living hero. While he was being fêted, crowned with laurel leaves made in gold and inset with precious stones, it was understandable that he would be convinced of his absolute power to legislate. When the time came to have the constitution approved, things had changed significantly. In Bolivia, Sucre still held enough sway to have Congress approve it, but this was not the case in Peru. This was one of the main reasons why the Liberator returned to Lima not wanting to miss the opening of the new congress. He knew that the biggest opposition came from Arequipa and was particularly worried by the return of Luna Pizarro. It was clear that the liberal cleric, who had been so influential in the creation of the 1823 Constitution, had no desire to have a new charter enacted.

Political maneuvering made it possible for the Peruvian Congress to be dissolved and a plebiscite on the constitution to be called for. Even as provincial electoral colleges gave their approval to the charter in great numbers, Bolívar soon realized that his project could not survive long. In Venezuela, he had powerful political enemies, and his illusions of a grand Andean Union were dashed as he became aware of the strength of local politics in his native land. If it was not possible for Colombia to be united, it was much less likely that an even more ambitious union of three republics could survive. In October 1826, Bolívar wrote to Santa Cruz, as a friend and mentor, saying that Santa Cruz should abandon the idea of having the constitution enacted. Instead, he should become the head of the opposition and act only as he thought best for Peru.[25] In spite of these reservations, Santa Cruz and Sucre were able to have the constitution enacted in both Bolivia and in Peru. They succeeded in having the discussion on possible federation advance enough so that by November, Bolívar himself once again thought it possible.

The notion of a federation appealed to most parties, at least in theory. The difficulties, however, were close to insurmountable, because there were as many different ideas of how to make the federation possible as there were parties involved. Bolivia was really only interested in a loose union and in ensuring that it would gain control over Tarapaca, Tacna, and Arica. Many Bolivians were also adamant that the capital should be moved further south, ideally to Cuzco. This last point was unacceptable to the elites in Lima, who thought that union with Bolivia was a good idea as long as it was more of an annexation of territory and a return to colonial practices. In southern Peru, there was a third option that appealed to most: the creation of a separate state, with Arequipa as its capital. This idea had been fielded early on by Luna Pizarro, and Bolívar saw it as a good solution that could bring balance to the region. Although he had been such a staunch enemy of the Bolivian Constitution, Luna Pizarro had advocated the creation of a federation. This, however, was not enough to save him from being sent into exile, or from the wrath of Santa Cruz.

The press in Arequipa championed the idea of establishing a federation of provinces, following on the path of the United Provinces of the River Plate. Copies of a paper called *El Zancudo* – the mosquito – that promoted this idea arrived in Lima in October. Santa Cruz immediately wrote to Prefect La Fuente, asking him to prevent these ideas from circulating. He sent a trusted lieutenant to Arequipa to observe the situation and take action if La Fuente had been involved.[26] La Fuente protested his innocence and adamantly denied what some Colombian generals had said happened: that some men had sworn the independence of Arequipa in his house, and its separation from the general union. Whether La Fuente was implicated, or even whether these ceremonies ever actually occurred, is not as important as the fact that regional sentiment in Arequipa was strong. People in the province felt that the union

[25] Letter from Bolívar to Santa Cruz, Popayán, 26 October 1826, in *Bolívar y Santa Cruz Epistolario*, p. 60.

[26] Letter from Santa Cruz to La Fuente, Lima, 19 October 1826, and to Bolívar, 23 October 1826, in *Archivo Histórico del Mariscal Andrés de Santa Cruz*, pp. 216–20.

was not providing for them and that they were sending money to Lima while receiving little in exchange. Once news arrived of a projected federation with Bolivia that would have given away Arica, Tacna, and Tarapaca, public opinion in Arequipa became even more incensed.[27]

The situation was complicated not only in Arequipa, but also in Puno. The prefect there tried to obtain support for the constitution, but faced an indigenous uprising. Considering the general climate in the south, Santa Cruz wrote to Gamarra in early November 1826. In this intimate letter, in which he addressed Gamarra as "dear friend," he explained the situation and asked him to try to find out as much as he could about these plans. Santa Cruz made it clear that he did not support the idea of dividing Peru and that this option would only be acceptable if it was presented as a sine qua non condition by Bolivia.[28] Bolívar in his letters from November of that year told Santa Cruz that he did consider the division of Peru an advantage. All of these conflicting positions made the federation impracticable; it essentially had failed before ever being implemented.

In spite of this opposition, the constitution was enacted to celebrate the second anniversary of the battle of Ayacucho in December 1826. It was not to last very long. Only a month later, a mutiny in the army barracks in Lima called for the return of the 1823 charter and the end of Colombian intervention. When Bolívar heard the news, he wrote to Santa Cruz that he understood the gravity of the situation, that he knew Santa Cruz was his dear friend, and that the people of Peru were not ungrateful, nor were they his enemies. He said that he only wanted the happiness of Peruvians, and that they should follow the laws best suited to them. He wrote that he did not care for the Bolivian Constitution, and that if Peruvians' desire was to burn it, they should indeed send it to the flames.[29] Bolívar had renounced the presidency of Colombia and was preparing to face enemies from all quarters, not least Peru.

The end of the Bolivian Constitution was in fact brought by the Colombian troops that still remained in Peru. At the end of January 1827 they organized a mutiny, stirred by the liberal propaganda arriving from New Granada, discontent with the Venezuelan leadership, and lack

[27] Letter from La Fuente to Bolívar, Arequipa, 18 December 1826, in *Memorias del General O'Leary*, Tomo X, Caracas: La Gaceta Oficial, 1880, p. 195.

[28] Letter from Santa Cruz to Gamarra, Lima, 12 November 1826, in *Archivo Histórico del Mariscal Andrés de Santa Cruz*, pp. 227, 228.

[29] Letter from Bolívar to Santa Cruz, Caracas, 8 June 1827, in *Bolívar y Santa Cruz Epistolario*, p. 75.

of pay.[30] A day later the municipal corporation of Lima met, in spite of having been suppressed by the Life-long Constitution, and agreed to return to the 1823 charter. Santa Cruz was at the summer retreat of Chorrillos, just outside Lima, when the troops took up arms, and he remained there as the municipal authority named him interim president. He arrived in Lima only two hours later and convened Congress to choose which constitution to follow. He was convinced this was the only honorable option and, following Bolívar's advice, he took on the challenge of leading the country of which he considered himself to be a citizen. To La Fuente, he wrote that he wanted to abandon public life as soon as possible, but that he would always remain a Peruvian citizen.[31] Not only did he consider himself Peruvian, but his then friend – but soon to be foe – Agustín Gamarra also believed him to be one. In a letter to La Fuente, the prefect of Cuzco assured him that at the moment the army should only be led by a Peruvian, and in fact at the moment it should be no other than either himself or Santa Cruz.[32]

The army was now at the center of politics, and it was particularly important to the way in which Santa Cruz, Gamarra, and La Fuente, the three most powerful men in Peru, understood politics. Much of their correspondence was dedicated to exchanging information on the organization of troops, the men most suited to lead each battalion, and how to maintain the loyalty of their soldiers. The three men had their bases of power in the south, and because their apprenticeship of war had been in the army in the Andean provinces, the army of the south was particularly strong. British traveler Samuel Haigh noted that Santa Cruz was always accompanied by military men. He wrote in his diary that whenever the president attended public functions, "he would travel in a coach drawn by four black horses flanked by a dozen dragoons in red uniforms, and hats similar to those worn by our royal guards . . . also in the theater he would have a military guard at the entrance and at the door of his box."[33]

[30] Letter from Santa Cruz to La Fuente, Lima, 31 January 1827, in *Archivo Histórico del Mariscal Andrés de Santa Cruz*, p. 242.
[31] Letter from Santa Cruz to La Fuente, Lima, 4 February 1827, in *Archivo Histórico del Mariscal Andrés de Santa Cruz*, p. 243.
[32] Letter from Gamarra to La Fuente, Cuzco, April 25 1827, in *Gran Mariscal Agustín Gamarra, Epistolario*. Edited by Alberto Tauro, Lima: Universidad Nacional Mayor de San Marcos, 1952, p. 67.
[33] Samuel Haigh, *Bosquejo del Perú entre 1826 y 1827*, in CDIP, XXVII "Relaciones de Viajeros," vol. 3, pp. 41–65, 61.

There was, however, a crucial difference in the way in which Gamarra and Santa Cruz understood their roles as leaders. In May 1827, Gamarra, an ardent Peruvian nationalist, began the process of distancing himself from Santa Cruz. Gamarra believed that Santa Cruz was not acting strongly enough against the country's enemies, but still accepted him as a fellow citizen. In the same letter in which he assured La Fuente that the country should only be led by a Peruvian, he complained of Santa Cruz's moderation: what Gamarra described as his need to promote public virtue.[34] Gamarra believed that military men should remain united against those whom he described as the "doctors" – meaning lawyers – who he believed detested the military. In spite of this, Gamarra chose not to take his place in Congress, as a representative of Cuzco, waiting instead for news of the political developments from afar. Santa Cruz claimed in his letters not to be interested in the presidency. He assured La Fuente that in spite of what most people thought, he had not taken command of the country to remain as its president, and that his only ambition was that a strong leader would be chosen so he could leave the country.[35] Days later, General José La Mar was elected to the presidency, but because he was away in his native Cuenca, Santa Cruz remained in Peru, although stepping aside and leaving the running of government to Congress until La Mar's arrival.

Separated from political affairs in Peru and with a great desire to leave Lima, Santa Cruz was soon implicated in conspiratorial rumors in Bolivia. His relationship with Sucre had always been fraught; during 1827 it broke beyond repair. Santa Cruz had viewed Sucre with suspicion ever since the Colombian troops had mutinied in Lima. He had written to both La Fuente and Gamarra that they should be careful with Sucre, especially when he offered to come to Peru to help. In August, Santa Cruz wrote Sucre a strongly worded letter in which he declared, "I have not served the country where I was born, it is true, but I have not offended it by serving Peru and obeying those who have given me this mandate."[36] A month later, he wrote to the Prefect of La Paz assuring him that he had had no part in any conspiracy in Bolivia. Santa Cruz

[34] Letter from Gamarra to La Fuente, Cuzco, 25 April 1827, in *Gran Mariscal Agustín Gamarra, Epistolario*, p. 69.
[35] Letter from Santa Cruz to La Fuente, Lima, 5 June 1827, in *Archivo Histórico del Mariscal Andrés de Santa Cruz*, pp. 265, 266.
[36] Letter from Santa Cruz to Sucre, Lima, August 1827, in *Archivo Histórico del Mariscal Andrés de Santa Cruz*, pp. 275, 276.

was adamant that he did not even exchange letters with anyone outside of his immediate family.

Santa Cruz was seen as the natural head of a party in opposition to Sucre. The Venezuelan general had important enemies in both Peru and Bolivia, and by then the idea of a federation had been completely discarded. As the Bolivarian edifice lay in ruins and a new constitution was discussed in the Peruvian Congress, in January 1828 Santa Cruz was finally sent by the government of Peru on an official commission to Buenos Aires.

## RETURN TO BOLIVIA

Santa Cruz arrived in Chile in April and was forced to remain in Santiago, because early snowfall covered all Andean passes and further travel was impossible. At first, he was bitterly disappointed, but soon he realized this was a unique opportunity to observe the country that had experienced the least upheaval after independence. The political situation in Argentina was so unstable that his diplomatic assignment could not have been carried out anyway. His letters show how his observation of Chile attuned his ideas about government, and the way in which he was inspired by the country's stability and prosperity. He declared that in Chile everyone was not only free, but also moderate. Political debate, he argued, was possible because of the absence of "turbulent men."[37] Santa Cruz was also quick to point out that Chile, because of its geographical position, did not have to fear anyone and could instead take an offensive position in the Pacific.[38] In letters to his friends in Peru, he was even more candid and showed his envy for the calm and moderate political passions that characterized Chile. The general was surprised that, in the context of constitutional debate, there was dissent, but that it never resulted in the open confrontation so common in Peru. He put it down to the Chilean character, which he believed was seldom involved in disturbances.

The situation was quite different in Bolivia, where Sucre found his position more difficult every day. Colombian troops were anxiously waiting for their delayed salaries, and Santa Cruz's supporters were

[37] Letter from Santa Cruz to Domingo Cáceres, Santiago de Chile, 28 August 1828, in *Archivo Histórico del Mariscal Andrés de Santa Cruz*, pp. 301, 302.

[38] Letter from Santa Cruz to the Minister of Foreign Affaire of Peru, Santiago, 12 May 1828, in *Archivo Histórico del Mariscal Andrés de Santa Cruz*, p. 305.

discontented after his departure from Peru. Gamarra stationed his army at the border, and bellicose language peppered the exchanges between Peru and Colombia. In Peru, Bolívar and his acolytes were seen as the biggest danger. Gamarra accused Sucre of being a liability if he continued to attempt to be "a Colombian general, a subject of Bolívar and president of Upper Peru."[39] Days after this letter was written, after a prolonged press campaign, an uprising broke out in La Paz. Even though it was controlled, Sucre felt compelled to meet Gamarra at the lake. In March, both leaders agreed that all Colombian troops would leave as soon as a new congress was elected. The election rallied anti-Colombian sentiment, and during a second uprising, at the end of April, Sucre was shot. Gamarra crossed the Desaguadero, took the injured president prisoner, and forced the interim president to sign a peace treaty.

Sucre was allowed to recover, but was forced to officially relinquish supreme power to the Constituent Congress that met in Chuquisaca in August 1828. In his last speech, he asked all free men of Bolivia – he called them the sons of Bolívar – to work constantly to maintain their independence. He reflected on the many successes of his brief government, as well as on the difficulties it had faced, particularly in implementing the direct taxation that sought to replace Indian contribution. Sucre did not think that the charter Bolívar had produced was the one best suited for the country. He warned representatives to be wary of annexing the southern departments of Peru to Bolivia, because the federation between the two countries had not been accepted by Congress, and he did not think it was a sincere proposal.[40] After Sucre abandoned the country for good, Gamarra fulfilled his promise and left Bolivia as well. Soon after, at the end of August 1828, Congress elected Santa Cruz to the presidency.

This election forced Santa Cruz to confront his anxieties over his nationality. Before his election he had written to Gamarra, the only person he addressed with the informal *tu*, "you need no further proof that I am your best friend, nor that my wishes and my interests are for the union of two 'peoples' (Pueblos) that I love equally."[41] He added that he disliked being called a foreigner in Peru for the sole

---

[39] Letter from Gamarra to Sucre, Lampa, 11 December 1827, in *Gran Mariscal Agustín Gamarra, Epistolario*, p. 84.

[40] Antonio José de Sucre, *Mensaje del Presidente de Bolivia al Congreso Extraordinario de 1828, Chuquisaca 2 de Agosto*, Valparaíso: El Mercurio, 1828.

[41] Letter from Santa Cruz to Gamarra, Santiago, 22 July 1828, in *Archivo Histórico del Mariscal Andrés de Santa Cruz*, p. 327.

reason of having been born in La Paz. Santa Cruz explained he had dedicated all his effort and his very existence to Peru; his best friends, his family, and his closest relations where there. In this same letter, written when Gamarra was in Bolivia, Santa Cruz made it clear that this was not the right moment to talk about a union with Peru. He understood that the only way this could be achieved would be by convincing people of the benefits of such a union.

To his friend La Fuente, Santa Cruz wrote that he was afraid news of his election was to be confirmed, because even though he would be flattered, he would be heartbroken if he had to sever his ties with the Republic of Peru. His letter to his close associate in Lima, Simón Rávago, had the same tenor. In it he explained that he was torn between the wish to accept the votes of the country where he was born, and the desire and duty not to be separated from the place to which he felt most personally linked. Ten days later, he again wrote to La Fuente that although he thought it impossible to reject the presidency, he had no ambition to govern, and that he only wanted to continue helping the people. Crucially, he also declared: "I will never allow myself to be separated from Peruvian service."[42]

Just over a month later, he came to terms with having been elected president of Bolivia. In Peru, the climate of extreme nationalism during conflict with Colombia made it clear: he had no real role to play in Peru. To his friend Rávago he confided that he was only making a sacrifice and taking the post to ensure the existence of Bolivia, hoping he could improve the situation of his country.[43] He had, in a matter of weeks, come to terms with the impossibility of ruling Peru and became reconciled with the idea of being the Bolivian president instead.

While Santa Cruz was in Chile reflecting on whether to accept the presidency of Bolivia, Peru and Colombia began hostilities. Bolívar feared that Peru wanted to annex Bolivia. Gamarra's invasion of La Paz was therefore only the prelude to the larger conflict as Colombia declared war on Peru. The causes cited were the nonpayment of the debt from independence, a dispute over territory in the northern border, and Peruvian intervention in the ousting of Sucre. Most of the action

---

[42] Letters from Santa Cruz to La Fuente and Simón Rávago, Santiago, 3 and 8 September 1828, in *Archivo Histórico del Mariscal Andrés de Santa Cruz*, pp. 345–53.

[43] Letter from Santa Cruz to Rávago, Santiago, 24 October 1828, in *Archivo Histórico del Mariscal Andrés de Santa Cruz*, p. 361.

took place in the outskirts of the port of Guayaquil, pitting La Mar against Bolívar and Sucre. The main point of contention was which country should have control of the port of Guayaquil, as a reaction to what Peruvians considered the aggressive behavior of their northern neighbors. In reality it was also due in great part to La Mar wanting to dominate the area where he was born and incorporate it into Peru, and therefore drown all debate over his nationality, as well as to Bolívar's fear of Peruvian territorial ambitions, in both the north and south. Santa Cruz knew this area well because he had fought there in 1821 against the Spanish with Sucre. He wrote to La Mar and Gamarra with instructions based on his experiences that gave him a good idea of the strategy most likely to be employed.

From his camp in the north of Peru, Gamarra wrote to Santa Cruz. He explained that it had been his greatest wish that in the elections of the previous year Santa Cruz, instead of La Mar, could have been elected president of Peru. Had this happened, he assured Santa Cruz, he would now be the savior of Peru, and there would be no further talk of Gamarra's ambition for the presidency. Gamarra also made it clear that he hoped Santa Cruz would "calculate where you will be more useful to our common cause. We are going to save the country together."[44]

After much thought and anguish, Santa Cruz officially accepted the post of president of Bolivia in December 1828. He wrote to the vice president that he would sacrifice everything for the existence of his country of birth. As he traveled through southern Peru back to Bolivia, he received a letter from Bolívar, who assured him that in spite of the circumstances, he knew he was his sincere friend. Bolívar thanked Santa Cruz for having defended him while in Chile. He wished him the best as president of Bolivia and asked him to look after this country that was so close to his heart.

Santa Cruz left Chile only when the official permission arrived from the Peruvian government allowing him to keep his Peruvian nationality even as president of Bolivia. Once he had reached Arequipa, however, Santa Cruz no longer held this post. The turmoil that developed in the aftermath of Gamarra's intervention in Bolivia resulted in a mutiny that installed Colonel Pedro Blanco instead. Born in Cochabamba, Blanco had a career that was identical to those of Gamarra and Santa Cruz, having joined the army with Goyeneche and Pezuela, changing sides

---

[44] Letter from Gamarra to Santa Cruz, Piura, 4 April 1829, in *Gran Mariscal Agustín Gamarra, Epistolario*, p. 133.

in the early 1820s, then fighting in Junín and Ayacucho. According to his contemporaries, Blanco could not even sign his name and was an ideal candidate to support Gamarra in his quest to dominate Bolivia.[45] Blanco's presidency was extremely short-lived: just over a month after taking power, he was killed. In response to this, Vice President José Miguel Velasco dissolved the Conventional Assembly, calling for the return of Santa Cruz and elections to confirm him in his post.

On receiving the news, Santa Cruz again exercised caution and gave much thought to his next move. He wrote to his closest associates in Lima and assured everyone in Bolivia that he would take the presidency only if confirmed by the people. Meanwhile, he accepted a commission in the Peruvian armed forces to command the army of the south, organized after Gamarra left to fight in the north. In many of his letters, Santa Cruz declared that he believed peace and stability would be achieved only if a professional army was established and if the men who served in it were well looked after. Santa Cruz was convinced that anarchy was largely due to the demoralization of troops. To General Velasco he wrote that "the principle of order in the republic was the army and that utmost care should be given to its reorganization."[46]

Santa Cruz believed that the only way in which he could legitimately take the post of President of Bolivia was after his confirmation by the electoral colleges, called for in April 1829. To that effect, he remained in Arequipa in charge of the Peruvian army of the south. He was adamant that the constitution had to be reformed and that he had to have full backing to install the necessary reforms if he was to accept the presidency. To his supporters in Bolivia, he repeatedly wrote that he was willing to make all the sacrifices needed, but that he would do so only when his legitimacy could no longer be questioned. He insisted that otherwise there would be no point in taking over the presidency.[47] He did not have to wait for long , and by March, Santa Cruz was once again called to the presidency. He immediately wrote to the Congressional Commission in Lima seeking authorization to take the post, in order not to lose his Peruvian citizenship.

[45]  Quoted in Alvaro Perez del Castillo, *Bolivia, Colombia, Chile y el Perú: Diplomacia y Política 1825–1904,* La Paz: Los Amigos del Libro, p. 66.
[46]  Letter from Santa Cruz to General Francisco López, Arequipa, 24 February 1829, in *Archivo Histórico del Mariscal Andrés de Santa Cruz,* vol. II, p. 43.
[47]  Letter from Santa Cruz to General Francisco López, Arequipa, 24 February 1829, in *Archivo Histórico del Mariscal Andrés de Santa Cruz,* vol. II, p. 41.

Just as Santa Cruz prepared to take the presidency of Bolivia, Gamarra struck against La Mar in northern Peru and La Fuente did the same in Lima. Gamarra had said that the three men should be "three bodies in one soul." By June they were in control of a vast territory.[48] They had often talked informally about creating a larger country that would encompass all the provinces of their birth. It was at this point, however, that different interpretations of how the union between Peru and Bolivia should materialize emerged. Gamarra had capitalized on the defeat of La Mar in Colombia and deported him to Costa Rica. In Lima, La Fuente was "called" to power by the army and the people who were afraid of anarchy, whereas in Bolivia, after his confirmation by the electoral colleges, Santa Cruz was in charge. Throughout 1829 Gamarra did not write to Santa Cruz, and the latter became so distraught that he resorted to writing to Gamarra's wife, Francisca Zubiaga de Gamarra, who was still in Cuzco. Meanwhile, in Lima, La Fuente organized an election where he was confirmed as vice president and Gamarra as president.

Santa Cruz accepted his post as president of Bolivia only after the congressional commission from Peru confirmed that he would be able to maintain his Peruvian nationality. Although he was granted this privilege, it was made conditional on approval by Congress, which was not in session at the time. Once again, Santa Cruz's correspondence shows that he was anxious to maintain his links with Peru, although he came to understand that he would not be able to take over the presidency in Peru. Instead, he offered his support to Gamarra and La Fuente from Bolivia, assuring them that they could count on the 4,000 men Santa Cruz had in the newly organized army. He made it clear, however, that he would only cross into Peru if called by its people.[49]

The union of Peru and Bolivia was one of Santa Cruz's most cherished dreams, and he spent much energy working in conjunction with Gamarra and La Fuente to achieve this goal. Some, however, believe that he also worked independently through the Masonic Lodge he established during his time in Arequipa, which sought to segregate southern Peru. One of the members of the lodge "Independencia Peruana" broke his oath of silence and exposed its aims as the union of the southern

[48] The letter published by La Fuente is quoted in Jorge Basadre, *Historia de la República del Perú*, Lima: Historia, 1961, vol. I, p. 258.

[49] Letter from Santa Cruz to General Aparicio, La Paz, 1 July 1829, in *Archivo Histórico del Mariscal Andrés de Santa Cruz*, vol. II, p. 107.

provinces to Bolivia.[50] On 9 August 1829, two colonels in the Peruvian army, who were looking to improve their standing with the government, captured one of Santa Cruz's closest associates. They accused him of wanting to send arms to the pro-Bolivian prefect of Puno. Their correspondence was intercepted by the Peruvian government, and when it was deciphered, it was alleged that the letters written by Santa Cruz proved the General was working to take over southern Peru. The letters appeared to show that Santa Cruz intended to annex all territory up the River Pampas, in the department of Ayacucho. The authenticity of these letters, which came to light during the judicial case, is disputed even today by those in Santa Cruz's camp. The letters talk brazenly of the establishment of a federation in southern Peru, under the protection of Bolivia, yet no other letters written by Santa Cruz are so open about any plans of union. The day before the men in Arequipa were taken, Santa Cruz had written to both Gamarra and La Fuente. To the former he promised that he could have troops on the border by October and to the latter, he sent assurances that even though many of his friends and supporters wanted him to return to Peru to become president, this was impossible because of his commitments to Bolivia.[51]

It was in the aftermath of this episode that Santa Cruz began to talk about Bolivia as his *patria*. From now on, he made it abundantly clear, his responsibility lay with the country of his birth. In letter after letter, he assured all his correspondents that it was impossible for him to leave Bolivia. He believed that his future was intrinsically linked with Bolivia's prosperity, and no matter how many friends and relations he had in Peru, he could no longer consider abandoning his people. This was a marked change from the time of his reluctant acceptance of posts of responsibility in La Paz in 1825, his commitments to Peru in 1827, and the repeated doubts he expressed about taking the presidency, only a year before when he was in Chile as the Peruvian representative. Santa Cruz would not abandon his dream of uniting Peru and Bolivia, but after 1829 he was no longer interested in doing so from Peru. He now dedicated all his energy and efforts to strengthening and organizing Bolivia, which, like a modern-day Alexander, he sought to turn into the Macedonia or Sparta of America.

[50]  Alvaro Pérez del Castillo, *Bolivia, Colombia, Chile y el Perú Diplomacia y Política 1824–1904*, La Paz: Los Amigos del Libro, 1980, pp. 76–7.
[51]  Letters from Santa Cruz to Gamarra and La Fuente, Oruro, 8 August 1829, in *Archivo Histórico del Mariscal Andrés de Santa Cruz*, vol. II, pp. 133–5.

The creation of a new country had a great impact on Santa Cruz, who saw himself, and was considered by his peers, as Peruvian. In the years that followed the establishment of Bolivia, Santa Cruz had to come to terms with the fact that he was increasingly regarded as a foreigner in Peru. After his failure to secure the Peruvian presidency and his sojourn in Chile, he finally came to terms with being a Bolivian.

The process by which Santa Cruz embraced his new nationality was complex and had much to do with his realization that he no longer had a space in Peruvian politics. Once he took over the Bolivian presidency, he did so with all his energy, convinced that the best possible future was to be the leader of a strong country that could eventually be united with Peru. Although he wholeheartedly embraced his responsibility as president of Bolivia and worked hard to modernize the country, Santa Cruz always kept a flicker of hope that he one day would be in charge of Peru as well.

# CHAPTER 4

# The Genesis of the Peru-Bolivia

# Confederation

One of the most difficult issues to resolve after independence was that of identity. The problem was particularly acute in border areas, and individuals who felt ties to more than one new republic found it most challenging. This was the case for Santa Cruz. He had tried to remain linked to Peruvian politics, but eventually had to come to terms with being limited in what he could do politically in Peru, because his enemies had successfully portrayed him as a foreigner. Although he accepted the presidency of Bolivia and took to it with all his energy and determination, he was still convinced that it was possible and advantageous to unite Peru and Bolivia in a federation. Santa Cruz was not alone, and indeed there were many important links between these territories that made a union possible to imagine. Many people in southern Peru and northern Bolivia were convinced that they belonged together. Santa Cruz was persuaded that the union would become a reality only if Bolivia became strong. So he dedicated all his energy to consolidating his country and to strengthening the economy and the army. He believed that if he was able to end political wrangling and have the backing of an organized military, he would be able to convince Peruvians to join a mutually beneficial federation. Peru, on the other hand, was marred by instability, because Santa Cruz's ability as an administrator was matched by Gamarra's inability to maintain control in Peru.

While Bolivia prospered and remained at peace in the 1830s, the Peruvian government had to face a multitude of uprisings, as well as an openly hostile congress dominated by the liberals. Gamarra was unable to control the army. Once his constitutional period in power ended in 1834, and a rival military officer was made president, there was again civil war in Peru. This chapter charts how the country descended into chaos and how Santa Cruz intervened, taking every opportunity to try to create a federation. Instability was so acute that Santa Cruz was called to assist, and the first seeds for the union of the country were planted. He agreed to provide help on the condition that he be invited by the Peruvian people, preferably by the National Convention. But the situation escalated to such a degree that when the official invitation came, Santa Cruz refrained from accepting.

Calm returned to Peru, but only fleetingly. Months later, in 1835, a new, more confusing civil war erupted. This time Santa Cruz did take his chances and, with the support of the army he had created and trained, took control of anarchic Peru. This was the genesis of the Confederation that is explored in this chapter – born with nearly as much opposition as support. Santa Cruz was able to bring his project to fruition because of his sheer determination and the backing of elites in southern Peru who were key allies. They had been won over by the prospect of becoming the center of a powerful federation and free from the administrative control of Lima. Santa Cruz advocated the creation of a southern Peruvian state, and the great majority of the elites and people of Arequipa, Cuzco, Puno, Tacna, and Moquegua agreed. The Bolivian Assembly, dominated so completely by Santa Cruz's backers, happily accepted the union. The north of Peru was more difficult to convince, but given that most of his enemies were in exile and the Assembly was tightly controlled, the federation was approved.

## The Consolidation of Bolivia

Bolivian politics had been shaped by the county's relationship to Peru, but in the 1830s Santa Cruz and his government began paying more attention to its southern neighbor. The confrontations between the Federalists and the Unitarians in Argentina began spilling over the border. This was also an important turning point for Andrés de Santa Cruz, as he retreated from Peruvian politics and dedicated all his energy to the establishment of a strong government in Bolivia. The years following Sucre's expulsion by Gamarra's cronies in 1828 had been anarchic. Even this short invasion did not completely dampen the prospects of union with Peru. In the years that followed, the threat of attack from Peru remained open and obsessed Santa Cruz. He blamed Gamarra and his excesses for the economic ruin of Bolivia. To rebuild the country, Santa Cruz issued a blanket amnesty. He called the best qualified to serve in his administration, regardless of their previous political sympathies.[1] He focused on reorganizing finances and the law; but above all, to ensure that his country was protected, he set out to organize the army. He believed that it was only possible to consolidate his government by having strong armed forces. This was to be the guarantee against invasion.

One of his first steps was to write a new rule book for the army. He sent a copy of it to a friend in Arequipa, explaining that his aim was to ensure that the military was no longer the cause of problems, but instead their solution. Santa Cruz believed that to achieve stability, organization was needed. This is why he chose to have the military, as an institution, at the center of the state. One of his first moves was to get rid of difficult people. He then appointed younger men, who would train to become officers. Santa Cruz believed that soldiers would exhibit excellent discipline if they were well fed and clothed and were not subjected to arbitrary punishment. He believed that the success of this policy would be seen in the decrease of deserters each month. He kept his door open to both soldiers and officers, and he was receptive to their complaints.[2] Furthermore, an armory was set up in Oruro, where Santa Cruz ordered sixteen pieces of artillery to be prepared; eight should have what were described as trains to carry them into battle. He also gave instructions to give artisans in the area tools and raw materials to build 300 lances and produce all the equipment needed by 500 mounted lancers.

Not only was Santa Cruz interested in ensuring that there was enough material for the army to fight, but he also called the National Guard into service. Instructions were sent to Oruro and Chuquisaca stressing that the most important positions were not to be given to officers, but to honest citizens interested in maintaining public order. Santa Cruz believed that *civicos*, as they were called, could be of variable quality. He also gave instructions for the creation of a special battalion in Potosí. The employees of the mint were given the possibility to organize and look after their place of work. A month after these instructions were

---

[1]   Details of the *Ley del Olvido* can be found in *El General Santa-Cruz explica su conducta pública y los móviles de su política en la presidencia de Bolivia y en la Protección de la Confederación Perú-Boliviana*. La Paz: Tipografía Salesiana, 1924 [1840], p. 14.

[2]   Letter from Santa Cruz to Antonio Seoane, La Paz, 25 November 1829, in *Archivo Histórico del Mariscal Andrés de Santa Cruz*, Andrés de Santa Cruz Schuhkrafft, La Paz: Universidad Mayor de San Andrés, 1981, vol. II, p. 174.

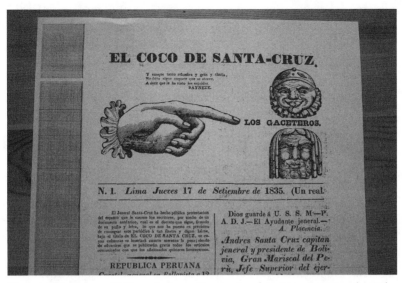

Figure 3. Newspaper *El Coco de Santa Cruz*, printed in Lima in 1835, from the collection at Yale University.

sent, eleven battalions and four cavalry regiments of the National Guard had been created. The enthusiasm for the cause was evident not only in La Paz, as could be expected, but also in Chuquisaca.

One of the National Guard battalions, composed of *literatos*, or men of letters, asked Santa Cruz to be their colonel. He happily accepted, because he considered the creation of such a force an example of patriotism and pride in the rule of law. Interest in the development of the guard was so strong, and the involvement of all classes in society so generalized, that even professionals such as lawyers, doctors, journalists, and teachers joined. In 1831, for instance, a newspaper called *The National Guard of Bolivia* was printed in La Paz. Next to the mandatory propaganda section, accusing Peru of all kinds of abuse, there were weekly articles on what was described as the science of war.[3] Young officers were counseled to learn the art of war from the Roman legions by reading the classics. Editors also recommended the study of the campaigns of Frederick the Great and Napoleon. The knowledge of contemporary war theory was evident: an author who published there made reference to the *Principles of Strategy* by Carl von Clausewitz, claiming he had read

---

[3]  *La Guardia Nacional del Bolivia*, No. 19, La Paz, 6 August 1831.

it in French.[4] The publication was clearly geared to the men of letters who were now involved in Santa Cruz's proudest creation: the National Guard.

All efforts to develop the armed forces were limited to ground troops, because it was clear to Santa Cruz that there was no point in investing in a navy. Instead, he believed Bolivia should seek the support of Britain and France in protecting its port. He argued in his letters that the creation of a strong military culture would ensure peace. Santa Cruz believed that the only way his nation would be respected by its neighbors was by becoming militarily strong.

Despite his claims of Bolivian patriotism, he invested heavily in dressing the members of the army with cloth purchased in Cuzco. His relationship to the cloth producers of this city was later tested when they attempted to increase the agreed cost from $3^3/_4$ of real to 5 reales. At this point he threatened to rescind the contract, but did not do so when the right price was agreed. This was his desired outcome, as he considered the cloth produced in Cuzco to be of better quality and more durable than any other.

Santa Cruz maintained relationships with many friends and relations in the Inca capital that were further strengthened with his marriage to his cousin, the Cuzqueña Francisca Cernadas, in late 1829.[5] Although she was the daughter of a former Audiencia judge from Cuzco, they were in fact married in Arequipa.[6] Santa Cruz assured his close friends that he had done so out of obligation because she was an orphan, but it did help that she was seen as virtuous. He claimed he had married out of commitment to the nation. He chose a woman from Cuzco as a spouse, even if differences with Peru over the control of Arica, which

[4]  This was most probably a translation of the *Two Letters on Strategy* addressed to the Prussian general-staff officer Major von Roeder on 22 and 24 December 1827, because his classic *On War* was published only after his death in 1831. There were at least a couple of German officers among those close to Santa Cruz, and many others who spoke fluent French.

[5]  She was the daughter of his aunt Eulalia Cámara, who had married a Pedro Antonio Cernadas Bermudez, details in his letter to Pío Tristán, La Paz, 11 February 1830, in *Archivo Histórico del Mariscal Andrés de Santa Cruz*, vol. II, p. 204.

[6]  Scarlett O'Phelan Godoy, "Santa Cruz y Gamarra: El Proyecto de la Confederación y el Control Político del Sur Andino." In *Guerra, región y nación. La Confederación Perú Boliviana 1836–1839*. Santiago de Chile: Gobierno de Chile, Universidad Andrés Bello y Centro de Investigaciones Diego Barros Arana, 2009 Carlos Donoso y Jaime Rosenblitt eds., p. 24.

had dogged Bolivia from its creation, continued. To defuse the conflict over the main trading port, Santa Cruz decided to lay the issue of Arica to rest and develop the port that had been assigned to the country at independence. This was the port of Cobija, nestled among the salty plains in the desert of Atacama. Santa Cruz passed decrees to divert all trade to this new port. He was hopeful that with the development of a customs house, there would be a good stream of income and government would not have to depend entirely on the tax paid by the Indians. The success of this measure was immediate. In February 1830, Santa Cruz assured the official in charge of the customs house in Cobija that trade in Arica had been completely paralyzed, thanks to the new laws.[7] Santa Cruz hoped that in two years, the port at Cobija would develop so much that it would become the most important port for the country. He considered that they should endeavor to achieve this even if Bolivia did eventually gain control of Arica. Measures were also taken to build defenses to protect Cobija from potential sea attacks. On a visit in 1832, Santa Cruz personally oversaw the digging of wells to provide the desert with water, and soon afterwards he declared Cobija an open port where ships did not have to pay import taxes.[8]

According to his supporters and even his enemies, management was one of Santa Cruz's greatest strengths. He was hands-on and kept abreast of all the major issues in the country. He was particularly keen to ensure that financial matters were managed as efficiently as possible. To this effect, he wrote letters to his administrators when he felt that the numbers did not add up, and expected them to explain themselves fully. Suspicion of wrongdoing was enough for Santa Cruz to replace officials with others whom he felt he could trust more. In Cobija, for instance, Santa Cruz installed a man whom he affectionately called *Indio*.

To be able to control all aspects of government, he devised a system by which he would be constantly traveling throughout the country. He divided his time between La Paz and Chuquisaca as evenly as possible, as well as spending some time in the other important cities. He began his first journey in late April 1831, taking the road to Yungas, then on to Cochabamba and Chuquisaca, not returning to La Paz until the end of the year.

[7]  Letter to General Lopez, La Paz, 4 February 1830, in *Archivo Histórico del Mariscal Andrés de Santa Cruz*, vol. II, p. 201.
[8]  *El General Santa-Cruz explica su conducta pública y los móviles de su política en la presidencia de Bolivia y en la Protección de la Confederación Peru-Boliviana.* La Paz: Tipografía Salesiana, 1924 [1840], p. 35.

In addition to strengthening the armed forces, one of the areas that Santa Cruz wanted to foster was education. To do so he was adamant that the Spanish intellectual José Joaquín de Mora, whom he had met in Santiago and with whom his nephews had studied, should come to Bolivia to take charge of education policy. He offered Mora 6,000 pesos as a salary and to cover all of his transfer costs. The investment in education also included infrastructure. Primary schools were to open in every town, and in every canton in every province. All main cities were to have a university and schools for higher education, not only for boys, but also for girls. A national system of libraries was to be built. Technical training was not forgotten, with a school of mining opened in Potosí and a school of sciences in Oruro. This would oversee the creation of the first textile factory in Bolivia.[9]

Santa Cruz was aware that he needed a workforce with suitable skills to sustain his educational reforms, so he paid for a number of young men to travel to Europe and train in arts and sciences.[10] He also asked for support from the French consul in Chile, pleading with him to send qualified Frenchmen to be educators. A Mr. Segers was hired to create a series of schools for 3,000 pesos a year.

Santa Cruz was close to the French consul and was often in touch asking for support, not only with educational matters, but also for protection against Peru. He requested backing from the French navy to look after the port of Cobija and Bolivian citizens in the event of a Peruvian invasion. He also worked hard to obtain official recognition by the court in Paris, finally receiving it in mid-1831. To thank the French consul in Chile, Santa Cruz offered to send him some typical Bolivian animals such as vicuñas, llamas, alpacas, leopards, and parrots.

French official recognition may have been as important to Santa Cruz as receiving backing from Bolívar. A year earlier, he had written to the Liberator explaining that he had taken over the presidency, but had only been able to do so by rejecting Bolivar's 1826 Constitution. He detailed the way in which he had been appointed president, and how he had dedicated all his efforts to strengthening the executive. Congress had not been called into session, he said, because the scheming previous assembly had led to the dissolution of government and a state of anarchy.

---

[9] *El General Santa-Cruz explica su conducta pública*, pp. 40–42.
[10] *Mensaje de S. E. el Presidente de Bolivia a las Camaras Constitucionales de 1833*, p. 261.

He went on to portray Congress as a workshop for disorder and public disgrace. Santa Cruz presented himself as the savior of the country, which he described as a political skeleton, a cadaver he had revived by reestablishing the lost morality of the army. He proudly noted how the situation had been completely reversed in only eight months.[11] To Pío Tristán in Arequipa, Santa Cruz confided that he was fearful of the idea of installing a congress, even though he knew that sooner or later he would have to do so. He claimed that this fear was caused by the disorder he saw in the entire continent.[12]

Santa Cruz arrived in Chuquisaca to much acclaim in June 1831, and he finally saw a good opportunity to call Congress into session. He was still governing with an interim authorization from an assembly of dubious legality and wanted to ensure his legitimacy. He decided, however, to postpone this measure once again because he thought it best to advance with the organization of the country, and because he feared the representatives would hinder rather than help his attempts to build a solid state. Soon enough, however, he changed his mind again, and on 24 June 1831, he installed an assembly to which he proudly presented a detailed picture of his achievements. In his public address to Congress, he not only listed the many public works he had begun, such as the construction of roads and bridges that began economic regeneration after decades of war, but also enumerated the new laws he had drafted, the support given to schools, and his innovation in the tax system.

Santa Cruz spent most of his time as president trying to improve the administration of the country. The most important aspect for him was the reorganization on the army. He made this such a high priority because he was convinced that the Peruvian president, Gamarra, wanted to invade Bolivia. He accused the minister sent from Lima of trying to foster rebellion within the country, and wrote several letters to Gamarra asking him to reconsider his bellicose language. To counter these perceived threats, Santa Cruz sent a special mission to Peru, with the aim of finding a peaceful solution to the simmering confrontation. He also began an aggressive epistolary offensive, writing to all his friends, acquaintances, and former allies in Peru, stating Bolivia's

---

[11]  Letter from Santa Cruz to Antonio Seoane, La Paz, 25 November 1829, in *Archivo Histórico del Mariscal Andrés de Santa Cruz*, vol. II, pp. 196–7.

[12]  Letter from Santa Cruz to Pío Tristán, La Paz, 11 February 1830, in *Archivo Histórico del Mariscal Andrés de Santa Cruz*, vol. II, p. 204.

position and asking for their support. He assured General Miller, for instance, that "Peru was his affective homeland, the land where he had achieved honor."[13] At the same time, he wrote to all his friends in Colombia, and especially to the newly appointed president of Ecuador, Juan José Flores, seeking an alliance against a possible Peruvian invasion. The conditions set by Gamarra to settle a final border treaty with Bolivia were, according to Santa Cruz, tantamount to a declaration of war. These messages continued to be exchanged as Santa Cruz wrote to his close friend and relation Juan José Larrea – an important landowner and politician in Cuzco – assuring him that he would never declare war on Peru or take up arms unless he was forced to do so by Gamarra.[14]

The special envoys Santa Cruz sent to Peru had been instructed to organize a conference between the two presidents, taking advantage of the fact that Gamarra had traveled to Cuzco to quell a rebellion. Negotiations on the possible meeting near the lake were to begin as soon as possible, and many letters were exchanged. Santa Cruz wrote to the Peruvian president, reminding him of their childhood friendship and expressing his hope that they would be able to resolve their differences.

Their meeting was not a success, however. Gamarra continued to ask for import duties to be lowered to four pesos per transaction, for Bolivia to cede territory around the lake without any indemnity, and for Peru to pay what Santa Cruz described as an imaginary debt for having helped them gain their freedom from Spain. Santa Cruz found these conditions unacceptable. He took them as confirmation that Gamarra wanted to remove him from power. Santa Cruz was, in fact, primarily interested in gaining control over the port of Arica. To that effect he wrote to his minister in Peru, Casimiro Olañeta, instructing him to be careful and to keep his interest in Arica a secret. Santa Cruz was convinced that they would never gain control of the port by asking for it, but instead would have to acquire it as compensation for something else. He told Olañeta that Peru would be reluctant to let Arica go for many reasons, not least because Vice President La Fuente was from Tarapacá, a territory south of Arica. Peru, Santa Cruz concluded, would only see the port go under very extreme circumstances.[15]

[13] Letter from Santa Cruz to Miller, Chuquisaca, 2 October 1830, in *Archivo Histórico del Mariscal Andrés de Santa Cruz*, vol. II, p. 237.

[14] Letter from Santa Cruz to Larrea, Chuquisaca, 27 October 1830, in *Archivo Histórico del Mariscal Andrés de Santa Cruz*, vol. II, p. 266.

[15] Letter from Santa Cruz to Olañeta, La Paz, 3 February 1831, in *Archivo Histórico del Mariscal Andrés de Santa Cruz*, vol. II, p. 305.

Although most of the attention of the Bolivian government was centered on its border with Peru, from 1831 onward the politics of the Argentine Republic and indeed the effects of the wars between the Federalists and the Unitarians began to be felt on Bolivia's southern border. Santa Cruz was close friends with Arenales, the governor of the province of Salta, under whose command Santa Cruz had served during the wars of independence. Santa Cruz therefore offered his support against the threat of the *caudillos* who were on the verge of taking over Arenales's province. The allies of the governor of Salta, the Unitarians, wanted to see the Argentine Republic united with a centralized administration. So Santa Cruz sent Arenales some of the weapons he had brought into Bolivia in case of war with Peru. He then invited the governor of Salta to bring some of his elite troops into Bolivia, to protect them from the threat of the enemy hordes. This was also a strategy to strengthen his rearguard, because Santa Cruz thought it would be useful to have more armed men within his territory. The offer was not accepted. Once the Unitarians were defeated, however, many prominent families from Salta who had supported the Unitarians fled to Bolivia for a long period of exile. After the victory of the Federalists and their fierce *caudillo* Facundo Quiroga, the southern border was no longer peaceful, and Santa Cruz used this fact to argue that he needed to maintain a large army to protect himself.

Military strength was a main point of contention between Peru and Bolivia. Disagreement over how many soldiers each country should have was at the center of the difficulties in agreeing on the final text of a peace treaty. This was compounded by the desire to sign a more encompassing peace agreement that would also include Ecuador and Chile. The fragile balance of power in the region had shifted with the death of Bolívar in 1830. The possibility of a larger Andean Union was buried with him. The perception in Peru was that without Bolívar in Colombia, Santa Cruz was weaker in Bolivia. In this context, negotiations with Olañeta stalled. Back in Bolivia, Olañeta accused Gamarra of having tried to convince him to rebel against Santa Cruz.[16] To prevent war, Chilean mediation was sought, and a new mission was dispatched to Arequipa. With a large Peruvian army stationed in Puno, the representatives who traveled to the other side of Lake Titicaca finally signed a preliminary peace treaty, and negotiations for a commercial agreement began. The

---

[16] *Manifiesto del Ciudadano Casimiro Olañeta, Ministro Plenipotenciario de Bolivia cerca del Gobierno del Perú*, Paz de Ayacucho: Imprenta de Educandas, 1831.

representative needed more than a year to reach the agreement, but still after all that discussion the final documents were not acceptable to both sides. Santa Cruz had initially agreed to reduce his force to 1,000 men, if Peru limited theirs to a proportional smaller number. The final treaty, however, stipulated that Peru would have 3,000 men, and this was unacceptable to Bolivia. In spite of this, the treaties were agreed to in principle, although those clauses were left to be discussed further.

Even though he was obsessed with the possibility of a Peruvian invasion, and dedicated to the development of the armed forces, Santa Cruz never lost sight of his main endeavor: the building of a strong state in Bolivia. He dedicated most of his energy to developing new laws for all areas of government. In 1831, a new constitution was enacted. It was accompanied by new legislation: new civil and penal codes, which aimed to end the colonial legal system. This was one of the lasting legacies of Santa Cruz's time in office; the new laws revolutionized government and are still known as the *crucista* legislation. The constitution, which was reformed in 1834, had several important innovations. Among them was the provision that all Bolivians had a duty to contribute a proportion of their wealth, and to sacrifice their possessions and even their lives, if the country was in danger. In this constitution, Santa Cruz enshrined in law the idea of an itinerant capital. Congress was to decide where government would ultimately reside, but in the meantime this was an interesting way to solve a contentious issue of which city in Bolivia should be the capital. The president was in charge of all military matters, but could only engage the National Guard in their provinces of origin, unless he had the approval of Congress. Presidential power was limited: he could detain a person for only 48 hours, he could not require individuals to give their property to the state without compensation, and he could not travel without a minister. To further aid transparency, the constitution had an article guaranteeing civil liberty, property, and equality at court for every Bolivian. All citizens, and this included Indians, could give their opinion in any forum, and there was complete freedom of speech and of the press. The constitution noted, however, that any group of individuals that made petitions in the name of the "sovereign people" would be considered seditious. The constitution was signed by all the deputies, who included at least one with an indigenous background: Manuel María Urcullo, representative from Chuquisaca.

To build a strong state, Santa Cruz reorganized the tax system. He saw no need to abolish the Indian head tax, now known as "contribution." This was the state's most important source of income, and

Santa Cruz had seen firsthand how the governments of Peru and Bolivia, after abolishing it in 1825, had backtracked when they found themselves bankrupt. Instead the Bolivian president wanted to reform the contribution, and to do so, he enacted a new *Reglamento* in 1831. He organized a *revista* to review the situation of all contributors, with the aim of updating the outdated records from 1784 that were still being used. Each canton, in each province, had to list the number, name, age, and sex of all family members who were subject to the tax, noting the differences between the *originarios* and *forasteros*, because only the former had the right to access communal land. These numbers were to be reviewed every five years.[17] In his speech to Congress in 1831, Santa Cruz described Indians as "commendable for so many reasons, they deserve the just protection of their rights."[18] He claimed to have reduced many of the taxes they had to pay and demanded other measures to be taken to improve the conditions of these citizens, whom he described as hardworking and moderate. After Santa Cruz's reform, the only taxes to be paid by Indians were the contribution, the sales tax known as the *alcabala*, and the tithe paid to the church. His long-term aim was that every Bolivian would contribute through some form of tax.

Taxation was only a piece of the larger economic reform that Santa Cruz saw as the cornerstone of his administration. He believed that all other reforms hinged on the state's ability to fund initiatives. He noted in his speech to Congress that, when he had taken power, both civil and military employees had not been paid for over seven months.[19] His first measure had been to raise a voluntary loan – although, under the circumstances, it is difficult to ascertain how "voluntary" these types of loans really were. A year later his tax reforms had been so successful that his government no longer operated at a deficit. Having been the last country in the continent to gain its independence, Bolivia was the only one not to be saddled with external debt, because when they became a republic, the money markets in London had dried up, and no one was lending to the new emergent states anymore. The internal debt had been reduced to 1 million pesos by 1833, a third of the value owed in 1829. In order to achieve this, the government purchased most of the debt by setting up a central office in Chuquisaca where the paper debt

---

[17] Reglamento de Contribuciones, La Paz, 1831.
[18] Andrés de Santa Cruz, *Mensaje del Presidente de Bolivia a la Asamblea Nacional en 1831*, La Paz: Imprenta de Educandas, 1831, p. 6.
[19] See *El General Santa-Cruz explica su conducta pública*.

was exchanged for government-owned land.[20] Another strategy was to develop the economy and to incorporate trade and agriculture from the low-lying eastern provinces into the mainstream. To do this, new roads were built and missions reestablished so as to gain contact with the people Santa Cruz described as "tribes."

According to early twentieth-century Bolivian historian Alcides Arguedas, Santa Cruz was extremely fond of self-laudatory celebrations of his triumphs. In his book, Arguedas describes how the president's birthdays were celebrated with feasts that lasted for three days or more. Streets were decorated with triumphant arches and banners; nightly fireworks spectacles were held in the main plazas, and the sound of tolling bells filled all public spaces. Troupes of *cholos* and Indians danced in the streets and paid their respects to the president, next to the corporations of the city. There were bullfighting matches for the populace, while the more select public attended banquets, masses, and dramatic art performances. Newspapers were filled with articles celebrating the "Great Citizen, restorer of the *Patria* and Constitutional President." Arguedas argues that Santa Cruz even held his children's christenings with the whole diplomatic corps, his cabinet, the curia, and the representatives of the municipal government in attendance.[21] Santa Cruz was enamored of his own success and felt that his name ought to be considered among those of the great. As an example, he promoted the idea that the legislation passed during his period in government should be known as *Crucista*, even though most of the actual drafting of the law had been in the hands of his ministers: Olañeta, Antequera, Llosa, Guzmán, Urquidi, and others.

There is no doubt, however, that the country had been changed for the better in the five years Santa Cruz was in power. He was both an authoritarian populist and a beneficent liberal, who wanted to control the political sphere but who also sought to introduce more liberal legislation that he believed would benefit the country.

## THE ROAD TO THE PERU-BOLIVIA CONFEDERATION

By 1833, thanks to Santa Cruz's hard and efficient work as an administrator, the country had changed to such an extent that it was

[20] Andrés de Santa Cruz, *Mensaje del Presidente de Bolivia a la Asamblea Nacional en 1831*, p. 8.
[21] Alcides Arguedas, "Los Caudillos Letrados" in *Historia General de Bolivia (El proceso de la nacionalidad) 1809–1921*, La Paz: Arnó editores, 1922, pp. 92, 93.

unrecognizable. Bolivia had become wealthy, strong, and organized, with a well-prepared army. Peru looked anarchic in comparison. Santa Cruz took advantage of the political instability north of the border and became increasingly involved in Peruvian politics. Gamarra had been president for as long as Santa Cruz, but had none of his success to show for it. Instead of consolidating the country, he had constantly battled rebellions, uprisings, and dissent. Vice President La Fuente was ousted in a putsch organized by Gamarra's wife. She was heavily involved in the running of the country and was known as *La Mariscala* because she often wore military uniform. While Gamarra was locking horns with Santa Cruz at the Desaguadero and controlling an uprising in Cuzco, his wife decided that the Vice President could not be trusted and had him sent into exile. According to his own reports, the president of Peru had to fight fourteen rebellions during his time in office. This was not all, as he also had to contend with the powerful opposition of the liberals in Congress. The liberal representatives had decided not to let Gamarra take complete control of government and so destroy what they considered the rule of law. They constantly challenged him and made every possible effort to limit his power. They were to a large extent successful. Gamarra wanted to retain some legitimacy and considered the legal process to be at its basis. He respected some of the limits the representatives imposed, even if he tried to circumvent them. One such occasion was when new representatives for a national assembly were elected in 1834. This body met to discuss the reform of the 1828 Peruvian Constitution, which had included a clause – one that was quite uncommon – that called for its revision six years after it was enacted. Gamarra hoped to influence the reform of the constitution, but because Congress was dominated by his enemies, this was highly unlikely. The assembly was made up mostly of liberals, and an old foe, Luna Pizarro, took the opportunity during the discussions to promote the idea of a federation with Bolivia. The liberal cleric, who had been so influential when the first Peruvian Constitution had been written in 1823, had opposed the union. But this had been when Santa Cruz was president of Peru in 1826. The situation was different now, and Luna Pizarro, who preferred Santa Cruz to Gamarra, now saw the federation with more favorable eyes.[22]

---

[22]  Both Santiago Távara in his *Historia de los Partidos* and Juan Gualberto Valdivia in his *Memorias sobre las revoluciones de Arequipa* note that Luna Pizarro had frequently mentioned the advantages of organizing a federation with Bolivia.

The constitutional presidential period was about to expire in Peru, and Gamarra could not be reelected. In these extraordinary circumstances, the assembly exercised its prerogative to choose a temporary successor to the presidency while new elections were called. Given the antipathy the liberals felt toward the incumbent, and their complete control over Congress, they chose a liberal. Luís José de Orbegoso was a member of the army but had always sided with Gamarra's enemies. He was appointed interim president, but those who were close to the outgoing president called the legality of the move into question. Peru was at the time divided between the liberals, led by Luna Pizarro, and the supporters of Gamarra, all of whom were members of the army. Although Orbegoso was an army officer, he was considered a weak leader by his fellow members of the military. Most of them believed that he was controlled by the liberals and by men of the cloth. Scarcely a month after Orbegoso was appointed, an uprising orchestrated by Gamarra's cronies broke out. It was led by his wife, the feared *Mariscala*, who, in full officer uniform with gold-tasseled epaulets and stirrups made of gold, headed the troops. To justify the rebellion, they argued that Orbegoso was in conversations with Santa Cruz to establish a federation.

What Gamarra's supporters in the army had not anticipated, however, was how unpopular they were – not only in the southern city of Arequipa, where General Domingo Nieto remained loyal to the constitutional president, but even in Lima, where the population of the city rejected the rebellion and forced the army to withdraw to the Andes. According to observers, much of the discontent was because many men had been removed from active service in the army and had not been given what they considered appropriate compensation.[23] These discontented erstwhile members of the armed forces organized the militias that fought against the army of Gamarra. Peru was once again divided, with some provinces loyal to Gamarra and others to Orbegoso. In the south, Cuzco and Puno sided with Orbegoso, but from the edge of the lake, Gamarra's crony Miguel de San Román organized an attack against Arequipa. His native north remained loyal to Orbegoso. The civil war ended when troops from both sides reconciled in the central Andes on the battleground of Maquinguayo. A mid-ranking officer who doubted that he was fighting for a just cause convinced his men to embrace their enemy instead of fighting. Isolated, Gamarra was forced to flee to

[23] See Juan Gualberto Valdivia, *Las Revoluciones de Arequipa*, Arequipa: Editorial El Deber, 1956, p. 23.

Bolivia. Once he was installed there, Luna Pizarro, who had never liked him and referred to him derisively as "the Indian," changed his mind about the federation with Bolivia. He was afraid that if Santa Cruz and Gamarra worked together, they would always be against him.[24]

Interestingly, all sides in this civil war at some point either asked Santa Cruz for help or were rumored to have done so. The letters and memoirs of the men who participated in these campaigns show how confusing it was for all of those involved to properly gauge what kind of support each side had at any given time. Fighting took place simultaneously in distant parts of the country, and communications were often interrupted and inaccurate. It was difficult to keep abreast of events; provinces changed sides repeatedly over short periods of time. There were confrontations in all the main cities of the Andes as well as in Lima. Control of the capital was important, although it was not enough to guarantee victory. The north, as usual in Peruvian history, was not involved in the fighting, which concentrated around the city of Arequipa, the mining center of Cerro de Pasco – where most of the silver was extracted – and the cities in the fertile valleys of Tarma and Huancayo.

Although most of the fighting took place in the Central Andes, it was there, after the Maquinguayo embrace, that the civil war ended. In spite of this, Arequipa, the area most convinced of the importance of constitutional government, continued to see fighting. The male population of the city joined the militia in droves. They purchased their own uniforms and even paid for their own guns. But, no matter how great their effort and dedication, it was clear that they stood little chance. They were up against an officer from Puno who was able to recruit large numbers of Indians at the edge of the lake. The people of Arequipa were unable to attack because they were not used to long marches, nor could they cope with high altitude. Aware of their weakness, leaders in Arequipa frantically and repeatedly wrote to Santa Cruz asking for help.

The president of Bolivia was eager to intervene, but only on his own terms. He agreed to send men only if asked by some elected body, be it the convention or the corporations of Arequipa. Santa Cruz did not want to become embroiled in the civil war. He especially did not want to do it only to be later accused of having intervened to further

---

[24] Francisco Xavier de Luna Pizarro, *Escritos Políticos*, edited by Alberto Tauro, Lima: Universidad Nacional Mayor de San Marcos, 1959. For the reference as Indian see p. 73. For his rejection of the union with Bolivia see pp. 89, 91.

his own interests. By February, he had the battalion ready but was still awaiting an official invitation. He noted that having his troops close to the border was enough to distract the enemy in Puno, ensuring that Arequipa would not be threatened. This worked temporarily, but on Easter Monday 1834, enemy troops were at the edge of the city. French traveler Flora Tristán left a detailed description of the events that surrounded the battle that took place outside the city of Arequipa. In her diary she describes how the members of the army, convinced that the enemy would wait for reinforcements from Cuzco before attacking, drank and played cards while the enemy troops congregated close to the city. The troops besieging the city, however, realized that they had camped in an area without access to water or food, and that the only way not to perish was to engage in battle. There was much confusion and initially it seemed that the defenders of the city had triumphed; a capitulation was prepared, but it was not signed, and a second battle was fought. After some crucial mistakes by the cavalry of Arequipa, the city was abandoned by the men who fought for Orbegoso and taken by those who supported Gamarra.[25]

In the meantime, Santa Cruz had received formal documents from the Peruvian National Convention granting him extraordinary powers to intervene in aid of the government. This time he politely declined, saying that the situation in Bolivia had changed: there was strong opposition to sending troops to Peru, and even the State Council had recommended that he not do so. In private letters he explained that he was so unwilling to act because he did not trust Peruvian leaders with his men and feared that they might become trapped in a situation outside his control.[26] Given the events that ensued, it was understandable that Santa Cruz was reluctant to send forces. Nieto later accused Santa Cruz of failing to help because Nieto had not called for a federation while in Arequipa. Nieto claimed this was why the Bolivian president had not sent the 100,000 pesos and 2,000 soldiers he had initially promised.[27] This accusation, however, does not stand up to scrutiny. Letters show that it was the Peruvians who repeatedly asked Santa Cruz for troops

[25] For a detailed description see Flora Tristán, *Peregrinaciones de una Paria* (1833–1834), Lima: Ed. El Lector 2003 [1838], pp. 309–30.
[26] Letter to Manuel del la Cruz Méndez, La Paz, 26 March 1834, in *Archivo Histórico del Mariscal Andrés de Santa Cruz*, vol. III, p. 151.
[27] Domingo Nieto, *Memoria de los hechos que justifican la conducta pública que como general del ejército peruano ha seguido en la época que comprenden los años del 34 al 39*, Lima: Imprenta el Comercio, 1839.

and money. Nevertheless, it was also the case that Santa Cruz wanted to use this situation of extreme uncertainty to push his planned federation forward.

In a letter to his agent in Lima, Santa Cruz explained that he knew the convention was discussing a federation of three states. This meant that Peru would be divided into two. He believed this to be convenient for two reasons. The first was that Bolivians would then appear as the protector of a people in difficulties. The second reason was more telling. Santa Cruz noted that if Bolivia ever decided to leave the federation, Peru would remain forever divided and would no longer be a threat to Bolivia.[28] Peruvian politicians would later give this danger of separation into two states as one of their main reasons to oppose the confederation. Both the elites and the majority of the people in the provinces of the south – mainly Cuzco, Arequipa, and Tacna – supported the creation of a new southern state, because they were all eager for their cities to become its capital.

The possible union was so popular that even Gamarra was willing to play the federation game. In May 1834, with his prospects for success greatly diminished, his envoys approached Santa Cruz to discuss the terms of intervention.[29] The federation was no longer the main issue in contention. After the embrace at Maquinguayo, civil war ended, and the majority of those defeated were exiled to Bolivia. There was no further talk of federation in Peru. Santa Cruz wrote that the most fitting revenge against his Peruvian enemies had been to provide them with the best possible hospitality in Bolivia.[30]

Order was restored in Peru by June. To celebrate peace, the convention asked Orbegoso to lead public ceremonies to enact the 1834 Constitution. He agreed in spite of having assured the people of Arequipa that he would travel to their city to personally thank them all for their support in the civil war.[31] The Peruvian president delayed his trip and

[28] Letter to Manuel del la Cruz Méndez, La Paz, 11 March 1834, in *Archivo Histórico del Mariscal Andrés de Santa Cruz*, vol. III, p. 146.

[29] Letter to Manuel del la Cruz Méndez, Chuquisaca, 11 May 1834, in *Archivo Histórico del Mariscal Andrés de Santa Cruz*, vol. III, p. 160.

[30] Letter to Manuel Lorenzo de Vidaurre, Chuquisaca, 11 June 1834, in *Archivo Histórico del Mariscal Andrés de Santa Cruz*, vol. III, p. 167.

[31] Letter from Orbegoso to Nieto, Lima, 4 June 1834, in *Archivo B. Mackenna* vol. 221, copy held at the Instituto Riva Aguero in Lima, Colección Félix Denegri Luna.

dedicated all his energy to the celebration of the enactment of the constitution, which had in fact been ready since before the uprising.

In his correspondence, Santa Cruz dismissed this new charter. Because of its liberal design, which gave the legislature a great deal of power, he considered it to be a hundred times more demagogic than the 1828 Constitution it replaced. The president of Bolivia was convinced that the departments of southern Peru would not abide by it, and it would soon be discarded.[32] He was, on the other hand, convinced that the changes he had made to the Bolivian Constitution had significantly improved it. He considered that his greatest success had been making the meetings of the legislative biannual.

Even though peace had returned, the possible federation with Bolivia was still being talked about in Peru. In Lima, most believed that the separation of the southern provinces would be imposed from Puno. Orbegoso admitted in a letter to Nieto that his views were not different from those of Santa Cruz, but that he would never agree to anything that was outside the constitution.[33] This was in fact no longer a problem. The second article of the 1828 Constitution had banned possible unions and had been included in the as a reaction to the 1826 lifelong Bolivarian experiment. This prohibition was not included in 1834 – a result of the work of Luna Pizarro, who had come around to the idea of uniting with Bolivia.[34]

The enactment of the new charter was celebrated in the Peruvian capital. In the months that followed these ceremonies, Orbegoso worked at establishing his power. He promoted many officers, but was unable to pay their salaries. Toward the end of the year, he began his presidential campaign. Orbegoso traveled south to gain the support of the provinces that had so bravely fought for his cause. He left the capital in November, and two months later a mutiny took over the castles in Callao. It was commanded by Felipe Santiago Salaverry, the officer Orbegoso had left in charge of the city, who now installed himself as interim president.

This situation gave Santa Cruz a renewed opportunity to move his federation forward. Just as he had predicted, Peru was once again

---

[32] Letter from Santa Cruz to Mariano Amaza, Chuquisaca, n/d 1834 [inserted between 24 July and 17 September 1834], in *Archivo Histórico del Mariscal Andrés de Santa Cruz*, vol. III, p. 190.

[33] Letter from Orbegoso to Nieto, Lima, 11 July 1834, in *Archivo B. Mackenna* vol. 221.

[34] For more on constitutional differences see Jorge Basadre, *Historia de la República del Perú*, Lima: Historia, 1961, p. 347.

engulfed in anarchy. The north supported Salaverry, who put forward a nationalist plan that aimed to bring the country closer to Chile and to reassert the capital's control over the rest of the country. The south, meanwhile, backed Orbegoso, who was in Arequipa at the time. In spite of these advantages, Santa Cruz proceeded with caution. He was standing for reelection to the presidency. Congress was to meet in mid-1835, and Santa Cruz did not want to run any unnecessary risks. In his letters to his confidant General Felipe Braun, he cautioned him to be patient and to assess the situation dispassionately.[35] Gamarra, who was still in Bolivia, did not lose a minute organizing his return to Peru. He went as far as to write to friends of the president of his desire to help in what he described as a needed federation. In April, the people of Cuzco and Puno declared themselves independent. This gave Gamarra a golden opportunity to take control of the situation.

Santa Cruz, certain that this was the perfect moment to advance his project, wrote to Braun indicating that he should contact Gamarra. Braun was to assure him that he was the first choice to lead the uprising, but that he should not yet travel to Peru because resentment still lingered after the revolution from the previous year. At the same time, Santa Cruz got in touch with Orbegoso, the man he considered not only the easiest to manipulate, but also the one with greatest constitutional legitimacy. In his letter, Santa Cruz explained that he would not allow Gamarra out of Bolivia and assured Orbegoso that he would provide help if needed based on the treaty signed the year before. Evidently Santa Cruz was in contact with both Peruvian leaders at the same time. He was candid with Gamarra and told him that he wanted to send him to Peru to take charge of the projected federation, but that he could not trust him and feared that once in Peru, he would side with Salaverry.[36]

It is difficult to understand what motivated Santa Cruz to send Gamarra to Peru, considering his distrust. Santa Cruz sent Gamarra to Cuzco because he was convinced that only Gamarra could ensure that Cuzqueños would join the federation. Santa Cruz thought that otherwise he ran the risk that the commanders in Cuzco would back Salaverry, as they had done in Ayacucho. Santa Cruz asked Braun to work to persuade the people of Tacna and Arica to declare in favor of the

[35] Letter from Santa Cruz to General Felipe Braun, Chuquisaca, 7 April 1835, in *Archivo Histórico del Mariscal Andrés de Santa Cruz*, vol. IV, pp. 42, 43.

[36] Letter from Santa Cruz to Gamarra, Chuquisaca, 19 April 1835, in *Archivo Histórico del Mariscal Andrés de Santa Cruz*, vol. IV, p. 54.

federation. He wanted Braun to assure all their allies that they would have unconditional support if they backed the plan. Santa Cruz met Gamarra in Chuquisaca in early May. In a letter to Braun, he described the interview in detail, explaining how he had coldly offered Gamarra 4,000 men on the condition that Gamarra declare for the federation. The Peruvian leader had demanded 40,000 pesos instead. Santa Cruz assured Braun that he knew Gamarra too well to trust him, and that he would send him to Cuzco but expect nothing of him. Instead he wrote to Orbegoso and proceeded with their negotiations.[37]

Santa Cruz later explained that he allowed Gamarra to return so he would lead the resistance against Salaverry. Santa Cruz believed that a divided Peru would be beneficial to the establishment of a federation between three states.[38] Gamarra, on the other hand, explained he had only accepted a return sponsored by Santa Cruz because they had agreed to create a Republic of Peru divided into three states: north, center, and south. The Republic would have the Peruvian flag, and Bolivia would cease to exist, becoming the southern state. Santa Cruz was to obtain the consent of Arequipa and Orbegoso.[39] Gamarra's first action after crossing the border was to write to Orbegoso. He declared in his letter that the thousands of letters he had received from all over the republic assured him that people wanted a federation.[40] Once he reached Cuzco, Gamarra addressed his compatriots, preparing them for war, but never mentioned his conversations with Santa Cruz. Disappointed by this lack of public commitment, Santa Cruz resumed negotiations with Orbegoso. He assured him that he had only allowed Gamarra back to Peru because Cuzco and Puno had declared for Salaverry.

In his *Memoirs* – written on his deathbed and published 100 years later – Orbegoso made it clear that he had only accepted the treaty with Santa Cruz because he had no other option. He was adamant that it was not an agreement between equals. The cooperation treaty, signed on 15 June 1835, was later ratified in Arequipa. Orbegoso later claimed

[37] Letter from Santa Cruz to General Felipe Braun, Chuquisaca, 6 May 1835, in *Archivo Histórico del Mariscal Andrés de Santa Cruz*, vol. IV, p. 76.

[38] *El General Santa-Cruz explica su conducta pública*, pp. 70–1.

[39] *El General Gamarra a sus compatriotas*, Costa Rica, 1835. A copy of a letter by José Joaquín Mora written on 19 May 1835 corroborates this version; it is inserted in Paz Soldán, p. 23.

[40] Letter from Gamarra to Orbegoso, Lampa, 17 May 1835, in *Gran Mariscal Agustín Gamarra, Epistolario*, Alberto Tauro ed., Lima: Universidad Nacional mayor de San Marcos, 1952. p. 258.

that he had not approved the treaty until two weeks later, when he personally met Santa Cruz at the border. He asked those who condemned him to consider the options open to him at the time, with Salaverry in charge of most of the country, Gamarra in Cuzco, Santa Cruz in Puno, and Orbegoso himself in control of only a small number of troops in Arequipa.[41] In Arequipa, in August 1835, he had given a different account of the reasons for signing the treaty. In his manifesto, Orbegoso claimed that the majority in the south favored a federation. Faced with such difficult circumstances he wanted the people to choose their future, so he had called on the Bolivian president so the Republic could be pacified and a congress called.[42] Santa Cruz, at this point, negotiated openly with both parties at the same time. He wrote to Gamarra that in Arequipa, Orbegoso was ready to declare for the federation, and that this was enough proof that Gamarra had no support there.[43]

In his letters, Santa Cruz repeatedly asked Gamarra to declare for the federation. The official papers backing this plan were not forthcoming, however, so Santa Cruz became ever more anxious. Moreover, the perceived need for the official declaration for the federation only grew when Gamarra took control of the forces on the border that had recently sided with Salaverry. From Lampa, the Peruvian ex-president assured Braun that he would declare for the federation once in Cuzco. He claimed that he had been unable to do so because he needed to gain the trust of the men he was now commanding.[44] Gamarra was never going to be accepted by the people of Arequipa. They made this clear to Santa Cruz, assuring him that if he took Gamarra's side, the city would declare for Salaverry. The elites of Cuzco and Puno were, on the other hand, adamant that they would only endorse the federation if they maintained their independence from Arequipa. Aware of these difficulties, Santa Cruz tried to obtain advantages from both sides, while the official treaties that allowed him to intervene in Peru were still in the process of being finalized.

[41] *Memorias del Gran Mariscal Don Luis José de Orbegoso*, Lima: Gil, 1939, p. 88.

[42] *Exposición que hace el Presidente Provisional de la República Peruana Luis José Orbegoso de las razones que le obligaron a solicitar de la república boliviana auxilios para pacificar el Perú.* Arequipa: Imprenta de Francisco Valdez, 1835, pp. 13–14.

[43] See letters written between 26 May and 5 June 1835 from Santa Cruz to Gamarra and Orbegoso, *Archivo Histórico del Mariscal Andrés de Santa Cruz*, vol. IV, pp. 91–100.

[44] Letter from Gamarra to Braun, Lapma, 1 June 1835, in *Gran Mariscal Agustín Gamarra, Epistolario*, p. 259.

This was the moment of truth, Santa Cruz knew how close he had finally come to implementing his projected union between Peru and Bolivia. Gamarra, his former friend and companion, had temporarily claimed that he would support Santa Cruz, but it was now clear that he would do no such thing. The elites in the southern provinces in Peru were divided, but the vast majority backed the idea of the union, and each of the provinces wanted to use its support as leverage to obtain the best possible terms for incorporation. Santa Cruz had to strike a difficult balance to keep many of the players on his side and to limit the power of those against him. This, however, was a difficult battle, and one that he had to continue waging all throughout the process of creating the confederation and even during his attempt to consolidate it. It was ultimately a battle he could not win: he only managed to gain the support of some core groups in southern Peru and northern Bolivia. His enemies, on the other hand, were able to successfully organize against him, even though he had made every effort to convince the people from the regions of the merits of his intervention in Peru.

To justify his actions, a long document was produced by Minister Mora and signed by Santa Cruz. In it they argued that they had to intervene in Peruvian affairs because Salaverry's government was a direct threat to Bolivia. They referred to the declaration made by Britain when it justified its attack on France in 1793. Just like the British, the Bolivians claimed a need to protect themselves from the new political system.[45] Mora and Santa Cruz stated that Bolivia had chosen not to participate in its neighbor's affairs the previous year and had refrained even after being called by all the leaders and invited by the Peruvian Convention. Mora and Santa Cruz explained that they had not intervened because they had no ambition to control Peru. They stressed they had only taken action because they had to defend their country and help a neighbor in need. They described the regime in Lima as tyrannical and stressed that the only reason for their intervention was to maintain the rule of law and return order to a country that was being ravaged. Santa Cruz's penchant for the legalistic was evident in this case as he reiterated that he had the approval of Orbegoso, the provisional president of Peru.

It was nevertheless true that Salaverry had unleashed violence not seen since the wars of independence. He was quick to send his enemies to the firing squad; the mortality rates of officers in this war were striking.

---

[45] *Exposición de los motivos que justifican la cooperación del gobierno de Bolivia en los negocios políticos del Perú*, La Paz: Imprenta del Colegio de Artes, 15 June 1835, pp. 3–9.

Nevertheless, the real purpose of Santa Cruz's intervention in Peru was, as he detailed in a long letter to Olañeta, to create the federation. In this letter, he explained that Bolivia's independence depended on it; the union would divide a country that would otherwise always aspire to control them. It was clear that the president of Bolivia considered this a good enough reason to intervene, even if Salaverry had not been a real threat.[46]

In late June, on the same day that Santa Cruz wrote to Gamarra informing him that he had signed a treaty with Orbegoso, Gamarra joined forces with Salaverry. After defecting, Gamarra wrote to Santa Cruz's principal minister assuring him that he had intended only to serve his country.[47] In spite of signing an agreement with Salaverry and writing to him in endearing terms, calling him "my godson," Gamarra still asked Santa Cruz for muskets and gunpowder. The two former school companions continued writing letters filled with bitter irony, never abandoning the intimate address of *tu*, a form that neither ever used in any of their letters to other correspondents. This form of address is indeed largely absent in the nineteenth-century epistolary form, which shows the closeness of their relationship. In fact, it seems that more than anything else, Gamarra and Santa Cruz were playing a complicated game of chess, each trying to outwit the other at every step. Even after it was clear, although unacknowledged, where each of them stood, they continued the charade, stating that they only wanted to mediate in the conflict between Salaverry and Orbegoso. In early July, both spoke of the prospect of meeting in Vilque to discuss their options. Both stood firm on their positions: Santa Cruz wanted two assemblies to be called to vote on the proposed federation and division of Peru into two states, whereas Gamarra was adamant that no such division should take place.

Letters continued to travel between Puno and Cuzco. Even on 24 July, when Santa Cruz openly declared that he knew Gamarra had sided with his enemies, he still spoke of the possibility of them working together if Gamarra could travel north to fight on his behalf.[48] Salaverry urged Gamarra not to confront Santa Cruz in battle before the troops

[46] Letter from Santa Cruz to Olañeta, La Paz, 17 June 1835, in *Archivo Histórico del Mariscal Andrés de Santa Cruz*, vol. IV, p. 112.

[47] Letter from Santa Cruz to Gamarra, La Paz, 21 June 1835, in *Archivo Histórico del Mariscal Andrés de Santa Cruz*, vol. IV, p. 114. Letter from Gamarra to Government Minister, Cuzco, 26 June 1835, in *Gran Mariscal Agustín Gamarra, Epistolario*, p. 261.

[48] Letter from Santa Cruz to Gamarra, Puno, 15 July 1835, in *Archivo Histórico del Mariscal Andrés de Santa Cruz*, vol. IV, p. 156.

he was sending arrived. But having an army of the regular size and at least 1,000 Indians armed with traditional weapons, Gamarra engaged in the battle of Yanacocha in early August 1835.[49]

Yanacocha was the first major victory for the Bolivians. They triumphed even though their enemies had done all they could to obtain the support of the Indians in the area. In the highlands near the battleground Gamarra had distributed sixty arrobas of coca leaf. According to observers, this amount of coca was enough to gain the backing of 8,000 to 11,000 men. At the time of the battle, however, these Indians did not fight; according to reports, as soon as firing broke out, they abandoned their positions.[50] Clearly, Indians were not interested in supporting a faction simply in exchange for coca. They turned up to the battle, having accepted the coca; this was the minimum that could be expected of them. But they had no real reason to fight for Gamarra. He had made no genuine effort to engage with them in a meaningful way, and he had only wanted them as auxiliaries.

Santa Cruz had delayed battle as long as possible. He feared Salaverry, but did not want to intervene before the Bolivian Congress gave its approval and reelected him president.[51] Santa Cruz had even written to Gamarra on the eve of the battle, asking him to reconsider his position. He asked Gamarra to accept the federation, Gamarra had vigorously endorsed in Chuquisaca, when he asked for Santa Cruz for support to return to Peru.[52]

Defeated, Gamarra fled to Lima. Salaverry hoped that he would take charge of the State Council while Salaverry prepared to travel south and face Santa Cruz. Gamarra did not think this was a good idea. He had no intention of serving under the younger Salaverry, so he left for exile. His first stop was Costa Rica; he then relocated to Guayaquil and finally to Chile.

Salaverry now controlled the Peruvian navy. Taking advantage of his maritime power, he launched an attack against the port of Cobija. In less than a week, the navy had destroyed all the hard work the Bolivians had

[49]  Basadre, *La Iniciación de la Republica*, vol. I, p. 327.
[50]  Charles Walker has studied most of the primary sources available in Cuzco on this battle and has a detailed description of the events in *Smoldering Ashes: Cuzco and the Creation of Republican Peru*, pp. 213–15.
[51]  Letter from Santa Cruz to Gamarra, Puno, 28 July 1835, in *Archivo Histórico del Mariscal Andrés de Santa Cruz*, vol. IV, p. 165.
[52]  Letter from Santa Cruz to Gamarra, Tinta, 10 August 1835, in *Archivo Histórico del Mariscal Andrés de Santa Cruz*, vol. IV, p. 172.

expended to build a town in the desert. Meanwhile, Salaverry advanced by sea, taking control of Arequipa. Just before he entered, all those in prominent positions abandoned the city, retreating toward Puno or Moquegua. No one in these cities in the south thought that it was either possible or useful to confront Salaverry without reinforcements from Santa Cruz. Once again following the traditional ideas of war at the time, they thought it better to retreat than to fight at a disadvantage.

Similarly, in Lima, the caretaker government left by Salaverry relocated to the fortresses in Callao. In December, after twice being overrun by bandits, the municipal authorities declared in favor of Santa Cruz and Orbegoso. At this point, reduced to controlling Arequipa and the navy, Salaverry found himself in a position similar to that of Orbegoso a year earlier. The difference was that Salaverry was trapped in deeply hostile territory. He fought valiantly and until the bitter end, but was defeated in the battles of Uchumayo and Socabaya. He escaped after the campaigns, but was taken prisoner by General Miller, who assured him that he would be safe. The Englishman was, however, unable to plead effectively for the defeated General's life, and Santa Cruz sent Salaverry to the firing squad.[53]

This was to be one of the most controversial actions taken by the Bolivian president while in Peru. Some contend this was the moment when Santa Cruz lost any legitimacy he might have had. With Gamarra in exile and Salaverry dead, the road was completely open for Santa Cruz to put his plan into action. Legislation was put forward to create a confederation. A congress met in southern Peru to swiftly implement it, and another followed some months later in northern Peru. Santa Cruz was called to become the Confederation's protector.

## Establishing the Confederation

With his enemies out of the picture, Santa Cruz's main goal was to create a new state that would unite Peru and Bolivia. In the weeks that followed the battle of Socabaya, while in Arequipa, Santa Cruz became increasingly aware that there were strong interests backing the union of the two countries as a centralist republic, but not as a federation. Santa Cruz opposed this from the start, believing that it was too risky. He saw that his enemies would portray the union as the takeover of one

---

[53] The debate on whether Miller could have saved Salaverry has long continued; see Manuel Bilbao and Robert Delayney for more details on this issue.

country by the other, and so he repeatedly defended the idea of creating a federation, which he believed possible only if Peru was to be separated into two smaller states. This division stood at the center of his policy. His letters spell out the reasons why he was so adamant this was the best course of action. Santa Cruz feared that the confederation might fail, and he was convinced that once two states existed, Peru would never be able to reunite. This, Santa Cruz believed, would be best for Bolivia.

Calls for a union of the two countries came from many provinces. The people of Arequipa expressed their desire to be joined with Bolivia. Cuzqueños, on the other hand, made it clear at an early point that their support was only for a federation rather than union. Santa Cruz agreed with the people of Cuzco and considered that an assembly was the only proper way to decide the matter. A month after Salaverry's defeat, representatives for the four southern provinces met at the edge of Lake Titicaca in the town of Sicuani to discuss the issue. Santa Cruz was of the same mind as the Cuzqueños: he feared that if these southern provinces were simply annexed to Bolivia, Santa Cruz would face constant battles with the north of Peru to keep control of them. Only if the north rejected the federation would he consider union a possibility. Santa Cruz was prepared, if that happened, to incorporate into Bolivia all the territory south of the Apurimac river. To him the most important issue was that the giant of the north would be divided.[54] In a letter to the vice president of Bolivia, Santa Cruz referred to the dismemberment of Peru and how they would no longer have to fear being "gobbled up" by their northern neighbor. He expressed his confidence that Peru would never again be joined as one country.[55]

Success in Sicuani gave Santa Cruz confidence that his project would be fully endorsed. Once the assembly had agreed to secession from Peru, a new independent state was created as Southern Peru. Because of the similarity in name and its short time in existence (1836–9), this political entity has seldom been considered an independent state. This was, however, the way Santa Cruz described it and conceived of it. In time, a new flag was designed combining the colors of the flags of Peru and Bolivia, and the hope was the new state would develop its own

---

[54] Letter from Santa Cruz to Hilarión Fernández, Arequipa, 28 February 1836, in *Archivo Histórico del Mariscal Andrés de Santa Cruz*, vol. V, pp. 101–2.

[55] Letter from Santa Cruz to Mariano Enrique Calvo, Sicuani, 20 March 1836, in *Archivo Histórico del Mariscal Andrés de Santa Cruz*, vol. V, p. 119.

national identity to rival the ones found in the other member states of the federation.

In spite of the good progress made at Sicuani, only a week after independence the citizens of Moquegua announced that they wanted to be incorporated into Bolivia. Tacna, Arica, and Tarapacá followed suit. This was an embarrassment for Santa Cruz, showing that acceptance of the new state was incomplete and offering a further complication for Santa Cruz: accepting the southernmost provinces into his country would finally have resolved the issue of the most suitable port for La Paz. But Santa Cruz was adamant that Bolivia should not accept the annexation of these provinces. He believed they should only be taken if the confederation project failed, not now when success was so tantalizingly close. Accepting these provinces into Bolivia would have been seen as an insult by the people of Arequipa, who would suffer heavy territorial losses.

Santa Cruz wrote to Orbegoso saying that he understood that the people of the north were interested in a union, just as in Tacna and Arequipa. He reiterated his decision for the federation, assuring Orbegoso that in the long run the fusion being proposed would cause more problems that it would solve. Santa Cruz could never consent to a Peruvian takeover of Bolivia.

In the southernmost provinces of Peru, the demand for union with Bolivia was linked to the desire of certain areas such as Tacna and Moquegua to become independent from Arequipa. Their incorporation into Bolivia would ensure this: they could not be included in any of the provinces already in existence, so they would have to become provinces in their own right. Santa Cruz understood this well and was therefore opposed to the possibility of dismembering the department of Arequipa to annex Tarapacá, Tacna, and Moquegua. He was also against the union proposed by the people of northern Peru, because it was not the confederation he envisioned, but an annexation.

Santa Cruz was especially disappointed with the southern provinces, because their initiative made his political situation in Arequipa and Puno more difficult and showed that opinion was not unified, although Santa Cruz assured everyone that a federation was the only option and that there would be no territorial shifts. He then proceeded to promote the port of Arica and the city of Tacna as the new centers, even though there was no official recognition of where the capital was to be located and both Cuzco and Arequipa believed that they were destined to become the principal city.

Finding a balance among the interests of Cuzco, Puno, Arequipa, Tacna, and Moquegua was not as easy as Santa Cruz had initially envisioned. But his resistance to the annexation of provinces and his dedication to the cause of the federation began bearing fruit by April 1836. Back in La Paz, he used the press and public meetings with supporters to prepare public opinion for the union and was able to assure them that opinion in Cuzco and Puno had changed in his favor. Not so easy to defuse was the opposition to the confederation project in Lima, where many feared that the only reason to create a new state was to snatch Arica from Peru.[56] The inhabitants of Lima could not fathom the idea of no longer being the capital, whereas the people of Cuzco openly courted Santa Cruz when he was in their city. They wanted him to return them to what they considered their rightful place as capital of this large federation. They envisioned it as following from the Inca Empire, so naturally they were best placed to be the center: after all they had always considered their city to be the "earth's navel." Part of their strategy to convince him of their importance was to receive the victorious general with all the fanfare they could muster. Santa Cruz described in his letters the public festivities, followed by bullfights, dances, and comedies, that lasted for days and far surpassed any way in which he had ever been celebrated in Bolivia.

In spite of all this, Santa Cruz was in no mood to decide on the possible capital of the federation. His mind was instead preoccupied with the fear that the assembly that was to meet in the north of the country, in the town of Huaura, would not ratify the separation of the southern republic. He also worried about the growing opposition to his project from all the neighboring countries, because émigrés, including Gamarra, La Fuente, and Pardo, were starting to work against him in both Guayaquil and Valparaiso. In contrast to the policy of inclusiveness Santa Cruz had championed when he took control of Bolivia in 1828, he adopted a quite different strategy in Peru. He considered that the circumstances were not comparable and that it would be impossible to set up the federation while the men who were most bitterly opposed to it were still in the army. He also stated that he had to be firm in Peru, where excessive indulgence had often been misinterpreted as weakness, resulting in more political instability.

---

56  Letter from Santa Cruz to Calvo, Pomata, 31 April 1836, in *Archivo Histórico del Mariscal Andrés de Santa Cruz*, vol. V, p. 171.

Throughout his campaign, Santa Cruz endeavored to keep firm discipline in his army. He had succeeded in great part because his men were highly trained, well equipped and were always paid on time. This made it possible for him to take control of a large territory without being seen with hostility. Instead of sacking and looting the towns they occupied, the Bolivian armed forces contributed to the local economy by buying food, employing tailors, and purchasing vast amounts of cloth for uniforms. In all his letters, this obsession with providing material support to his men can be seen at the core of Santa Cruz's strategy in the departments of Arequipa and Cuzco. The people in these provinces could compare his way of conducting war with that of their enemies, who confiscated their goods and made no promises of ever paying them back. This was one of the great differences between Santa Cruz and other *caudillos* of his time. He was adamant that the only way in which his men could maintain advantage in the battlefield was to have the support of the local population and to be happy and contented in their positions. With complete control of the south of Peru, Santa Cruz sent all the troops whose tour of duty ended back home to Bolivia. He did so to fulfill the promise made to the men when they had been recruited that they would only serve for a given time and would then be allowed to return home.

During those two months in Cuzco, Santa Cruz took an interest in administrative matters and awarded key positions to those who had helped him. In May 1836, he made Luna Pizarro Dean of the Cathedral of Arequipa in return for all the help he provided in setting up the Confederation.[57] Indeed, in a private letter to Santa Cruz in April 1837, when Luna Pizarro was working to defend the interests of the Confederation against the aggression of both Ecuador and Chile, the cleric described the union between the two countries as one that had existed since their origin in the times of what the author described as primitives, with close connections in language and social customs, all common inhabitants of an area that was not divided by nature.[58] Santa Cruz also spent some time developing his ideas for how the union should work politically. These ideas were different from those that had formed other existing federations: he repeatedly pointed out that his experiment would differ from the one put in practice in North America.

---

[57] Luna Pizarro, Letter to the Dean of the Cathedral of Arequipa, 4 May 1836, *Escritos Políticos*, p. 94.
[58] Luna Pizarro, Letter to Santa Cruz, Lima, 4 April 1837, *Escritos Políticos*, p. 97.

He candidly described Peru as having disappeared to become two independent states, federated with Bolivia. The three, he wrote, were one body that maintained its individuality and its independence.[59]

Santa Cruz remained in Cuzco for a couple of months, until he received confirmation that the Bolivian Congress had ratified the confederation project and elected him president for a second term. Although there had been no real danger that either would not be passed by the assembly in Tapacarí, Santa Cruz still did not want to be too far from his core constituency in La Paz, in case he had to return in haste. He was concerned about the three deputies from Chuquisaca who had expressed what he described as "demagogic ideas."[60] Once he had been ratified in his post in Bolivia, he left Cuzco for a brief sojourn in La Paz before embarking on a long trip to northern Peru, where he expected his federation to come to fruition.

Instead of immediately going to Lima, Santa Cruz decided to await the results of the Assembly of Huaura in the highlands, just a couple of days' journey east of the capital. He did not want to arrive in the ancient viceregal center of power as a guest, with no political mandate, having to attend endless public appearances required by etiquette. He was much happier in the city of Tarma, from where he could easily travel back south or to Lima, depending on the results of the assembly. He did not think it was politically wise to be at the meeting of the representatives of the north, as he had been when those of the south had met, because he did not want to be accused of having put them under any pressure. His aim was clear: he wanted the Assembly of Huaura to recognize the agreements of Sicuani and to declare an independent country under his protection. He had been reassured that in spite of the opposition of Lima – because the city did not want to cease being the capital of a vast country and supported the idea of a union – many people had great faith in him as a person. He hoped to capitalize on this faith once the agreements in Huaura had been reached.

The assembly met in Huaura on the historically charged date of 28 July, when the country was celebrating fifteen years since San Martín's declaration of independence in Lima. Just as in those days, the country was divided along an invisible line in the environs of the river Pampas,

[59] Letter from Santa Cruz to Vicente Pasos Canqui, Huancayo, 13 July 1836, in *Archivo Histórico del Mariscal Andrés de Santa Cruz*, vol. V, p. 238.
[60] Letter from Santa Cruz to Braun, Cuzco, 11 June 1836 in *Archivo Histórico del Mariscal Andrés de Santa Cruz*, vol. V, p. 214.

where the Andean valleys of Junín transform into those of Huanta. The south of Peru, just as before, chose to remain closer to the territories that had once been known as Upper Peru. The same cities and provinces that had declared independence from Spain in 1821, and had fought bitterly for the union with the provinces that had now declared themselves as a separate republic, met to discuss the federal project. Lima and Trujillo were thrust into the same position they had held during the process of independence.

Although the elites in this area had always endeavored to maintain Peru as a union, on this occasion their representatives relented and gave their backing to the federation. Given the circumstances, it was hardly surprising that the ideas of Santa Cruz triumphed. The deputies had been carefully selected, and Orbegoso, in spite of all his deathbed protestations, had worked to ensure that only those who supported the federation were elected to represent the departments of Lima, Trujillo, and Tarma.[61] With little option but to acquiesce, in late July 1836 the representatives in Huaura endorsed the creation of the southern Peruvian state and gave permission to create a Confederation. Santa Cruz, ecstatic, wrote to his closest associates that they had finally prevailed. In little less than a decade they had transformed Bolivia from a backwater center of unrest to a beacon of political development. He prepared to travel to Lima and called a new meeting, this time of the representatives of the three states, to enshrine the Federal Pact. Santa Cruz foresaw this would take place in Cuzco between January and April. The future of the Confederation seemed bright as he entered Lima in August amid loud celebrations.

The path to the Confederation had not been easy. Santa Cruz had worked hard and was prepared when the opportunity arose. He finally struck when unrest in Peru was so widespread that his enemies had little choice of action and could not prevent him from achieving his goal. His dedication to the reorganization of the Bolivian army was at the center of his success. This was no longer a band of quickly assembled men, but a trained contingent who knew how to comport themselves in battle. The members of the armed forces were kept content by fair recruitment policies, appropriate salaries and pensions, and a well-defined and not too extensive time in service. In comparison, the armies of Gamarra, Orbegoso, and Salaverry were disorganized. Although they also wanted

---

[61] See letters from Orbegoso to Nieto, May 1836, copies held at the Colección Felix Denegri Luna.

to provide material benefits on a structured basis to the men fighting for them, they were not as successful. Because their regimes were seen as unstable, there was no guarantee that salaries and pensions would be paid in the future, and so the armies faced a constant threat of desertion.

The dedication of the people of Arequipa also made the Confederation possible. They supported the plan from its inception and never wavered in their desire to become independent from Lima. Cuzqueños were also in favor of a federation, but they did not support Santa Cruz as wholeheartedly, and many were prepared to back Gamarra if he offered them better conditions. Opinion in Bolivia was not as undivided as Santa Cruz had hoped, and some voices of dissent were heard. Santa Cruz was, however, still powerful enough to stifle those voices and prevail. He asked his trusted ally General Braun to ensure that a new newspaper was published to defend their cause.[62]

In northern Peru, there was little enthusiasm for the federation. The Protector, aware of this, attempted to provide the northern republic with funds for schools and libraries, as well as to send money to fund the army stationed in its main cities of Trujillo and Piura. It was clear that in this part of the Confederation a union could be tolerated, as long as Lima remained the preeminent city. Santa Cruz's internal enemies were silenced, albeit temporarily, while his backers loudly celebrated the coming of the union.

---

[62] Letter from Santa Cruz to Braun, Pacayal [Lima], 25 January 1837, in *Archivo Histórico del Mariscal Andrés de Santa Cruz*, vol. VI, p. 46.

CHAPTER 5

# The Rise and Fall of the Peru-Bolivia

# Confederation

The union of Peru and Bolivia had been a long-held desire for many people with divided loyalties, such as Santa Cruz. Since independence, there had been a vocal constituency advocating both federation and political union. The southern provinces, separated by the creation of the Viceroyalty of the Río de la Plata in 1776, were reunited between 1810 and 1825 when the armies raised in southern Peru intervened to prevent the Junta of Buenos Aires from taking control of the Audiencia of Charcas. In colonial times they had belonged to different administrative entities for only thirty-four years. During the wars of independence, they were brought back together for fifteen years, and when the Confederation came into being, only a decade had elapsed since they had become separate republics. For many, the union of Peru and Bolivia was no more than a return to a comfortable status quo ante. Arequipa, Cuzco, Tacna, Puno, and La Paz remained the provinces historically most committed to the union, whereas those who had opposed it continued to view it with distrust. This chapter explores the process by which the Confederation came into being as well as the sources of its support. It also examines the difficulties the Confederation encountered and seeks to understand the opposition to it.

The union was never universally popular, but in spite of this Santa Cruz was able to silence the opposition in Bolivia and obtain the support he needed. In the north of Peru and in Lima in particular, the project was never seen sympathetically, especially because a shift of power to the south seemed an inevitable, yet fiercely disputed, matter. The influence of Bolívar's thinking was plain to see. Santa Cruz had been inspired by the 1826 Constitution and shared with his mentor the belief that a charter was the best way to create a viable political union. The title of

Map 3 – 1830s.

Protector, used before by San Martín in Peru, brought to mind the idea of benevolent overseer, distanced from the more controversial one of Dictator, used by Bolívar. In effect, the way Santa Cruz envisioned it, the Protector was to be at the very center of the union holding it together. There were, however, noteworthy innovations in his conception of federalism. The Confederation was conceived differently from other federations because it was to be a union among three different states. Each would maintain its national identity. This was stressed by the development of national markers, such as the flag and coat of arms that had recently been created for the Republic of Southern Peru.

The Confederation had internal and external enemies. The ones from within were particularly opposed to the division of Peru: some, mainly Peruvians, because they considered that the country would be greatly weakened; others, generally Bolivians, because they thought Peru would be strengthened, with two votes against only one for Bolivia. Even though most of its support came from southern Peru, elites in this region were divided among themselves. The greatest external adversary of the union was Chile. Its government opposed the Confederation from its inception, and its leaders were convinced that if the Confederation were to succeed, they would always be in danger from its aggression. Part of the problem was linked to trade and the commercial policy implemented by Santa Cruz, but the fear of being absorbed by a more powerful regional player must not be discounted. The Confederation was conceived to provide a space in which each member could maintain its own nationality. It was designed as a supranational union of nations, where different national identities could coexist. Many prominent players who had come of age during the wars of independence and who, like Santa Cruz, had conflicting issues with their identities found this an ideal space. This was because it allowed particular nations to live side by side in a larger unit that was inclusive of the different nationalities from which it was made up.

## CREATION AND SUPPORT FOR THE PROJECT

Elites and popular sectors in Arequipa gave the Confederation unwavering support. Commercial ties in the whole province and not just the city had motivated many to fight to maintain their links to the Altiplano, particularly to the Potosí market, since the end of the colonial period. Now that the project was finally a real possibility, these sectors were once again behind Santa Cruz. In exchange, they expected to be well

rewarded. Other provinces in southern Peru also saw the Confederation favorably, but the people of Cuzco were more divided. Gamarra,
their favorite son, had been able to garner support there. The majority,
including those with links to Santa Cruz's family, were willing to participate in the federation if their interests were protected. The people
in these provinces wanted to improve their situation vis-à-vis Lima, but
they also wanted to ensure that their deal was better than that of their
neighbors. So Santa Cruz had to tread carefully in order to maintain
support. He also received crucial backing from Great Britain, which at
the time was Peru's most important trading partner. The British, however, were also in it for their own interest, and they managed to sign a
favorable trade agreement with the Confederation.

Assemblies held in the small towns of Sicuani, Tapacarí, and Huaura
gave Santa Cruz the chance to unite the three states into a federation.
In his correspondence, he described the union of three independent
states that he envisioned. It would not follow the example set by the
United States, but would be a new take on the Federation of the Andes
designed by Bolívar. On 28 October 1836, while Santa Cruz was in Lima,
the Confederation was created by decree. Each of the three states was
to name three plenipotentiary ministers who would meet in Tacna to
finalize the details of the union. At the last minute, Tacna, not Cuzco,
was selected because it was more central and easy to access from all
three states. People from Lima could sail quickly and safely, and those
in Bolivia were only a few days" travel away. The ministers that were
to represent each of the states were not elected, but chosen by Santa
Cruz. In his selections, Santa Cruz respected the traditional colonial
hierarchical system of representation. He chose a judge, a priest, and
a member of the military for each state. Each individual was elected
because he had shown his commitment to the cause and represented a
traditional corporate body.

Bolivian representatives prepared a first draft of the federal proposal
in December 1836. It included the idea of the executive as a lifelong
appointment with the title of His Highness. Santa Cruz rejected this,
convinced that it would have no backing.[1] This was one of the few issues
on which Santa Cruz deviated from the Bolivarian experiment. His
Bolivarian-inspired plans for political union had long been established.

---

[1]    For more details on the creation of the Confederation see Phillip Taylor Parkerson, *Andres de Santa Cruz y la Confederación Peru-Boliviana, 1835–1839*, La Paz:
Editorial "Juventud," 1984, p. 132.

The draft from March 1837 was in essence the same text on which he had agreed with Gamarra in 1835. When ministers finally met in April, this was the draft discussed. It was approved with no changes, but this exercise in rubber-stamping did generate some debate on the nature of the union. The representatives from Southern Peru brought the question of the debt to the table, because they considered that Bolivia was indebted to Peru for having financed and fought for their independence. This had long been a contentious issue; Bolivia rejected any financial responsibility. They argued that they had been forced to fight for their independence for over a decade against troops sent from southern Peru. The irony that Santa Cruz had been among those who defended the king with troops and men from southern Peru against those seeking independence in the Audiencia of Charcas was not lost on his opponents.

This was the only contentious issue in the meeting. After two days of intense but fruitless discussion, the demand for debt repayment was dropped. The pact was approved by all the representatives, with no changes made to the Bolivian proposal. The Congress of Tacna finally gave the union a legal basis on 1 May 1837. The final document was not as long as other constitutions, but it was conceived as one, stipulating the way government should be organized. Changes could be made only by an assembly with representatives from the three states.

Indeed, this experiment was quite different from the other kinds of federations that had been attempted in South America. The three states, as constituent components of the Confederation, would be governed independently and remain sovereign. Only foreign affairs, the armed forces, and general economic interests would be controlled by the Supreme Protector. This leader was elected for a ten-year tenure and could renew the term indefinitely. So, not only would the reign be for an extensive period, but most of the power was concentrated in one man. The Protector would be in charge of selecting the senators for the federal assembly, as well as the presidents for each of the member states. This structure not only resembled Bolívar's 1826 "vitalicia" Constitution, but also the 1819 Angostura Constitution with its hereditary Senate.

The federal legislature, composed of deputies elected for six years by the electoral colleges and lifelong senators, would meet every two years. This body would elect the Protector from a list of candidates sent by the state legislatures. There would be no direct elections for the federal government. As Antonio Zapata has pointed out, the lack of

representation in this arrangement, as well as the limits it imposed on
the career progression of the officers in his army, was one of the greatest
problems Santa Cruz had to contend with.[2] No federal judicial authorities would exist. Each of the states would retain complete responsibility
for judicial affairs. If there were accusations against ministers, members
of Congress, or any other federal bureaucrats, a special tribunal could
be called into session with judges from each of the member states. Each
state would therefore retain full responsibility for its internal affairs,
and only external issues were delegated to the federal government. Crucially, this was also the case with taxation. States retained complete
control of collection and revenue, and the federal state was financed
by subventions proportional to income. The two Peruvian states would
divide the responsibility to pay external debt between them, whereas
Bolivia would not recognize any obligation to pay any part of it.

The Confederation, similarly to the federal project proposed by
Bolívar a decade earlier, was to ensure that, in spite of their independence, states would maintain their nationalities while also having a
supranational identity. For that purpose, a whole new series of symbols
were put forward. The process started with the newly created State of
Southern Peru. The new flag design combined elements from those of
Peru and Bolivia. There would be a green and red horizontal line to the
right and a vertical red one to the left. On the red section there was
a yellow flaming sun with four stars representing the provinces of the
southern state. The Confederate flag was all red, incorporating the color
that was common to the flags of the three member states. At the center
was the coat of arms of each state and a crown of laurel.

The flags and coats of arms were important symbols. They made Santa
Cruz's intention of building new states very clear. Although conceived
as a federal union that gave each of the states much freedom, the
Confederation had an extremely centralized inner structure. Most of the
power was in the hands of the Protector. It was his sole responsibility
to appoint men to all important posts. He was not hindered by any
elected officials and did not even have to respond to a supreme court,
or in fact to any judicial body. This was what Santa Cruz meant when
he explained that his federation was different from any seen before. It

---

[2]  Zapata, "La política peruana y la confederación Perú Boliviana," pp. 109, 110. In
     *Guerra, región y nación. La Confederación Perú Boliviana 1836–1839*. Santiago de
     Chile: Gobierno de Chile, Universidad Andrés Bello y Centro de Investigaciones
     Diego Barros Arana, 2009 Carlos Donoso y Jaime Rosenblitt eds.

combined a loose union of states that retained many options for self-government with a strong executive power at the center of the union. The Protector was, to a large extent, the federation itself. This doubtless came straight from Bolívar.

Santa Cruz was proud of his creation. He wrote to some of his former comrades in arms from the wars of independence, who had been close to the Liberator, explaining how the Confederation made it possible to avenge the memory of Bolívar, who had died in the port of Santa Marta in 1830 when he was on his way to exile.[3] Bolivarian inspiration was important; it could be clearly seen all over the institutional design. The project nevertheless responded to a wish the southern provinces of Peru had cherished for a long time: to become, on the one hand, more autonomous and, on the other, to maintain their links with Bolivia, particularly the department of La Paz. From pre-Hispanic times these areas had shared much. In fact, to this day the Aymara people live divided between countries in the environs of Lake Titicaca. The Incas had expanded their control along the mountains and valleys of present-day Bolivia, reaching all the way to the large esplanades of the pampas. Today, in northern Argentina, Quechua is still spoken in communities descended from the people who were transported there in Inca times. These linkages between the peoples surrounding the lake, from the Pacific to the Pampas, were greatly strengthened during the colonial era when the economy of the region developed to provide for the largest mining city of the Americas: Potosí. During the late eighteenth century, this constant communication allowed social discontent to spread quickly among these provinces. Túpac Amaru's rebellion, for instance, had immediate impact, and similar uprisings broke out in La Paz and Oruro, areas that were socially and economically integrated with Cuzco.

The Confederation was built on this very long common history. Not only did the provinces have many reasons to remain united, but the ones in southern Peru had long desired control over their administrative matters. As discussed in chapter 1, an important issue during the Great Rebellion in 1780 had been the colonial system of *audiencias*. There had never been a judicial court in Cuzco. Establishing it was probably the

---

[3] Letter to Tomás Heres, Tacna, 18 April, 1837, *Archivo Histórico del Mariscal Andrés de Santa Cruz*, Clemencia Santa Cruz de Siles Salinas; Andrés de Santa Cruz Schuhkrafft; Lima: Universidad del Pacífico, 1991, vol. VI, p. 134, and 17 May 1837, p. 182.

only tangible victory of the uprising. Many advocated for the Audiencia's jurisdiction over all the provinces in the south. A strong regional sentiment was evident in these territories south of the river Pampas, and the wars of independence had provided another fruitful moment for its development. Many in the cities of Cuzco and Arequipa invested heavily in an attempt at military control of the provinces south of Lake Titicaca. As the situation changed during the wars, there was further integration between the areas under the jurisdiction of the Audiencia of Cuzco and the ones under the Audiencia of Charcas. The north and south of Peru, on the other hand, became more distant from each other after independence was declared in Trujillo and Lima. For nearly four years, southern Peru, and what later became Bolivia, were the only areas loyal to the king of Spain. Political proximity did nothing but strengthen these already-existing linkages. It is important to consider that when the Confederation was proposed, only a decade had elapsed since independence and the formal end of the union in the southern Andes. The process of setting up new republics had been difficult, and there had been several attempts to federate the newly established states.

Santa Cruz was not acting in a vacuum. Even his nemesis, Agustín Gamarra, agreed that it was best to unify the two countries. Gamarra, however, believed that Bolivia should simply be annexed to Peru. Many provinces in the south of Peru had longed for a formal union between the two countries for several decades, so they supported the Confederation. In spite of the shared goal of unity, there were serious discrepancies in how to implement it. Provinces had different notions of what constituted a good federal arrangement. During the months of open confrontation, Santa Cruz capitalized on this. He gave few details of how the union would function, and this allowed people in each province to imagine the federation in the way best suited for them. Santa Cruz gave no details on how the union was to be implemented until he was able to actually do so. This strategy of leaving the details of the Confederation open to different interpretations was successful.

Another way in which Santa Cruz tried to maintain support in areas in which he intervened was by not enforcing military recruitment and by keeping control of his own troops. Santa Cruz achieved this by ensuring that his men were paid on time and were allowed to return to their provinces of origin as soon as their commitment to the army had ended. The ability to maintain the loyalty of his men was one of the key reasons behind his triumph at the battle of Yanacocha, when Gamarra was defeated on his home territory. Santa Cruz's letters show how much of his attention was focused on establishing a long-term relationship with the communities that provided him with men for his army. It was clear to him that his project hinged on his ability to control his men. He sought the support of an army instead of depending on guerrilla forces. In times of acute economic difficulty, Santa Cruz preferred to pay the military rather than civil servants, and he used some of the strategies he had learned from the Spanish to fund his forces, such as asking members of the elite who supported him to help sustain battalions of 600 men.[4]

Regular payment, the commitment to short periods of service, and the return to their communities on finishing their time were all central to the experience of service in Santa Cruz's army. Those fighting also considered timely provision of goods such as uniforms to be extremely important. This was so central to the relationship between the leader and his men that when Santa Cruz heard that some of his soldiers were being forced to pay for uniforms and armament that had been taken by deserters, he immediately wrote to the commanders in charge and asked for this situation to be resolved.[5] The uniforms produced in Cuzco were of such high quality that Santa Cruz had continued ordering them, even when he was using the strongest nationalist rhetoric in Bolivia. Artisans and cloth producers had therefore much to gain with the Confederation. Together with food producers and elite members linked to his wife's family, they made up the core of Santa Cruz's support in Cuzco.

Gamarra's home town, the same city that had not long before backed Santa Cruz's fiercest opponents, now received him with open arms. As soon as Santa Cruz arrived in September 1835, weeks of public celebrations followed. Not only were many in the city and province making a large profit out of the Confederation, but some harbored the hope that Cuzco's importance would finally be recognized and it would be made capital of the federation. Santa Cruz was eager to maintain this hopeful spirit, and he combined a policy of removing Gamarra's backers from office with the promotion of those whom he considered

[4] Letter from Santa Cruz to Ramón Herrera and to Pío Tristán, Tacna, 23 April 1837, in *Archivo Histórico del Mariscal Andrés de Santa Cruz*, vol. VI, pp. 142, 147.

[5] "Instrucciones al Coronel Geronimo Villagra," in *Archivo Histórico del Mariscal Andrés de Santa Cruz*, vol. VI, p. 163.

to be working in favor of his regime. To raise income in the province, he devised a scheme by which those who were renting property from the state would provide half of their payment in advance as a loan to the government.[6] This was seen with much sympathy as a great step away from the arbitrary collections that had characterized the Gamarra (1829–34) and Salaverry (1835) regimes.

Santa Cruz had taken Cuzco from the control of its favorite son in mid-1835 for several reasons. His better military organization enabled him to win, even though he had fewer men. At the time of battle, it was more important to have a committed army than numerous loosely held auxiliaries who were unwilling to fight. Also, Santa Cruz was no stranger to Cuzco. He had his own support base organized by his in-laws and could count on the liberals, who detested his opponents and had long tried to get rid of them. Ultimately, the way in which he played the regional card benefited Santa Cruz greatly. Once Gamarra abandoned his pledge to fight for Cuzco's primacy and gave his backing to Salaverry, the representative of the Lima elite, many in the city of his birth believed that he was no longer protecting their interests.

The moment Santa Cruz controlled Puno and Cuzco, the rest of southern Peru fell like a house of cards. One of the places where he had most support was in the department of Ayacucho. In the highlands of Huanta, Indians who became known as Iquichanos had resisted the newly established republic in 1826 and 1827; Santa Cruz had fought against them when he was briefly President of Peru. In 1834, the Iquichanos had sided with Orbegoso, who reached an agreement with them, offering to recognize many of their claims against the state in exchange for their support against Gamarra.[7] The Indians in this area organized guerrillas and in return were treated as citizens by the liberal government. One of their most important demands had been an exemption from tribute payment for six years. The arrangement was not finalized with Orbegoso, because Salaverry took over. The Iquichanos nevertheless refused to pay, and Santa Cruz capitalized on these differences. His agents in Ayacucho worked hard to gain the support of these Indians, even though he had once fought them himself. Once

---

[6]   For more details on this scheme and the reception of Santa Cruz in Cuzco see Luis Miguel Glave, *La república instalada. Formación nacional y prensa en el Cuzco 1825–1839*, Lima: IEP, 2004, p. 198.

[7]   For more on the Iquichanos and their participation in the 1834 conflict see Méndez, *The Plebeian Republic: the Huanta Rebellion and the Making of the Peruvian State (1820–1850)* Durham NC: Duke University Press, 2005, pp. 192–205.

he took control of the area, Santa Cruz passed an executive decree exempting them from the payment of tribute as long as they remained loyal to his regime.[8] This was an astute move that allowed him to retain the support of the Iquichanos and consolidate his control of the whole province of Ayacucho without much effort. The Indians in this region remained loyal to the Confederation throughout its existence, providing Santa Cruz with an important buffer between the northern and southern states. The division between north and south had traditionally been at the river Pampas, just north of the department of Ayacucho: precisely where the Iquichanos lived.

In the south, Arequipa proved to be the province most dedicated to the federation. Previous attempts to create a union had been launched there, and people of all backgrounds supported it. Just like their counterparts in Cuzco, the elites of Arequipa had long fought to join together with the areas of the Altiplano. Their principal aim in both cases was to keep trade flowing with the mining city of Potosí. The people from these provinces had raised armies and sent their most prominent men to fight in Upper Peru when the Junta of Buenos Aires sent its armies in 1810.

The most important port for Bolivia was located in the province of Arequipa. Arica and the neighboring town of Tacna depended greatly on the trade and transport of goods to the highlands and did not want policies that would distance them from Bolivia. Not only the elites but most of the population in the province of Arequipa had sacrificed much to defend Orbegoso. During the civil war, in spite of twice being occupied by enemy troops, they had never relented in their determination to sustain what they considered the legal order. In June 1835, the Peruvian president asserted that with the defeat of their enemies, security had been achieved. As a reward, all farmers should return to their homes. He assured them that the army would not be allowed to recruit in the countryside.[9] Moreover, a year later personal and property taxes were abolished in Arequipa. In April 1836, the tax collected on milling, an important source of revenue in this wheat-producing area, was returned to the control of the municipality.[10] Clearly Santa Cruz

[8] Ibid., p. 202.
[9] Sarah C. Chambers, *From Subjects to Citizens: Honor, Gender, and Politics in Arequipa, Peru, 1780–1854*, University Park: Pennsylvania State University Press, 1999, p. 226.
[10] Ibid.

continued courting the support of the city where he was held in high esteem by the popular sectors as well as by the elites.

Similarly to Cuzqueños, the people of Arequipa were in favor of the Confederation not merely because they wanted to further their trade linkages with Bolivia. Arequipeños also wanted to increase their independence from Lima and become the center of the new admin-istration. There was, however, much competition between Cuzqueños and Arequipeños, and they often changed their allegiances to ensure the best possible treatment from whichever side they thought would give them a better deal. The people of Arequipa hated Gamarra and any increase in Cuzco's power so much that they would have sided with Salaverry if Santa Cruz had given Gamarra his support. Divisions within the province of Arequipa were also evident. The southern cities of Moquegua, Tacna, and Arica wanted to become part of Bolivia as a strategy to become independent from Arequipa. The antipathy of the people of these cities toward the capital of their province was so great that they would rather belong to another country than remain under the control of Arequipa.

Acutely aware of these differences, Santa Cruz aimed to navigate them as best he could. He tried to minimize the conflict between Cuzco and Arequipa by providing people with enough benefits, mostly eco-nomic, that they would not complain. In the case of the cities in the Department of Arequipa, he did eventually create a new province. To diffuse confrontation between Cuzco and Arequipa over where the capital should be, he called the representatives to confirm that the Confederation would meet in Tacna.

In Peru, support for Santa Cruz came nearly exclusively from the southern provinces that became the state of Southern Peru. In Bolivia, he was backed by the people of his native La Paz, Oruro, and certain sectors in Potosí. Further south there was much less enthusiasm for his project. In the administrative city of Chuquisaca – now more frequently being referred to as Sucre – there was open opposition to his venture. Having the backing of the most populated and economically integrated areas in Bolivia was crucial to Santa Cruz's ability to control opposition, ensure that Congress ratified all his actions, and maintain a completely subordinated military machine on which he could rely completely. He was acutely aware of the importance of the press, and he repeatedly asked his allies to ensure not only that positive articles were published, but also that entire newspapers were financed to support the Confederation, especially in Northern Peru and Bolivia.[11] His control over the army was in large part dependent on his masterly eye for administration. His ability to keep his men clothed, fed, and content, because they tended to travel with their woman companions on campaign, made possible his venture in Peru.

Santa Cruz also counted on the support of many of the generals and officials with whom he had fought on the royalist side. The most prominent was Pío Tristán, under whom he trained between 1809 and 1813. Tristán was the head of one of the most important families from Arequipa. He supported the Confederate project with great conviction, unlike his brother Domingo, who abandoned the army as soon as Gamarra was sent into exile. Pío Tristán had remained on the royalist side until after the capitulation at Ayacucho and had briefly been viceroy when he was the Intendant of Cuzco in 1824. Tristán had fought for nearly two decades to maintain the union between southern Peru and the Audiencia of Charcas. Although a wealthy man, he was fluent in Aymara, a language he had learned when he had accompanied his father on campaign against Túpaj Katari in the 1780s.[12] This elite southerner returned to political prominence during the Confederation. He was once again made a general and became president of the Southern State in October 1838.

Santa Cruz had known many of the Bolivian generals for a long time. Some, such as José Miguel Velasco and Ramón Herrera (who was described as Chilean or Argentine), had, like Santa Cruz himself, been royalists before changing sides. Others, such as Carlos Medinacelli or the Argentine Jerónimo Villagra, had remained loyal to the crown until Ayacucho.[13] Among those of the highest ranks, several had fought for independence from the beginning. Bolivians José de Ballivián and José María Urdinea and Peruvians Domingo Nieto and Francisco Vidal were among them. Prominent Peruvian ex-presidents Luís José de Orbegoso and José de la Riva-Agüero also supported Santa Cruz. Both came of aristocratic families from northern Peru and Lima, and both had served

---

[11] Letter from Santa Cruz to Tristán, Arica, 1 March 1837, in *Archivo Histórico del Mariscal Andrés de Santa Cruz*, vol. VI, p. 82.

[12] For biographical details on Pío Tristán see Manuel de Mendiburu *Diccionario Histórico Biográfico del Perú*, Lima: Imprenta Solis, 1876.

[13] For more details see Celia Wu Brading, *Generales y Diplomaticos: Gran Bretaña y el Perú, 1820–1840*, Lima: PUCP, 1993.

in the colonial militia and joined the independence movement on the arrival of San Martín.

The largest contingent among the army officers who backed the Confederation were foreign born. This included men from other parts of the Americas, such as Argentines Francisco de Paula Otero and Mariano Necochea – whom Santa Cruz had met when he joined the patriots after his defeat in the battle of Cerro de Pasco in 1820 – and Venezuelan Trinidad Morán, with whom he had fought in the battle of Pichincha in 1822 and who had married and settled in Arequipa. Even more prominent in Santa Cruz's army were the Europeans who supported him. Many had traveled to South America after fighting in the Napoleonic wars. Some such as the German Otto Felipe Braun, and Irishman Francis Burdett O'Connor had fought with Bolívar, while Irishman John O'Brien and Englishman William Miller had come to Peru with San Martín. In his memoirs, O'Connor remarked that it was among the foreign born that Santa Cruz found his most loyal supporters, partly because these men could not aspire to become bigger political players than they already were.[14]

Having such backing from foreign soldiers, it was not coincidental that the Confederation also had the approval of the United States, France, and Great Britain, the most influential nations on the Pacific. Santa Cruz had a particularly close relationship with the regime of Louis Philippe of Orleans. The French king had even made him a member of the French Legion, a great honor for a foreign dignitary. France had been the first country to recognize Bolivia as an independent republic, and even though they did not sign a treaty with the Confederation, they were important supporters of Santa Cruz's regime. The United States had a great interest in trade with countries in the Pacific and was quick to recognize Santa Cruz as the best trading partner available. His relationship with Great Britain was mediated through an old companion in arms, Belford Hinton Wilson. Wilson, who had been an aide-de-camp to Bolívar and was at the time the chargé d'affaires in Lima, was instrumental in the signing of a trade agreement between the Confederation and Queen Victoria.

Wilson was the son of an important politician of liberal inclination. His father had done much to support the efforts of the American colonies

---

[14] Francis Burdett O'Connor, *Un irlandes con Bolívar. Recuerdos de la independencia de América del Sur en Venezuela, Colombia, Bolivia, Perú y la Argentina por un jefe de la legión Británica de Bolívar*, 3rd ed. Caracas: El Cid, Editor, 1977, p. 266.

to obtain independence from Spain. He had sent his son to Bolívar, in the hope that he could further his career with an appointment to the Colombian army, because he did not have enough funds to obtain such a commission in the British Army. Wilson met Bolívar in 1824 and, with the rank of captain, fought in the battles of Junín and Ayacucho. He was close to the *libertador* and in 1826 was given the task of taking the Bolivian Constitution to Sucre.[15] Wilson remained with Bolívar until his death in Santa Marta in 1830. He then returned to England to attempt once more to obtain a diplomatic post. Two years later, he succeeded and was sent to Lima – to a country dominated by the enemies of his mentor. In his correspondence with the Foreign Office, Wilson was open about two things: his dislike for Gamarra and his conviction that a federation in the Americas would never be successful. His experience in Colombia had taught him that the system was not practicable. Wilson thought highly of Santa Cruz, a fellow Bolivarian, but he dismissed as futile his ideas of creating a durable union between Peru and Bolivia. Wilson believed that the best solution was to divide Peru into two republics. In spite of this, Santa Cruz was able to convince him of the viability of his plan. Eight months after condemning the idea as impossible, Wilson wrote to the British Foreign Minister recommending that the crown give all its support to the project.

Santa Cruz was persuasive, and his arguments were backed by the benefits the British would obtain in exchange for their support. Gamarra had implemented protectionist trade policies, raising tariffs up to 90 percent. His main purpose was to ensure that local manufacturing, especially of textiles, could compete with the cheaper imports, which were mainly British. Another important goal for Gamarra had been to create an incentive for traders to lend him money. He offered heavy tax discounts to those who funded his regime, and he succeeded quite well. Even foreign traders were forced to participate, desperate as they were to trade, and they provided 57 percent of the loans.[16] British traders were particularly opposed to this practice, believing that local traders held an unfair advantage.

The disagreement over trade policy was, however, greatest with Chileans. In 1832, tariffs on the products they exchanged with Peru rose to unprecedented levels. Soon there was no more Chilean flour

---

[15] For a study of Wilson and his relationship to Peru see Celia Wu Brading, *Generales y diplomaticos*, pp. 97–171.

[16] Ibid., p. 137.

in the markets in Peru. Instead they were flooded with flour coming from the United States. Chile stopped stocking Peruvian sugar and brought the product from Brazil instead. Orbegoso, who understood the needs of the sugar-producing economy of northern Peru, drafted a treaty with Chile that Salaverry implemented. Wilson argued in his consular reports that this agreement was highly prejudicial to Peru, because they could not produce more than a third of the sugar needed by Chile. The British Consul argued that the Chileans would continue to trade with Brazil while controlling the Peruvian flour market.

With few options to finance themselves, the governments of Orbegoso and Salaverry retained high taxation as a way to force traders to lend them money. Once Santa Cruz took over, this changed. He introduced trade legislation that he had drafted for Bolivia a decade earlier. Foreign traders benefited most. The British obtained special favors, such as a monopoly over the trade in the port of Islay, in Arequipa, which ensured that the French were not allowed to trade there. In June 1837, a treaty was signed that was extremely favorable to Great Britain. Santa Cruz wrote to Wilson assuring him that no one else would have been able to obtain such conditions from him.[17] Indeed, the ministers of the Confederation who had been negotiating had refused to accept some of the most controversial issues. One of them was giving Great Britain the status of "most favored nation." This meant all British merchandise had to be taxed as Peruvian. The agreement was reciprocal, of course, but Peru as yet had few products that it could export to Britain.

The Confederate government's desire to gain the backing of powerful allies was clear. Six months before the trade treaty was signed with the British, a similar one had been agreed with the United States, which was also granted the status of "most favored nation." This treaty had not caused such a public outcry. The difference was that the British naval forces were given the right to disembark, in order to protect their nationals, without first seeking permission from the president. Santa Cruz's faith in the naval power of the British and his belief that they would protect him from the Chileans lay behind his apparently naïve openness to the British traders. Santa Cruz felt that it was important to keep his foreign allies happy. He was convinced that their support

---

[17] Letter from Santa Cruz to Wilson, Lima 1 June 1837, copy found in *The National Archives of Great Britain* FO61/45, quoted by Wu Brading, *Generales y diplomaticos*, pp. 204–5.

and official recognition protected the Confederation against its fiercest enemies.

## THE ENEMIES OF THE CONFEDERATION

The Argentine Confederation and Chile were unimpressed by the idea of the union of their northern neighbors Peru and Bolivia. The main reason for this was geopolitical. Both countries feared the possibility of a strong union that threatened their interests. The question of trade was also central, particularly in the case of Chile. The commercial policy set forward by Santa Cruz, so well received by the foreign traders, was viewed by the Chilean government with great distrust. The Confederation's greatest nemesis did not relent in its efforts to destroy the union between Peru and Bolivia until it succeeded in crushing any hope of creating a larger country.

Santa Cruz was aware of the opposition he was likely to face from Chile and Argentina. But he was confident that he could overcome it by flaunting his international connections and advocating peace. This proved to be a miscalculation. Chile had no intention of tolerating the creation of a strong union north of its border. An excellent excuse to pursue this relentless policy was provided by Peru itself, when they allowed a misguided attempt by a deposed Chilean president, Ramón Freire, to attempt to return by sea to regain power. Freire bought some recently decommissioned Peruvian fighting ships and set sail to southern Chile from Callao. The regime in Santiago presented this event as Peruvian aggression, a *casus belli*. The refusal by president Orbegoso to honor the trade agreement he had negotiated with Chile in 1834 (which was finally signed by Salaverry) should not, however, be underestimated as a cause for war.

As soon as Santa Cruz found out the expedition was on its way to Chile, he knew that it would bring him trouble. He had little faith in its success, he had not sanctioned it, and he had not even been close to Lima when the exiled Chilean ex-president embarked. Santa Cruz complained bitterly to those who had allowed it to happen, explaining that it would be used as a weapon to accuse the Confederation of interfering with Chilean domestic policy.[18] Yet in spite of his public

---

[18] Letter from Santa Cruz to Manuel de la Cruz Méndez (his minister in Santiago), Jauja, 17 July 1836, in *Archivo Histórico del Mariscal Andrés de Santa Cruz*, vol. V, pp. 251, 252.

protestations that he had nothing to do with the Freire affaire, Santa Cruz did later instruct his agents to provide all possible covert support to his cause and particularly to the Indians of southern Chile who were intent on attacking the government.[19] In this context of deep distrust, all efforts by Santa Cruz to limit the damage were fruitless. The regime in Santiago had decided that they would destroy the Confederation, no matter the cost.

The Chileans saw the union as the biggest enemy to their stability. Chile was governed by conservative president Joaquín Prieto. In reality, however, the man who ran the country was Diego Portales. A wealthy merchant, he eschewed the idea of being president and was instead its general minister. Portales did not want to be limited by office and instead controlled the country from his ministry. Portales believed in the importance of "a strong government that should be led by men of virtue that could direct citizens on the path of order and progress."[20] Similarly to Santa Cruz, he considered a strong organized government as the basis for peace and prosperity. Portales confided to Admiral Manuel Blanco Encalada, who was preparing the navy to fight, that they were "fighting for a second independence of Chile."[21] The minister believed they could not but be alarmed by the existence of a Confederation. In the long run, he was convinced, the common origin, language, habits, religion, ideas, and traditions Chile shared with the Confederation would doom Chile to being overpowered. He feared that Chile would follow Peru in becoming the Confederation's dependent. The only solution he saw was for the Confederation to disappear forever from the map of America.

Chile was at the time overrun with Peruvian exiles not welcome in the Confederation. Santa Cruz was partly to blame for this. In contrast to his policies for the inclusion of former political enemies that helped him pacify Bolivia, he refused to accept his Peruvian foes in his government.[22] In his letters he repeatedly wrote about the importance of showing strength; he believed Orbegoso and La Mar had proven to

---

[19]  Letter from Santa Cruz to Trinidad Morán, La Paz, 29 March 1837, in *Archivo Histórico del Mariscal Andrés de Santa Cruz*, vol. VI, p. 110.

[20]  John A. Crow, "Democracy of the Oligarchy" in *The Epic of Latin America*, New York: University of California Press, 1992, p. 641.

[21]  Letter from Diego Portales to Manuel Blanco Encalada, Santiago, 17 September 1836, in *Epistolario de don Diego Portales, 1821–1837*, 3 vols. Santiago: Imprenta General de Prisiones, 1936–37, pp. 452–4.

[22]  Letter from Santa Cruz to Blas Cerdeña, La Paz, 24 March 1837, in *Archivo Histórico del Mariscal Andrés de Santa Cruz*, vol. VI, p. 102.

be too weak. There were two opposing factions wanting to capitalize on the Chilean hatred of the Confederation. One was headed by a former vice president and erstwhile friend and collaborator of Santa Cruz: none other than Antonio Gutiérrez de La Fuente. He had been in Chile the longest, as he had been exiled by Gamarra's wife in 1831 and had returned to fight on the side of Orbegoso in 1834, but he had gone back to Santiago after Santa Cruz's intervention. The other faction revolved around the writer and publicist Felipe Pardo y Aliaga. He had many important contacts in Santiago and was working to have his protégé Manuel Ignacio de Vivanco, a younger colonel in the Peruvian army, chosen to lead the Peruvian contingent that was to accompany the Chileans on their attack to Peru. Conspicuously absent from this milieu was Gamarra, who had taken refuge in Guayaquil. In spite of his efforts to influence the Ecuadorian president, who was also being lobbied by the Chileans to join them in their fight against the Confederation, the regime of Vicente Rocafuerte remained distant from Santa Cruz, but never openly declared against it. This was partly because the Protector was still held in high esteem by many in Ecuador because of his participation in the campaigns to liberate the country from the Spanish – but mainly because Santa Cruz's closeness to the late Bolívar, whose memory was still capable of uniting the men who had come of age under his shadow, prevented Ecuadoreans from openly opposing him.

The Argentine Confederation – the loose political association under the command of Juan Manuel de Rosas in the former United Provinces of the River Plate – could see the perils of a strong and consolidated country in their northern border. Following on the Chilean cue, the Argentine Confederation declared war on the Peru-Bolivia Confederation. The Argentines argued that they feared an attack from the newly created country, because the many political exiles within its borders could use this as an excuse to return. Although many of the opponents of Rosas and other *caudillos* from the region had taken refuge in Bolivia, there was no intention of increasing its territory by expanding its borders to the south. Nevertheless, this was a distraction. Santa Cruz had to divert some of his troops in the Altiplano to defend the border with Argentina. Having come of age during the wars of independence, he knew all too well what a gaucho invasion could mean to his homeland, even though he also knew that they could only attack between the months of April and June.[23]

---

[23] "Instrucciones a S.S.I. el General en Jefe del ejército del Sur," La Paz, 28 March, 1837, in *Archivo Histórico del Mariscal Andrés de Santa Cruz*, vol. VI, p. 106.

Argentina's strategy against Bolivia was the same as it had been during the wars of independence: to take the southernmost province of Tarija. Chile threatened Peru from the sea, just as they had done in the 1820s. The navy had taken Salaverry's side, so after his defeat, when Orbegoso was returned to power by Santa Cruz, the majority of officers were relieved from their duties. Most vessels were decommissioned. It was a couple of these ships that the Chilean ex-president had leased in his ill-advised attempt to return to power. Nevertheless, Santa Cruz felt protected by the treaty he had signed with Great Britain. He believed that it was enough to guard the Confederation, and was extremely surprised when, the day after he had sent a circular to all the governments in America detailing the creation of the Confederation, the only three ships remaining in the Peruvian Navy were captured by the Chilean vessel *Aquiles*.[24] The Chilean captain explained that this was a preemptive measure. He claimed to have been following instructions to obtain guarantees that the Confederation had only peaceful intentions toward Chile. The British naval officers stationed in Lima and the British Consul considered this to be an act of treason.

Santa Cruz was livid. His first reaction was to arrest the Chilean chargé d'affaires and order Chilean ships to be attacked. He soon realized that this was not a useful tactic, so he gave the diplomatic agent his passport and asked him to leave the country.[25] Peace negotiations followed aboard a British vessel, under the aegis of Her Majesty's consul Belford Hinton Wilson. Santa Cruz agreed to allow the Chileans to retain the captured ships until a final arrangement was reached by both governments. Although he was aware that he was giving the Chileans a great advantage, Santa Cruz argued that there were sound reasons for him to do so: first because he considered peace to be not only desirable but necessary, and second to silence his critics in Chile who argued that his intention was to attack them.[26] Santa Cruz allowed the Chileans to take control of the sea. He did so because he wanted to consolidate his hold over the Confederation. As important as this consolidation was,

[24] For details of the naval history of the period see Jorge Ortiz Sotelo, *Perú y Gran Bretaña: política y economía (1808–1839) a través de los informes navales británicos*, Lima: PUCP, 2005, pp. 169–208.

[25] Letter from Santa Cruz to Moran, Lima, 22 August 1836, in *Archivo Histórico del Mariscal Andrés de Santa Cruz*, vol. V, p. 312.

[26] For this see his letters to Nieto, Lima, 29 August 1836, in *Archivo Histórico del Mariscal Andrés de Santa Cruz*, vol. V, p. 337, 338, and Braun, same day, in *Archivo Mariscal Santa Cruz*, leg. 1836–1866, quoted in Parkerson, p. 170.

Santa Cruz had left the ocean open to his enemies, which limited his options once war was declared.

Based on his experience in the wars for independence and his trust in the backing by the foreign naval powers in the Pacific, Santa Cruz did not consider the control of the sea to be enough for the Chileans to defeat him. The difficulties he had faced in 1823, when he had attempted to overpower the royalists by using seaports, had led him to believe an organized army was the most important thing in the Andes. He was under the impression that Chile did not have a proper army. He believed they lacked officers, but above all he was convinced they did not have money – what he called "the soul of war." He did worry that the enemy would land in the north, his perceived weakest point, but was reassured once it became clear that Ecuador would not intervene.[27] Santa Cruz was confident that his powerful army was a good deterrent to the Chileans, who would be forced to attack unimportant ports. He did not consider them to be a match to his well-paid and trusted army.

This was a miscalculation. Portales was once again instrumental in preventing his government from accepting the peace proposal. Indeed, when the agreement arrived in Santiago, preparations were already in full swing to send an expedition to Peru. In October, a commission headed by the president of the supreme court and Admiral Blanco Encalada was dispatched to negotiate peace aboard five fully armed vessels. Their instructions were simple: they were to obtain the dissolution of the Confederation at all costs.[28]

The Peruvian government refused to enter negotiations with a blockaded port. The Chilean representative responded by noting that war had practically been declared. The representative of the British Navy managed to convince Blanco Encalada to take a less hostile attitude. The Chilean Admiral only agreed to negotiate peace so trade could resume. A truce was agreed to; however, it lasted only a few weeks, until the Chilean Congress sent its approval to declare war against Peru. Chile established a blockade of all ports, exactly as they had done during the wars of independence from Spain. The Confederation retaliated by opening all its ports to foreign vessels.

Although the Confederation had the backing of Britain, France, the United States, and the Vatican, when push came to shove not one of

---

[27] Letter from Santa Cruz to Braun, Lima, 12 December 1836, in *Archivo Histórico del Mariscal Andrés de Santa Cruz*, vol. V, pp. 483, 84.
[28] Ortiz Sotelo, *Perú y Gran Bretaña*, p. 175.

them was willing to take action to defend it. Santa Cruz trusted the British fleet to be a deterrent to Chile. He counted on their support in case of a direct attack. To combat the Chilean blockade, all ports were open to foreign vessels, including the small ones between Callao and Arica that were used only for local intracoastal trade. Blanco Encalada assured the British admiral that the neutrality of his fleet would be respected. Throughout 1836, trade by foreign merchants continued without difficulties. Santa Cruz was even invited to travel by sea aboard a British vessel from Lima to Arica to open the Southern-Peruvian Congress. Unable to find suitable dates for his trip, he sailed aboard a French ship instead, returning to Lima on a British navy frigate. This was a successful coup that showed the level of international support his government enjoyed. Chileans had no recourse but to complain about the lack of respect for neutrality. The British government later apologized to the government in Santiago for having overstepped their neutral position. Two things became clear with this episode, on the one hand, Santa Cruz had the backing of the men on the ground – consuls and the naval officers; on the other hand, it was also clear that London in particular, as well as the commander of the British naval forces in the Pacific, were disinclined to take sides and wanted to maintain neutrality at all costs.

Officially, Santa Cruz made every effort possible to maintain peace, but he also made sure that Chilean wheat was kept out of markets in the Peru-Bolivia Confederation.[29] He knew that this was the greatest possible "hostility" toward Chile that he could undertake. This made Prieto and Portales in particular ever more adamant that they could not allow the Confederation to prosper. They were convinced that its very existence was a threat to the balance of power in the region. They argued they had as much right as Bolivia to intervene in Peru in times of crisis. To make their point more boldly, they accused the Bolivian minister of interfering with domestic politics and threw him out of the country. The Chilean government engaged with newly arrived Casimiro Olañeta, although they never acknowledged him as a representative of the Confederation and simply accredited him as the representative of Bolivia. Olañeta's brief was to try to convince the Chilean government

---

[29] "Instrucciones reservadas que servirán al conocimiento del presidente del consejo de ministros del Estado Nor Peruano," in *Archivo Histórico del Mariscal Andrés de Santa Cruz*, vol. VI, p. 65.

of the Confederation's peaceful intentions. He was also to make contact with the Peruvian opposition in exile and give them the impression that if they were to change sides, they would be welcome to return. Santa Cruz asked Olañeta to tread very carefully. He did not want his enemies ever to be able to say that Santa Cruz had tried to bribe them. What he did want was to ensure that they knew they would receive a handsome financial reward if they changed their policy. This was a remarkable brief, especially considering that Olañeta had been sent to Chile on his way back from Europe because Santa Cruz did not trust having him in Bolivia. Bolivian historians have even stated that Olañeta had openly told Portales that he opposed the Confederation and wanted to see "*el cholo*" fail.[30]

It is interesting how much this epithet was used against Santa Cruz in the context of the war with Chile. The word has been recorded as having been used by Olañeta and Portales, and this was also how author and publicist Felipe Pardo y Aliaga described Santa Cruz in his writing. He had done so at least since 1835, when he had been Salaverry's minister. At the time he had produced the newspaper *El Coco de Santa Cruz* – roughly translated as "Santa Cruz the bogeyman." Pardo was born in Lima in 1806 but spent most of his youth in Cuzco, where his father, who hailed from the Peninsula, held an important post in the colonial administration. When his father was taken prisoner by rebels during the 1814 revolution, Pardo was only a child. He was lucky not to have been orphaned at the time, because the army in which Santa Cruz and Gamarra served defeated the rebels. Pardo returned to Peru in 1828 after studying in Spain and realizing that he would never obtain a diplomatic post there, despite his father's connections. He began his political career in Lima by becoming part of a circle of conservative writers and thinkers who backed Gamarra's first government because they longed to have a strong leader. Pardo edited several official newspapers, and in 1830 he was sent as a secretary to the diplomatic mission that was negotiating a trade agreement with Bolivia. There, in the aftermath of the confrontation over the possible secession of the southern provinces to Bolivia, he became personally acquainted with Santa Cruz. He soon realized that they were firmly established at opposite ends of the political spectrum.

[30] For detail on Olañeta's mission in Chile see Parkerson, *Andres de Santa Cruz, y la Confederación Perú-Boliviana, 1835–1839*, La Paz: Editorial Juventud, 1984, pp. 175–83.

Although Pardo's political enmity with Santa Cruz began in this period, it was not until much later that he used his pen to discredit him using racial taunts. By 1835, Pardo made repeated references to his large mouth, calling him *cholo jetón*. He called Santa Cruz names such as Alejandro Huanaco that brought to mind his Andean origin and his aspirations to create a new Macedonia in Bolivia. He also made fun of Santa Cruz's predilection for France, ridiculing him as a would-be Bonaparte.[31] It is interesting to note that Pardo used this strategy when he was working for Salaverry, and not before, when he was serving Gamarra, who was also of mixed heritage and came from Cuzco. Pardo described Gamarra as a cultured man who spoke Quechua, Aymara, and French.[32] Yet Pardo used only the most racially offensive language toward Santa Cruz after Pardo was sent into exile and was defending the regime from what he considered was an invasion. In Chile, Pardo was once again closest to the most conservative Peruvian Creole exile groups.

Portales supported Pardo, making him quite powerful. It seemed possible that Pardo's preferred candidate would accompany the Chilean expedition, being prepared to fight the Confederation. In the end, Portales backed the faction headed by La Fuente. The Peruvian former vice president trumped the choice because he was more experienced and had numerous contacts. He had initially asked only for financial support for an all-Peruvian force, but this had not been approved because Portales feared that a badly prepared, unsuccessful campaign against the Confederation would only strengthen Santa Cruz. The eventual agreement granted Chile excellent conditions. If successful, Peru would recognize the debt incurred during the wars of independence, all the costs of the campaign against the Confederation would be covered, and a navy was never to be developed in Peru, because Chile feared that they would always have a larger army. Chile would also be allowed to keep the vessels they had taken. All commercial policies implemented by Santa Cruz would be rescinded and the agreements signed with Salaverry reintroduced. Chile would be allowed to occupy the ports of Callao and Islay

---

[31] See his letrilla *Para Muchachos* (1835) and his many poems in *El Coco de Santa Cruz* (1835). For a discussion of Pardo's use of race see Cecilia Méndez, "Incas Sí, Indios No: Notes on Peruvian Creole Nationalism and its Contemporary Crisis," *Journal of Latin American Studies* 28 (I), pp. 197–225.

[32] Felipe Pardo y Aliaga, "Semblanzas Peruanas" in *Boletín de la Academia Chilena de Historia (Santiago)*, vol. 32, 1945, p. 66.

until Peru paid all the debt.[33] In return, Chile would help the Peruvian exiles defeat Santa Cruz and would recognize Orbegoso as president. A caveat was added to the agreement: Portales made it a condition that Gamarra and his supporters were to be excluded from the expedition. If Gamarra was later elected president, the Chileans would accept him, but only after free elections. Details of the agreement became public because Gamarra's backers in Chile were so furious at their exclusion from the expedition that they leaked all of the details. The conditions imposed in this agreement were so Draconian that many, including Felipe Pardo y Aliaga, lived to lament having backed the Chilean expedition against the Confederation.

Before the actual war began, an equally virulent battle raged in the press. Santa Cruz used the information obtained on the agreement to discredit the campaign as one that would destroy the nation. Portales, on the other hand, had been careful to prevent any discussion in the Chilean press of Santa Cruz's many attempts to find a peaceful solution to the conflict. He also framed the war against the Confederation as one of national survival against attack by foreign enemies. In spite of this, there was some discussion in Chile of how Portales used the threat to unify the whole country, and how he presented all his opponents as being against the nation itself.[34] Indeed, not everyone in Chile was against the Confederation. The diary of a Chilean soldier at the time candidly speaks of the generalized opposition to the war.[35] British Consul Hugh Wilson, in Tacna, assured the Foreign Office that the prospect of war was highly unpopular in Chile. He claimed that both natives and foreigners were against it, "but the government is so despotic and there is such a system of 'espionage' established that people are afraid to speak their real sentiments."[36] Peruvian newspapers explained that the campaign

[33] Cónsul Belford Hinton Wilson reported this to the Foreign Office on 18 May 1837 and claimed to have little doubt as to the accuracy of these accounts; see *National Archives of Great Britain*, FO 61/45, p. 20.

[34] For a discussion in the Chilean press of this issue see Ana María Stuven, "La palabra en armas: patria y nación en la prensa de la Guerra entre Chile y la Confederación Perú-Boliviana, 1835–1839" in *La República Peregrina: Hombres de armas y letras en America del Sur, 1800–1884*, edited by Carmen McEvoy, Lima: IEP, 2007, pp. 407–41.

[35] Considering that this soldier was very much in favor of the war, this is an interesting source; Antonio Barrena Lopetegui, *Vida de un Soldado: Desde la toma de Valdivia a la Victoria de Yungay*, Jorge Javier Molina Hernández, ed. Santiago de Chile: RiL Editores, 2009, p. 160.

[36] Thomas Crompton, Islay, 14 April 1837, FO 61/48, p. 118.

against Santa Cruz was being presented by Chileans as a nationalist crusade, when it was little more than an attempt by a particular group to cling on to power.

Opposition to Portales and his project was in fact so strong that in June 1837, he was killed. He had been visiting troops preparing to travel to Peru when he was kidnapped by disgruntled army officers. In their manifesto, they declared that they did not want to wage war with Peru; rather, they wanted to stop the abuse of power, which they described as "absolute despotism."[37] Sixty-two officers asserted that this war was the product of the hate of just one man – a man who, acting above the law and the constitution, wanted war at all costs, even when peace was being offered by his opponent. When the army officers realized that they had no possibility of succeeding and taking over the government, they decided to kill the powerful minister anyway. After their defeat, most were tried and executed on 4 July, a day chosen, according to some, because it resonated with all those who fought for the cause of liberty.

The rebels had hoped that the death of warmongering Portales would diminish appetite for war. They were mistaken. After this death, the entire nation rallied behind president Prieto, and there was no more room for political opposition to the armed intervention against the Confederation. Santa Cruz was presented as having had a dark hand in the matter. He always denied having any involvement, even though he hoped Portales's death would mean the end of the Chilean intervention. A month after Portales was killed, in spite of all Santa Cruz's efforts to broker peace with British support, the Chileans sailed for Peru.

## THE FIRST RESTORATION CAMPAIGN

In mid-September 1837, 2,792 Chilean troops and 402 Peruvian exiles sailed from Valparaiso aboard four ships. Santa Cruz expected them to attack in the north, where the Confederation was viewed with little sympathy. The Protector felt that this was his weakest point. He had therefore stationed most of his troops north of Lima. Blanco Encalada, who was sailing from the south, stopped first in Cobija, where the British and French naval forces had secured the port and its residents were protected against any attack. The same happened in Arica,

[37] *Acta de la reunión de Jefes y oficiales acantonados en Quillota en 3 de Junio de 1837*, inserted in FO 61/45, p. 348.

where the British marines landed at the port to look after the property of the British merchants; no goods were taken from the customs house. The expeditionary troops finally disembarked in Quilca, a port close to Arequipa. They went on from there, planning to attack the city. Blanco, who had gained his naval experience during the wars of independence, was convinced that he needed to control this region to swiftly defeat the Confederation. Although he had been born in what later became Argentina and his brother had been born in Chuquisaca, Blanco Encalada had settled in Chile. He had risen to a prominent position and considered himself to be Chilean. Having been part of the navy that kept the royalists at bay, he knew that although conducting the war by sea would allow him to blockade the enemy, it could never defeat the powerful land forces of the Andes.

Blanco Encalada thought that he needed a different strategy from the one used during independence. The Peruvian exiles had led him to believe that Santa Cruz was unpopular in the area. They were all convinced that control over this region would allow them to attack and destroy the core of the Confederation. The plan was to break the line of communication between the Altiplano and the coast. To succeed, this plan needed to be put in practice in conjunction with an attack from Argentina, which would force Santa Cruz to fight on two fronts. Reinforcements would be unable to come from northern or central Peru, because it would be divided in half. Blanco estimated the Confederate troops to number around 2,800 men. He calculated that 1,500 would be forced to remain in the Argentine border, because there hostilities had already been declared.

It is paradoxical that he chose Arequipa for the attack. This was the core area of Confederation support. It was in Arequipa that Salaverry had found his death. It was there that Santa Cruz had been repeatedly called to intervene, not only by local politicians, but also by Orbegoso himself.

La Fuente had been prefect of Arequipa and was married to a member of the local elite. He led Blanco to believe that they could easily get the backing of the most important citizens. In fact, when they arrived, most of the prominent inhabitants had left. The leader of the Confederation government in the city had allowed everyone wishing to leave to take with them all they deemed important, thus preventing the newly arrived forces from accessing goods and money. Santa Cruz had left clear orders that all his men should conduct the "war of resources," which meant that the enemy would be allowed to disembark and enter the territory and, once inland, they would be left without food or provisions.[38] A British-born officer in the Chilean army wrote that he was surprised to see women running away from him when he disembarked in Arica. He also reported having heard that Santa Cruz "was more popular than had been represented in Chile."[39] He was impressed by the troops, which he described as "well officered, and under good discipline."

The most prominent members of society and the Confederate army had retired inland from Arequipa. This made it extremely difficult for the invading troops to obtain enough provisions to feed all their men. Santa Cruz was not pleased when he heard that his men had abandoned the city and had made no effort to defend it, even though it was standard practice of war at the time never to give battle when at a disadvantage. One should fight only when there was as much certainty as possible that the enemy could at least be met under equal conditions.

Santa Cruz, who was in Bolivia when the invasion took place, traveled as fast as he could toward Arequipa. To prevent the enemy from marching north, which was his greatest fear, he spread rumors that there had been a rebellion further south. The Chilean expeditionary force, however, was not able to move anywhere even if it had wanted to. Santa Cruz had left clear instructions that the enemy should not be attacked but allowed to disembark and enticed to intern themselves in the country, to be trapped without resources.[40] This was exactly what happened: after traversing the desert from the coast to Arequipa, the enemy were exhausted and unable to recruit any reinforcements to cover for those who had fallen ill. All their attempts to reequip their troops were unsuccessful. Santa Cruz, on the other hand, had set in motion a campaign to entice Chilean soldiers to abandon the fight. He offered them incentives to either return to Chile or establish themselves within the Confederation.[41]

The Chileans could not count on any help from the outside. They were trapped in the valley of Arequipa, unable to offer battle with any reasonable chance of winning. Consul Wilson, who had been in Peru

---

[38]  Letter from Santa Cruz to Braun, 27 April 1837, in *Archivo Histórico del Mariscal Andrés de Santa Cruz*, vol. VI, p. 152.

[39]  Thomas Sutcliffe, *Sixteen Years in Chile and Peru from 1822 to 1829 by the Retired Governor of Juan Fernandez*, London: Fisher and Sons, 1841, p. 451.

[40]  There are many references to the "war of resources"; see "Instrucciones al Señor Coronel Villagra," Tacna, 4 March 1837, in *Archivo Histórico del Mariscal Andrés de Santa Cruz*, vol. VI, p. 87.

[41]  Parkerson, *Andrés de Santa Cruz*, p. 229.

during the wars of independence, wrote that he had never seen such a "national spirit" among Peruvians. He claimed not to have seen it even when they fought the royalists. This unity against the Chileans was generalized and made it difficult for the invaders to rely on men or provisions, according to Wilson.[42] The British aide-de-camp to Blanco Encalada, Thomas Sutcliffe, noted in his memoirs the indifference with which this "supposedly liberating army" was received. He explained how difficult it was to obtain any kind of help, and how few people joined the ranks of the Peruvian legion once they disembarked.[43] Santa Cruz sent his representative to negotiate a peace treaty, when his enemies were at their lowest point. Blanco, who had already tried to find a peaceful solution, found in Santa Cruz a willing interlocutor who was just as eager as he was to avoid unnecessary battle. Much as he had acted in Lima a year earlier, the Protector believed that the best way to continue building his project of union was through peace. He was convinced that Chile would eventually understand and accept that the Confederation harbored no ill feelings against them and represented no real threat.

During the Chilean occupation, Vice Consul Thomas Crompton, who was based in Islay, came to the aid of British merchants and residents in Arequipa. According to his dispatches, his advice to Blanco Encalada proved pivotal in obtaining the peace agreement. Crompton had been friends with the general for the better part of twenty years. The vice consul believed that Santa Cruz also deserved credit for his extreme moderation in granting such generous terms, notwithstanding his great superiority.[44] Considering the conditions under which the treaty was negotiated, Santa Cruz was indeed extremely generous. His only desire was that the Confederation's existence be accepted by Chile. He even offered to pay the Peruvian debt to Chile with interest, and agreed not to take any measures against the Peruvians who had accompanied the Chileans in the invasion. Santa Cruz allowed Blanco Encalada to use the three ships that had been taken the previous year, and were due to be returned to Peru, to transport his troops back to Chile. In exchange, Santa Cruz would be cleared of any responsibility in the failed invasion of the previous year. Chile was to accept the Confederation, and the treaty was to be guaranteed by the British government.

[42] Belford Hinton Wilson to Palmerston, Lima, 28 October 1837, FO 61/46, p. 192.

[43] Sutcliffe, *Sixteen Years in Chile and Peru*, p. 466.

[44] Thomas Crompton to Palmerston, Arequipa, 20 November 1837, FO 61/48, p. 148.

Santa Cruz was convinced that this was the best course of action. He believed peace was "a hundred times more important that the greatest victory."[45] He did not want men to die in battle. He was convinced that a magnanimous attitude toward his enemies, especially considering his absolute superiority and the assurance of victory, was proof of his strength and of his desire for peace. The Confederate army assembled at the outskirts of Arequipa, toward the end of 1837, was unassailable. More than 6,000 properly trained men, who were provided with uniforms and promptly paid, were far superior to the nearly 2,500 ragged recruits and militia members that had managed to make it from Chile. These men had traveled by sea, and then by foot over the punishing road from the desert coast to Arequipa, so they were in no shape to fight. Santa Cruz was once again generous, considering his great numerical and tactical advantage. He sent Blanco Encalada, a man who was a close friend of the invading general, as commissioner to propose peace talks. It is an important fact that most men involved in this conflict had fought on the same side, during the wars of independence, and knew each other well.

War was waged by former comrades in arms. Sutcliffe, the British-born officer in the service of Chile, described this in great detail. In his memoirs, he wrote of how surprised they were by the reception Santa Cruz was given in Arequipa, just as they were by the deference that even the wealthiest Peruvians showed toward him. After the peace negotiations, they all met for a banquet. The men who only a day before had been at the brink of fighting to the death were now dining together as the old comrades in arms they were.

The issue of nationality was indeed quite complex for most of them. The only Chilean by birth who was present at the table was Ramón Herrera, the president of Southern Peru; he was a close associate of Santa Cruz. Blanco Encalada had been born in what had become Argentina, even though he headed the Chilean contingent. British officers were found on both sides, although most fought for the Confederation and were prominent officers in Santa Cruz's army.[46] The Confederation emerged as a possible response to growing nationalist sentiment. This had started to take shape with the wars of independence but still took some time to develop. The men who sat around the table continued

[45] Letter from Santa Cruz to Braun, quoted in Parkerson, *Andres de Santa Cruz*, p. 232.
[46] Sutcliffe, *Sixteen Years in Chile and Peru*, p. 475.

to believe that war was fought among gentlemen. In this case, it was a war fought between friends. This was something they had already experienced during the wars of independence, especially those who, like Santa Cruz, had served both sides.

Blanco Encalada thought that a good way to end the disagreement between Chile and the Confederation was to select a number of men of each side and have them meet in battle in a prearranged spot. The winners of the contest would be considered the victors of the war. Blanco was sure that the Confederate army would retain their advantage because they were much better soldiers. His offer was, nevertheless, rejected.[47] Wilson agreed with Blanco in his assessment of the Confederate army and his complete trust in it: he thought it was capable of conquering any enemy. Indeed, Santa Cruz had continued to use the policies he had implemented for Bolivia in the Confederate army. One of the first measures his government took was to reorganize the National Guard in every city in the union. He reformed the army first by granting leave to all those who wished to retire, giving them a proper pension. He then gave amnesty to all those ranked captain or lower, even if they had fought for his enemies. In 1837 when the Chilean threat was evident, Santa Cruz gave several decrees prohibiting the forcible recruitment of troops. He believed there was no use in having men who had joined the service in such a way.

It is puzzling, given the complete military superiority over the Chileans, that Santa Cruz exhibited such generosity in the terms he agreed to in the peace treaty signed in the town of Paucarpata, on the outskirts of Arequipa. Some believe he did so because he was confident that he would always prevail militarily and thought that his generosity would cause the Chileans to come around and accept his union of Peru and Bolivia. In his correspondence, Santa Cruz was adamant that he chose peace over war because he wanted to show the Chileans that he had no expansionist agenda. The chief negotiator for the Confederation was Chilean-born Ramón Herrera, and his counterpart was Blanco Encalada, a man born in Buenos Aires. The first article stated that there would be perpetual peace and friendship between Chile and the Confederation, and all previous disagreements would be forgotten. In article two, both sides apologized for their past actions. The subsequent articles went on to state the terms of return of the Chilean troops and

---

[47] Celia Wu reconstructs this episode with the letters between Blanco Encalada and Ramón Herrera; see *Generales y Diplomaticos*, p. 148.

stipulated when the Peruvian boats would be returned. Considering the circumstances in which the Chilean troops found themselves in Peru, the treaty was extremely generous; the Confederation not only agreed to repay debts to Chile, but declared that it would not pursue any compensation for the aggression so far. All individuals, no matter their origin, would be forgiven for having fought against the Confederation. Britain would guarantee the terms of the treaty. As Vice Consul Hugh Wilson wrote in December 1837, the peace treaty was so well received in the Confederation that he was certain Santa Cruz would remain in power for many years hence.[48]

Santa Cruz agreed; he felt so confident that he began to demobilize his men. Troops in Peru were reduced. Some of the Bolivian National Guard battalions that had traveled to Arequipa were sent back home, and others were sent to the southern border with Argentina. This was done partly because Santa Cruz had blind faith in the agreement with Chile, and partly to save money. The Protector wanted to use those funds for economic development. He envisioned reform at the local level and the repayment of long-standing debts, including those owed to the British. The Protector aimed to radically change the way in which government was conceived, as he had successfully done in Bolivia. He made every effort to pay salaries on time, reduce graft, promote trade, and work toward gaining international creditworthiness for heavily indebted Peru. Santa Cruz had implemented an aggressive policy of debt repayment, both internal and external, and was trying by all means possible to balance the books. He wanted to be able to pay civil and military employees promptly. In Lima, in November 1836, he had passed a decree that allowed landowners in the valley who held government debt to pay three quarters of their tax bill with debt paper and the rest in cash.[49] In August, he had asked all public employees who had been paid with government debt bonds to come forward to be repaid.

The backbone of his economic plan was the massive introduction of debased currency. Known as the *peso feble*, this coin contained a lower amount of silver. The effect this had on the economy was similar to what today would be achieved by printing more money. More cash

---

[48]  Hugh Wilson, FO61/48, p. 77.
[49]  Decree of 15 November 1836, http://www.congreso.gob.pe/ntley/Imagenes/ LeyesXIX/1836106.pdf.

flowed into the system, but the currency was devalued. This move was not viewed favorably by the British merchants, who complained bitterly to the vice consul in Islay, Thomas Crompton.[50] During the 1830s, the proportion of debased currency in Bolivia rose to 30 percent of the total money in circulation. This move allowed Santa Cruz much leeway in his fiscal policy and was the start of an inflationary process.[51] After finding this system useful in Bolivia, Santa Cruz began using it in Peru as well. In August 1837, he decreed that one fifth of all the coin minted in Lima should be of a lower grade and should be minted in smaller denominations.[52]

The Protector was convinced that reviving the economy was crucial for success. He hoped to reignite an economy that had been depressed for several years by increasing the monetary supply in Northern Peru. In Southern Peru the minting of debased coinage had already made a profit estimated at 200,000 pesos. Consul Wilson assured the Foreign Office that he had managed to convince Santa Cruz that this method was problematic; using his influence, he was eventually able to get the decree repealed.[53]

With his focus on reviving the economy and fending off the Chilean attack, Santa Cruz paid less attention to developments in Bolivia. Unrest and discomfort with the Confederation had escalated. Vice Consul Wilson had already reported from Tacna, in April 1837, that the idea of the Confederation had not been well received in Bolivia. He wrote to the Foreign Office that he had been told privately, by people of importance, that the projected Confederation "produced great discontent" in Bolivia because many feared that Peru, as the richer and more populous member, "would obtain a decided superiority." Wilson also asserted, "The Generals of the Bolivian Army also expressed their discomfort, because they considered that such form of government was too democratic, and they unanimously pronounced in favor of a monarchical

[50]  FO 61/48, p. 159r.
[51]  For more on the debased Bolivian currency see Alejandra Irigoin, "La fabricación de moneda en Buenos Aires y en Potosí entre 1820 y 1860 y la transformación de la economía postcolonial en el Río de la Plata" in *Moneda y Mercado. Ensayos sobre los orígenes de los sistemas monetarios latinoamericanos, Siglos XVIII a XX*, A. Ibarra and B. Haubserger, editors, Mexico: UNAM (forthcoming), p. 7.
[52]  Belford Hinton Wilson complained to Lord Palmerston about this on 3 August 1837, FO61/45, p. 326.
[53]  Belford Hinton Wilson to Palmerston, 22 September 1837, FO 61/46, p. 86.

government."[54] More symptoms of disquiet in Bolivia were noted by the British Consul in Lima. On September 1837, he included in his dispatch an extract of a letter between two British officers in the service of the Confederation, in which the officer in Bolivia cautioned his correspondent in Lima that there was opposition to the pact of Tacna, warning of "alarming stories afloat here [La Paz], and more so in Chuquisaca."[55]

These rumors were based on some fact. The same day the Chilean fleet appeared off the coast of Arica, a small garrison in the town of Oruro attacked the local authorities. Santa Cruz thought that this had been organized in combination with the Chileans and sent in reinforcements from La Paz. In the end this was not needed, because the uprising was put down by the local militia.[56] Although this action had little consequence, its leader escaped and established a guerrilla force deep in the lowlands of the province of Chuquisaca. This gave the group that was eager to work for the destruction of the Confederation a place in which to gather its strength. Moreover, it was a clear sign that backing for Santa Cruz's project was incomplete. This was also the case within the elites of Bolivia, as can be gleaned from the correspondence of Bolivian Vice President Calvo. In late 1837, he wrote to Braun, saying that he was so worried about the future of the Confederation that he thought it best to abandon his post.

The conflict with Argentina was of much greater interest to Santa Cruz than rumors in Bolivia. He was not willing to reach the same kind of generous agreement with Rosas as he had done with Prieto. Fighting in the southern border had started in August 1837, and, in contrast with Chile, here Santa Cruz did harbor a hope of territorial gains. Many in the border town of Jujuy were interested in joining Bolivia. They had deep connections with the area and in open municipal meetings had declared their intention to leave the Argentine union. Several border towns were annexed to the Confederation. A battle was fought in Argentine territory, but both sides claimed victory. The difficulties of the terrain and the greater threat of the Chileans distracted Santa Cruz. The Argentines concentrated on attempting to reach the Pacific coast via the Atacama Desert with the aim of joining up with Chilean forces.

---

[54] Hugh Wilson, "Remarks on the present system of Government under General Santa Cruz," Tacna, 29 April 1837, FO61/48, p. 37.

[55] Letter from Francis O'Connor to William Miller, 2 September 1837, copied in FO61/46, p. 83.

[56] Parkerson, *Andres de Santa Cruz*, p. 235.

After the peace of Paucarpata, signed on 17 November 1837, hostilities resumed. As they had done during the wars of independence, both sides tried to make territorial gains. After inconclusive attempts, however, the division remained more or less the same, with Tarija on the Bolivian side and Jujuy in the Argentine one. Santa Cruz hoped Braun would be able to advance to Tucumán, but cautioned him repeatedly not to venture on to the forests or to the pampas where the enemy would have a distinct advantage. Instead he advised Braun to limit his actions to the mountainous regions, where he would always prevail.[57]

At the beginning of 1838, Santa Cruz was back in La Paz, ready to begin what he envisioned would be the consolidation of his project. He trusted that the Chileans would accept the peace treaty, or that they would be pressured by the British Navy into doing so. He focused all his attention on the war on the southern border and on reorganizing the army. When he received news that President Prieto had rejected the peace treaty of Paucarpata and was preparing a second expedition to Peru, Santa Cruz realized that he needed to act quickly. Once again, he saw Northern Peru as the weakest point. Ecuador had a new president who had less sympathy for the Confederation and threatened to join Chile. Santa Cruz also had to contend with opposition within Bolivia and in northern Peru. The Confederation was beginning to show deep cracks. In the following year these grew to such a degree that it was no longer possible to keep the project alive.

The Confederation had only been possible because of the vision and dedication of Santa Cruz and the support of the elites of some key provinces. Santa Cruz, of course, had important backers, but had it not been for his overarching desire to return to Peruvian politics and to ensure that Bolivia had access to the port of Arica, it would probably have never come to fruition. Santa Cruz had now truly become the *caudillo* of the Andes, and he had used his power to unite the two countries to which he felt closest. His ability as an administrator made it possible for him to build a solid base from which to set the experiment in motion. The preceding disastrous administrations in Peru and its tendency to experience civil conflict – which in this period twice escalated to full-blown civil war – gave Santa Cruz a crucial set of opportunities for intervention.

[57] Letter from Santa Cruz to Braun, La Paz, 16 January 1838, in *El Mariscal Braun a través de su Epistolario*. Cochabamba: Editorial los Amigos del Libro, 1998, p. 120.

*Andrés de Santa Cruz, Anónimo (hacia 1860),*
*daguerrotipo francés colección A. Santa Cruz, La Paz.*

Figure 4. Portrait of Santa Cruz in old age. Daguerreotype circa 1860, reprinted with permission of Carlos Mesa Gisbert, in his reprinted *Santa Cruz: El Condor Indio*, by Alfonso Crespo, La Paz: Presidencia de la Republica, 2005.

In spite of his ability to create a union, his dedication and the great political imagination that allowed him to find creative answers to difficult practical problems were not enough to shield him from his enemies. A combination of dedicated internal and external foes threatened the very survival of the union.

# CHAPTER 6

# DEFEAT AND EXILE

The Confederate wars that raged between 1836 and 1839 mirrored, in many ways, the wars of independence. The close relationship between the south of Peru and the north of Bolivia remained the driving force for the union and was an extremely difficult area to penetrate either from the coast or from the south. In the 1830s – just as they had done two decades earlier – the men from the southern plains of what had become Argentina made an effort to reach these high valleys, and those attempting to do so by sea tried to take the coast of Arequipa. Also as before neither of these strategies was successful. The natural barriers – the deserts and high mountains – made access close to impossible, and the general support for the cause among the local populations made the core of the Confederation impregnable.

This chapter explores how once again, replaying a conflict already experienced, success was found by attacking Lima and establishing a strong military force in the northern Andes. Lima was an easy target and could not be defended, whereas the northern Andes provided a peaceful and relatively wealthy place from which to prepare for the campaign. This chapter examines how, even though the Confederate army was the better prepared, it was ultimately defeated. Santa Cruz had endeavored to retain its loyalty by paying his troops fairly. He was good at providing his men with food and clothing and he had developed a dedicated following among troops and officers. But regardless of this attention to organization, crucial momentum was lost during the long marches in adverse conditions undertaken in 1838 to cross the Andes from south to north. Once again, as the royalists in 1824, Santa Cruz found himself cornered when his support in Bolivia vanished.

This chapter also analyzes how, just as Pedro Antonio de Olañeta's defection had made the battle of Ayacucho such a success for those fighting for independence, the rebellion in Bolivia led by Generals José Miguel Velasco and José de Ballivián made Santa Cruz's position untenable. Both had been close to Santa Cruz and had followed a similar path in the army, beginning their career in the colonial militias and changing sides during the wars. Velasco had risen to preeminence early on and was the vice president when Santa Cruz was called back to Bolivia in 1828. Ballivián's career had taken off that same year during the invasion by Peruvian forces and continued its ascent in the following decade. He was so close to Santa Cruz that the Protector regarded him as a godson. Both Velasco and Ballivián had initially supported the Confederation, but they had grown wary of it. The situation faced by Santa Cruz closely resembled that of the royalists in 1824, with an uprising in Bolivia and with Chile once more using its navy to overpower its neighbors and to hold complete control over the Pacific.

At the heart of the conflict was the question of the most suitable port for Bolivia. This issue had dogged the country since its inception, and the Confederation offered a solution that allowed La Paz the best possible access to the Pacific without the port having to be ceded or taken from Peru. This chapter reviews the reasons why the support for this option came not only from Bolivia, but also from the southern Peruvian localities that would have seen their trade with the Altiplano, as well as its burgeoning transport enterprises, continue to grow in importance. The question of Pacific trade was a further reason why the enemies of the Confederation were so adamant that it should not be allowed to succeed. Valparaiso had seen its control over trade decrease, and its merchants worried that incentives provided by the Protector to all the main ports in the Confederation would result in further decline. Traders in Callao were also worried that if the center of the political union continued to shift south, their primacy as the main port would be challenged – something they fiercely opposed. Although there are conflicting reports over whether the northern ports gained or lost with the implementation of the Crucista trade laws, the elites in that region tended to side with Callao and Valparaiso, where they had their most significant trade partners. In fact, during the Confederation, the northern port of Paita grew in economic importance as it became a vital stop for North American whalers. In spite of some support for Santa Cruz in this area, most elites in northern Peru were not prepared to give up their well-developed trade relationship with Chilean flour producers who bought their sugar, even as North Americans continued to make inroads in the market for flour by providing it more cheaply.

The Confederation had many enemies who were united in their desire to defeat both Santa Cruz and his political project. In spite of their failure in 1837 during the first campaign that ended with the treaty of Paucarpata, they continued to fight against the Confederation, finally ending it in 1839. Although some attempts were made to revive it after its demise, these were never successful, and with the banishment of Santa Cruz to Europe in 1846, the dream of union was shattered. This chapter follows him into exile and sees how the disgraced leader was eventually rehabilitated and became a diplomatic representative to the most important courts in Europe; he was even successful in signing a Concordat with the Vatican. There was such general fear of Santa Cruz in Bolivia, however, that he was not allowed to return in the mid-1850s and had to campaign for the presidency from neighboring Argentina. Even after his death, it took more than a century for his remains to be returned to his native La Paz. The way in which he is commemorated and remembered in La Paz is quite different from the lack of interest shown toward him in the city of Sucre.

## THE UNRAVELING OF THE PERU-BOLIVIA CONFEDERATION

When Chile did not accept the treaty of Paucarpata, the survival of the Confederation depended entirely on the British Navy. A possible British attack on Chile was the only deterrent possessed by the Confederation, which lacked a navy of its own. Santa Cruz was confident that if matters escalated, the British would intervene. Not only had they recognized the Confederation as a fully fledged political entity, but they had guaranteed the peace treaty. Santa Cruz believed that fear of British intervention would make the Chilean administration to reconsider its position.

Both of these assumptions proved to be wrong. The British government was slow to condemn Chilean aggression; it asked its navy to remain neutral and broker a peace deal. The Chileans were emboldened by the fact that the British consul in Santiago and the envoy who had recently reached Bolivia did not favor the Confederation. In late 1837, Santa Cruz had not accepted the credentials of the British consul to La Paz, because he had spoken publicly against the union with Peru. In spite of this, the British representative remained in conversation with those who wanted to end the Confederation. The newly appointed consul knew Bolivia well; he had surveyed the country in 1826 during a fact-finding mission for the British crown. Letters from the British commanders in Santa Cruz's army to Wilson explained how this representative alienated himself from the Protector, and how he had openly challenged the Confederation.[1]

The situation in Chile was even more complicated, as can be seen in the correspondence between the British consul there and the Foreign Office. Santa Cruz had sent a minister to London to plead his case to Lord Palmerston, and his many letters show how José Manuel de Mora defended the Confederation and reminded Great Britain of its responsibility to honor its commitments. Mora made it clear that this was the only way in which the large debt Peru owed Great Britain could ever be paid. The Confederation's minister stressed its firm commitment to honoring these obligations and claimed that if the Confederation was allowed to demobilize its troops, it would be able to start repaying its debts immediately. Although Palmerston was guarded in his replies, he noted that Britain had no quarrel with Chile. He pointed out that at best Britain could maintain its neutrality and make every effort to broker peace. Queen Victoria's minister did write to his representative in Santiago, exhorting him to ensure that the Chilean government understood that Great Britain recognized the Confederation as a legitimate government with a freely elected president. He then wrote to the Chilean government explaining, in no uncertain terms, that they were obligated to respect the choices of another country and that Britain would stand behind the Confederation.[2] The Chileans were not impressed, and they continued their plans to launch a second expedition to destroy the union between Peru and Bolivia. Blanco Encalada was court-martialed and asked to explain his behavior during the campaign. The Peruvian exiles who had traveled with him, especially La Fuente, also lost favor.

In a timely fashion, after two years residence in Ecuador, Agustín Gamarra arrived in Chile in early 1838. The nationalist former president, born in Cuzco, was opposed to the federation proposed by Santa Cruz, not because he did not think Peru and Bolivia belonged together,

[1] Letters from Miller and O'Connor can be found among the papers Wilson sent to London; see FO 61/46.
[2] For a summary of these communications see Celia Wu Brading, *Generales y Diplomaticos: Gran Bretaña y el Perú, 1820–1840*, Lima: PUCP, 1993 p. 152.

but because he believed Bolivia should be annexed to Peru. Now Portales was no longer around in Chile, and La Fuente's incompetence provided an opening for Gamarra: as a recent arrival in Chile, Gamarra had not been involved, and therefore tainted by, the failure of the previous campaign.

While the Chileans prepared the new expedition, they captured a Peruvian schooner with Bolivian General Ballivián aboard, in disobedience of express orders not to travel by sea. Ballivián was taken prisoner to Valparaíso, where he escaped in a romantic fashion by jumping ship. He was pursued by his Chilean captors, but was granted asylum aboard a French vessel. The captain, however, did not take him to Confederation territory, so he changed ships to an Italian whaler that allowed him to disembark on the coast of Arequipa. Ballivián returned to Bolivia and began to work organizing the opposition. The circumstances of his capture and escape were so fortuitous that his enemies later claimed there had been foul play and that he had been working in combination with the Chileans all along.[3]

Chile claimed that it wanted a peaceful solution, in spite of this surprise attack against the Confederation and their continual preparations for a second invasion. They were no doubt encouraged by the British consul in Santiago, who did not engage wholeheartedly in negotiations seeking a solution to the conflict. The Foreign Office had already reprimanded him for not getting the Chileans to accept the peace treaty. The conditions set out by the Chileans were, once again, the nonrecognition of the Confederation. This was unacceptable to Santa Cruz, even if he was open to calling a new meeting of representatives to discuss the Pact of Tacna. A new negotiation of the agreement was nonetheless desirable, because it still had not been endorsed by the Bolivian Congress. Bolivian Vice President Mariano Calvo, who had become increasingly critical of the Confederation, asked Santa Cruz to reconsider the Pact of Tacna because he did not believe that the Bolivian Congress would ever approve it. Santa Cruz could not afford to have such open opposition in Bolivia and realized he had to call for a new meeting to reform the legal basis of the union. The situation had reached a difficult point, if even the vice president of Bolivia was against the ratification of the current Pact of Tacna.

[3]   For details of his escape and the theories surrounding it see Phillip Taylor Parkerson, *Andres de Santa Cruz y la Confederación Peru-Boliviana, 1835–1839*, La Paz: Editorial "Juventud," 1984, p. 258.

Santa Cruz pondered the best course of action at length, and finally
decided to call a meeting of the representatives of the three states. A
new debate on the Union would be held in May 1838, in Arequipa.
In a letter to Calvo, he made it clear that he did not consider the
Tacna agreement the only option. Instead, he wanted to make sure the
agreement would strengthen the Confederation.[4]

The timeline for the assembly was not realistic. In May, the Bolivian
Congress met in the city of Cochabamba – a success for Santa Cruz, who
had worked to prevent it from meeting in Chuquisaca, where opposition
to his plan was rife. He agreed to allow this Bolivian parliament to
establish the basis for a new pact for the union, because he recognized
that the one agreed on in Tacna contained many errors. A month
later, the Bolivian Congress had approved all of Santa Cruz's actions
and prepared a new blueprint for the negotiations on the Confederate
agreement. This was a reaction to what they considered the autocratic
nature of the previous arrangement.

The Bolivian Congress wanted a union of independent states that
would retain their constitutions and laws. They also stipulated that all
the power not conferred on the federal government would remain at
the state level. The federation was to be divided into three branches: an
executive, a bicameral legislative, and a judiciary in the form of a federal
court. Bolivian representatives were prepared to give to the federal
government responsibility for defense, foreign affairs, trade, and the
postal and naval services, but made it clear that the federal government
would have no ability to tax citizens and would levy only import and
export taxes. The head of state would be a Protector, who would stay in
office for ten years and could be reelected without limit. The greatest
change was that there be no hereditary or even lifelong tenure in power.[5]

Santa Cruz humored the Bolivian Congress, allowing it to debate the
best possible terms for the Union. Meanwhile, he worked hard to get
the economy of Southern Peru back on track after the Chilean invasion.
One of the first measures he took was to allow government debt held on
paper to be used to pay sales taxes on land and houses. This was the same
law he had enacted for Northern Peru. The British consul lobbied the
Confederation government to include the Anglo-Peruvian debt in this
law, and subsequently a new decree allowed those who held this debt to

4   Letter quoted by Parkerson, *Santa Cruz*, p. 262.
5   Parkerson, *Santa Cruz*, p. 263.

profit from this tax incentive.[6] According to the numbers provided by Consul Belford Hinton Wilson, it was not just the south that profited from the new commercial code, but also the north. He claimed that the revenue in the customs house of Huanchaco had grown by 48,653 pesos after the liberal code had been established in 1836, compared to the previous eighteen months under the commercial code of 1833. Wilson claimed that this could not be attributed to a more favorable situation, because during this time the Confederation had been engaged in a war with Chile, which logically should have led to a drop in income and not a drastic increase.[7]

In spite of the numbers Wilson presented, most historical accounts attribute the failure of the Confederation to frustrations in Northern Peru over the decrease in trade. Most studies have pointed out that the end of the trade between Chile and Peru had a devastating effect on this region. It is possible, however, that those who were losing the most now were the members of the elite who had traditionally gained the most from commerce with Chile, whereas the British traders were faring better.

The northern elite ultimately decided to abandon the Confederation. Indeed, the question that dogged Santa Cruz in Peru as much as it did in Bolivia was who was going to decide the policies in the particular states. The Peruvians –mainly the Northern Peruvians – were wary of any perception that they were being legislated for from Bolivia. President Orbegoso recommended that they adopt a federal system similar to the one debated by the Bolivian Congress.

There was growing resentment in Peru. People there thought it was unfair that the Bolivian Congress was allowed to provide their opinion on the Pact of Tacna, and in effect to destroy it. In an 1838 letter, Casimiro Olañeta informed Santa Cruz that the main political operators in Lima resented having been unable to express their views on the pact of union. Olañeta also wrote that many blamed Santa Cruz for having agreed to such a disadvantageous treaty in Paucarpata. His enemies believed that he had done so because he was concerned only with his personal glory.[8]

---

[6] Decree by Andrés de Santa Cruz, La Paz, 14 March 1838, in FO61/50, p. 56.

[7] Wilson, *Comparative Statement of the Revenue derived from the Custom House of Trujillo during two separate Epochs*, FO 61/50, p. 110.

[8] Letter from Olañeta to Santa Cruz, 16 January 1838, quoted in Parkerson, *Santa Cruz*, p. 266.

Santa Cruz was well aware that as long as he controlled Bolivia, the Confederation would be able to sustain such criticisms. He also counted on the support of many in Peru who despised the Chileans. As hostilities were resumed, he received the backing of many who, according to Orbegoso, did not want to be invaded once again. The president of Northern Peru argued that there was opposition to the Pact of Tacna, but that it could be resolved if popular elections were called for and the agreement was revised.

News on how much real support there was for the Confederation in Northern Peru was conflicting. According to Orbegoso, if some changes were made and a new pact was negotiated, Santa Cruz could count on the support of the people of Northern Peru, who opposed Chilean intervention. Most of the opposition came from those who were still close to Gamarra. The ex-president had moved from Guayaquil to Santiago, in the hope of leading the second expedition to Peru. He reported he had received many letters from Lima assuring him that he would have plenty of backing. In one of his letters, in March 1838, he explained to La Fuente that there would be "an explosion" if they disembarked in Lima.[9] Gamarra reported that it was proving difficult to gain the endorsement of the Chilean government, and in spite of their resolve to act against the Confederation, the lack of public enthusiasm for a new expedition made it harder to get a commitment to finalize the preparations. As late as May, Gamarra was still not sure when they would embark and whether the Chileans would actually let his faction of exiles participate.[10]

The Chilean government had found it extremely hard to recruit enough men to join the army. Gamarra wrote that President Prieto was against the so-called *enganches* – in which men were forcibly drafted into service – because he thought that those recruited in that way would not fight properly. Several foreign eyewitnesses reported that when the troops finally embarked, they had to be tied up to prevent them from escaping. In the end, it had not been possible to obtain the support of volunteers, and the unpopular draft had to be used. A Swiss traveler in Valparaiso reported that "there prevailed in Chile a feeling adverse to this campaign; so much so that most of the troops were

[9] Letter from Gamarra to La Fuente, Santiago, 12 March 1838, in *Mariscal Agustín Gamarra, Epistolario*, Alberto Tauro ed., Lima: Universidad Nacional mayor de San Marcos, 1952, p. 267.

[10] Letter from Gamarra to La Fuente, Santiago, 11 May 1838, in *Epistolario*, p. 273.

embarked by force.... The soldiers who were in wretched uniforms most of them wearing ponchos, and unarmed, were bound together two-and-two by ropes and absolutely driven into the boats."[11] This was echoed by an officer onboard the English vessel *Neptune*, chartered to carry Chilean soldiers, who wrote "The President of Chile arrived here yesterday without one "Viva." He saw the detachment here embarked *unarmed* at the point of the bayonet, by a Regiment they think trustworthy, but of whom I have doubts."[12] This was a complete contrast to what the leader of the expedition, General Bulnes, wrote to his brother, indicating that he had more than 5,000 fully equipped and trained men who traveled with "the enthusiasm typical of good Chileans."[13]

Once it was clear that the Chileans, accompanied by Gamarra, were on their way to Lima, the unease in the Northern Peruvian capital grew exponentially. The coast had been under blockade for a long time, and the situation was not very different from the wars of independence. As news arrived, there was more commitment to the Confederate cause because people feared the imminent threat, and the feeling of antagonism toward the Chileans was greater than that against Bolivians. Santa Cruz trusted that this hatred of Gamarra and the Chileans would be enough to guarantee the commitment of Orbegoso and General Nieto, who were still dithering. In fact, the president of Northern Peru had been in contact with the opposition until at least February, when he deported the main ring leaders of the opposition who remained in Lima.[14] General Nieto, always a reluctant supporter of the Confederation, remained committed to the idea of breaking away from the union and thought that the Chileans would then no longer have a reason or justification to invade northern Peru.

With this in mind, and backed by Nieto's troops, Orbegoso abandoned the Confederation project in July, with the Chileans at his doorstep. Orbegoso claimed that he had been forced to leave the union because Santa Cruz had failed to call for the assembly to revise the Pact of Tacna. Orbegoso was adamant that he had abandoned the Confederation because he had been pressed to do so by public opinion. He

[11] Johan Jacob von Tschudi, *Travels in Peru, during the years 1838–1842*, translated by Thomasina Ross, London: David Bogue, 1847, p. 28.
[12] Letter from Captain Elliot to Admiral Ross, copied in FO 61/50, p. 263r.
[13] Gonzalo Búlnes, *Historia de la Campaña del Perú en 1838*, Santiago: Imprenta de los Tiempos, 1878, p. 24.
[14] This was the case of Manuel de Mendiburu, whose memoirs provide excellent details of this period.

made it clear that he had tried to prevent a final separation until after the Chilean invasion, but this had been impossible because in the span of one week, four major cities in the north publicly rejected the union with Bolivia. Nieto occupied the capital a day after the Independence Day celebrations of July 28, and with the backing of his troops, Orbegoso decreed the secession of all of Northern Peru. Two of the generals serving under Nieto did not accept the legality of this declaration and, after accusing Orbegoso of high treason, they abandoned Northern Peru, leaving Nieto alone to confront the Chilean invasion.

Orbegoso later defended himself by claiming that he had not taken part in the July revolution, but had taken it over in an attempt to control it, because he believed that was better than simply abandoning the country to its invaders.[15] In his letters to Santa Cruz, Orbegoso said he had been forced to take this step because of the general opposition to the Confederation. He explained that people from Peru felt oppressed by the Bolivians and by the fact that foreign-made laws were arbitrarily imposed. The army had been reduced in size, and the best posts, both in the army and in the civil service, had been given to foreigners. Orbegoso went as far as to declare that he had done nothing that Santa Cruz himself had not done in 1827, when there was such open opposition to the Bolivarian Constitution.[16] Most of the antagonism toward the Confederation, at this point, stemmed from the idea that the union was the reason they were being targeted by the Chileans. Many clung to the belief that once those bonds were broken, there would no longer be any need for the Chilean intervention. This was behind Nieto and Orbegoso's thinking. Even when the Chilean forces arrived in Lima, Consul Wilson still tried to engage in mediation and prevent them from disembarking off the coast of Lima.

All these efforts were in vain, because it was impossible not only to return the Chileans to the negotiation table, but to prevent them from taking Lima. Santa Cruz wrote bitterly to Wilson; his trust in Great Britain had been futile, and their support ineffective. The naval forces stationed in the Pacific had followed the recommendations of the Foreign Office to the letter and had not intervened, no matter how much Wilson had tried to convince them of the need to take more direct

[15] Letter from Orbegoso to Otero, Lima, 30 November 1838, quoted in Búlnes, *Historia de la Campaña*, p. 27.
[16] Letter from Orbegoso to Santa Cruz, Lima, 3 July 1838, quoted in Parkerson, *Santa Cruz*, p. 271.

action. All diplomatic efforts proved to be useless; Chile was not prepared to relent in their drive to destroy the Confederation. Sympathy from the consul, and even from the minister in London, was not enough to obtain a real commitment to use force against a country with which Great Britain had no direct conflict.[17] Consul Wilson observed that a main reason why the people of Lima did nothing to defend themselves from attack was because they were shocked and dispirited by the rebellion. They did not trust Nieto, who most believed would betray them to the Chileans. Wilson was convinced had it not been for the rebellion and the "retirement into the interior of the Bolivian and part of the Peruvian Division in all about 3,500 men, no reasonable doubt can exist but that the Chileans would have been attacked and defeated by the Peru-Bolivian army."[18]

## The Destruction of the Confederation

Santa Cruz reacted calmly to the loss of Lima, even expressing relief. Not having to defend the Northern Peruvian capital was actually a blessing. His experience during the wars of independence had taught him that it was impossible to secure the city by sea without a powerful navy. It had also made it extremely clear that holding the capital was not necessary for the control of Southern Peru and Bolivia. Santa Cruz knew from personal experience that Southern Peru was impregnable, and he adopted a defensive position, with the aim of uniting Southern Peru and Bolivia. He wanted to maintain the independence of the newly created southern republic and keep it as a buffer. In his letter to Orbegoso, Santa Cruz accused him of causing the war with Chile by providing Santiago with an excuse for war, in allowing the Chilean ex-president to lease former Peruvian navy ships. He rejected accusations that he governed autocratically, referring yet again to the assemblies of Sicuani and Huara as having invested him with full powers to take the decisions he took. Santa Cruz refused to accept Orbegoso as anything but the president of Northern Peru, the post he had given him with the backing of the Huaura Assembly. As such, Santa Cruz asked Orbegoso to continue fighting the Chileans, assuring him that once peace had been restored,

---

[17] For more on this see Wu, *Generales y Diplomaticos*, p. 153.

[18] Letter from Belford Hinton Wilson to Palmerston, Lima, 14 September 1838, FO61/51, pp. 15–16.

he would once more call for the meeting of the assemblies to decide the fate of the Confederation.[19]

Once established as president, Orbegoso contacted the Chilean fleet and denied them permission to disembark. He explained that his government was no longer linked to the Confederation, so the Chileans had no reason to attack. Two negotiators sent by the Chilean President assured Orbegoso that their government had no interest in interfering in Peruvian politics; their only goal was to destroy Santa Cruz. Orbegoso remained firm and refused the Chileans permission to land until the terms of their presence in Peru had been agreed.[20] The Chileans ignored Orbegoso and in early August traveled some miles north to the bay of Ancón, where they disembarked. Once on land, they requested permission to travel inland, which Orbegoso again denied. Negotiations continued, but there was no resolution. The Peruvians were adamant that because they had severed all ties with the Confederation, the Chileans had no legal right to be in their territory. The pleas of the Peruvians accompanying the expedition did not help convince the Orbegoso regime to allow them to enter the territory, and hostilities soon began.

The Peruvians (whom Santa Cruz considered to be Northern Peruvians) had been in negotiations with both sides simultaneously, because Nieto and Orbegoso were unsure which side would give them the best conditions. Gamarra was not willing to accept Orbegoso in the presidency, so he proposed that Nieto be made interim president of a temporary council instead. On the same day this proposal was made, Nieto decided to return to the Confederation and reject the Chilean invasion.[21] Olañeta was able to convince Nieto by assuring him that the only reason the Chileans were so intent in their effort to destroy the Confederation was because they wanted to dominate trade in the Pacific and destroy the Peruvian economy. Olañeta claimed that Diego Portales himself had told him this when he traveled through Valparaiso on his way to Europe in 1833.[22] Apparently this was what swayed Nieto,

[19] Letter from Santa Cruz to Orbegoso, Cuzco, 20 August 1838, in *Eco del Protectorado*.

[20] Letter from Orbegoso to Búlnes, Lima, 7 August 1838, in Búlnes, *Historia de la Campaña*, p. 33.

[21] Manuel de Mendiburu was one of the negotiators and gave many details of what was happening behind the scenes in his *Memoirs* Lima: Archivo Instituto Riva Agüero Colección Félix Denegri Luna.

[22] Parkerson, *Santa Cruz*, p. 277.

as well as the Protector's firm commitment to call for a series of assemblies that would decide the future, as soon as their enemies had been brought under control. Olañeta promised that a division of the army would be sent to Nieto's aid and that after the confrontation, the port of Arica and the city of Tacna would be ceded to Bolivia as payment for their support. The Bolivian minister claimed that this would bring great benefit to the provinces and would not really affect Peru.[23] Nieto agreed to all the points except ceding the southern provinces. He argued that he had no mandate to do so, and that it was an issue that could only be decided by a Peruvian congress.[24] Once again the future of these provinces, and especially the port, was at the center of the debates between Peru and Bolivia.

These negotiations were taking place far too late, because the Chileans were on the verge of taking the capital, which they did the day after Nieto and Orbegoso had pledged to return to the Confederation. A scuffle took place on 21 August 1838, at one of the doors to the still-walled city of Lima, the *Portada de Guía*. It was one of the most disorganized and badly planned battles fought to that time. But it showed clearly that neither the Chileans nor their Peruvian allies had the backing of the people in the capital. The invaders took Lima, and after doing so, Bulnes – the Chilean commander – reintroduced the 1834 Constitution and called for free elections. Consul Wilson commented that the whole process had been a mockery, noting that carts loaded with the wounded were paraded in front of the very hall in which the call for the return of legality had been made. The British consul noted that only nine people of "disrepute" attended the meeting and "voted" for Gamarra, who was appointed president. According to Wilson, after the meeting, "these nine electors and 30 or 40 black or colored men and children of the lowest classes headed by a Chilean military band paraded the streets by torch light in celebration of this event."[25]

As soon as he was installed in the capital, Gamarra contacted Orbegoso, who had sought refuge in Callao. Gamarra tried every device to convince him to join his cause, even offering Orbegoso the presidency if he agreed to back the Chileans. Orbegoso refused. He also rejected all

---

[23] Letter from Olañeta to Nieto, Tarma, 10 August 1838, quoted in Paz Soldán, *Historia del Perú 1835–1839*, Le Havre: Lemane, MDCCCLXX p. 192.

[24] Letter from Nieto to Olañeta, Callao, 20 August 1838, quoted in Paz Soldán, *Historia del Perú*, p. 194.

[25] Wilson FO 61/51, pp. 18–19.

of Santa Cruz's offers to return to his side. Santa Cruz then appointed ex-president Great Marshall José de la Riva Agüero to take over the presidency of Northern Peru. At the end of September, a decree called for a meeting of the representative assemblies of Huaura, Sicuani, and Tapacarí, with the aim of confirming whether the people of each of these states still wanted to be united in a Confederation. Santa Cruz bluntly stated that the union had no reason for existence if it did not have the backing of its inhabitants.[26]

Once again, in Northern Peru there were at least three presidents with claims to legitimacy. Orbegoso, in the fortress of Callao, rejected the Chilean and Bolivian forces and claimed that Peru should be able to decide its destiny without the interference of either. In Lima, Gamarra was being propped up by the Chilean army and claimed to be legitimate after the election carried out by the assembly put together by the invading forces. Now Great Marshall Riva Agüero, the man who had held the presidency of Peru for the first time in 1823, claimed to be president of Northern Peru, named by Santa Cruz and vested with authority by the assembly of Huaura.

The situation was not in fact dissimilar to the one Peru had experienced only a decade before, during the struggle for independence: the Chileans controlled the sea and took the capital, and the south of the country was impregnable, as the Chileans had learned just a year earlier. Santa Cruz knew this and wanted to use the same strategy that had served the royalists so well. The Confederation was built on the closeness of southern Peru and the Altiplano; this had been its greatest strength. Chilean forces could not compete in the highlands, because they needed to traverse the desert coast to reach them. The north, by contrast, was much closer to Chile, and as in the early 1820s, it was prone to changing sides. Lima was an impossible city to defend; all the armies that tried, failed in the attempt. It was not simply that sea power was required, but also that once taken, it was equally difficult to defend from new attack, as the royalists, San Martín, Bolívar, Gamarra, and now the Chileans had found.

In 1838 it was not possible for the newly formed government of Gamarra, under the name of the "restoration," to keep hold of Lima. In November, they evacuated the city as Santa Cruz, seeing the weakness of his enemies, abandoned his defensive strategy and rode in with his army. Wilson noted that he "had never witnessed in America an equal

---

[26] El Eco del Protectorado Extraordinario, Tarma, 30 September 1838.

display of enthusiasm to that with which the People of Lima received as Liberator, H.E. General Santa Cruz and the army under his orders."[27] The backing Santa Cruz received from the population of Lima was corroborated by an eyewitnesses less invested in the Confederation than Wilson. The representative of the Pope in Bogotá, who sent regular colorful dispatches to the Vatican based on information gained on the ground, claimed that the people of Lima had warmly welcomed Santa Cruz back to the capital and joined his forces.[28]

Once established in the capital, the Protector's first measure was to ask the British Government, and Wilson in particular, to try to broker a peace agreement with the Chileans.[29] Even at this point, Santa Cruz wanted to obtain peace and believed that his Confederation should not be built on enemy blood. Once again, Santa Cruz's desire to negotiate was seen by his enemies as a sign of weakness. In a private letter to Wilson, Santa Cruz declared that he wanted peace and, rather than any glorious victory, would prefer a peaceful solution that would save the honor and the interests of all those involved.

Wilson initiated the peace negotiations, but it proved impossible to continue them because the Chileans would under no circumstances recognize even the past existence of the Confederation. Their sine qua non condition for peace was to revert to the situation of 1836, with Orbegoso as president. The Chileans were prepared to accept a Confederation only if it was created after they left, if new elections and new assemblies were called for. This, however, would have rendered the union between Peru and Bolivia nonexistent, and all of its actions and agreements null and illegal. This was not something Wilson could agree to, especially considering that the Chileans had not really proved their mettle in battle and had so far only dominated the seas and the capital.

Santa Cruz, however, was open to the idea of leaving Peruvians to decide in their assemblies whether they wanted to be part of the Confederation. He was not opposed to starting all over again and regaining the people's backing. The Chileans rejected his offer, claiming that they needed assurances that their navy would be allowed to grow.[30] According to the apostolic nuncio, the real causes for Chilean aggression were jealousy over commerce, fear that Peru would become powerful, and

---

[27] Wilson FO 61/51, p. 202.
[28] Letter from Gaetano de Bagnovo to the Pope, Bogotá, 25 January 1839, in *La Confederación Perú-Boliviana, el Mariscal Santa Cruz y la Santa Sede, documentos inéditos*, La Paz: Banco Central de Bolivia, 1977, p. 109.
[29] Wilson FO 61/51, pp. 320–2.
[30] Wilson FO 61/45, pp. 334–41.

the outright rejection of a possible monarchical government that could develop in the Confederation.[31]

After this failure to find peace, Santa Cruz took the offensive. He forced the Chileans to abandon Lima and regroup in the valleys of the northern Andes. This echoed the march Bolívar had been forced to undertake in 1824. Santa Cruz was now following in the footsteps of the former royalists – and with men on his side such as Pío Tristán and Riva Agüero, who like him knew firsthand what had happened then. Santa Cruz's greatest enemy, Agustín Gamarra, also had this experience. Santa Cruz had gone as far as he could in his attempt to obtain peace with the Chileans. He had abandoned his safe position in the southern Andes, but this had not been enough. The question remains, why did he do it? What motivated him to leave his stronghold to take over Lima, a city he knew he could not defend? It seems that he did so to try to force Chile's hand into negotiating peace. Santa Cruz later claimed to have been aware of the conspiracies taking place in Bolivia, and that this had been behind his bold attempt to fight the Chileans, so that he could better withstand an attack in his home turf.[32]

His letter of September 1838 to Vice President Calvo explained that he had had to attack because it was the only way to defend Bolivian interests. He reaffirmed his position on the Confederation: it should only continue to exist if there was a clear mandate from the elected assemblies. He made it abundantly clear that under no circumstances was he prepared to allow Peru to return to being one state. He argued that it would be much better for the three states to remain independent than to return to the status quo ante. This was no doubt the main issue in his mind when he set out to obtain peace with the Chileans by taking an offensive position and retaking Lima. Santa Cruz was aware the only way to prevent the union of Peru was through victory in battle. He agreed with Calvo that Tacna and Arica would be a great prize for all their efforts, but that Peru would never consent to leaving these territories in a peaceful manner. Yet he was also convinced taking Tacna and Arica by force was not sustainable, because they would have to fight continually to keep them.[33]

---

[31] Letter from Gaetano de Bagnovo to the Pope, Bogotá, 25 January 1839, p. 110.

[32] Wu, *Generales y Diplomaticos*, discusses the letter Santa Cruz wrote to Wilson onboard the *Samarang* in February 1839, p. 157.

[33] Letter from Santa Cruz to Calvo, 26 September 1838, in Calvo, *Oposición en Bolivia a la confederación Perú-Boliviana: cartas del vicepresidente Mariano Enrique Calvo y el Presidente Andrés Santa Cruz*, Sucre, Bolivia, Corte Suprema de justicia, 1996, pp. 40–1.

Throughout this period, the south of Peru remained committed to the Confederation. It was in these provinces that Santa Cruz found the backing he needed to fight. His support there was so great that he felt he had a secure base from which to fight the Chileans. In areas such as Ayacucho, there had been open acts of support for the Confederation, which added to the perception that the invasion had brought Peruvians together in their common hatred of the Chileans. In Lima, Santa Cruz was received with much enthusiasm, strengthening his commitment to fight. He was, however, unable to reach an agreement with Orbegoso, who claimed that the Protector had not honored his commitments. Santa Cruz tried to convince him and even visited him aboard the vessel where he had taken refuge, in an attempt to sway him toward his position. These efforts were fruitless, and in early December, Orbegoso sailed into exile. Many of the men who had supported him now abandoned Santa Cruz's cause, some joining the Chileans, others returning to private life.

At the start of 1839, Santa Cruz's position was dire. He had lost part of Lima's backing because, as the situation had worsened and the Chileans intervened, many thought he could no longer provide them with enough benefits. He received continual warnings from Bolivia about an imminent revolution. Even though he knew the best line of defense was to station his troops in the large inter-Andean valleys just north of the capital, between Chancay and Pasco, he was forced to march farther north. The enemy was encamped in the valley of Huaraz. This was one of the first areas to declare independence from the Confederation, and they had the full support of the local population. Santa Cruz felt compelled to engage there, because he feared that if he did not win a decisive victory, rebellion would break out in Bolivia. He was also afraid that the Chileans would carry out their threat of attacking Arica and send an expedition from the south, cutting off his communications with his core area of support in Bolivia. This was, in fact, the same strategy Santa Cruz had attempted in 1823 when he had tried to divide the royalist forces, but had only succeeded in reaching La Paz and Oruro before his troops were disbanded.

Short of options, Santa Cruz marched to the northern Andes at the most punishing time of the year, when heavy rainfall made the journey most difficult. It so impeded the transport of his men that he lost up to a third of his troops. Exhausted and much reduced in size, the Confederate army gave battle to the "Restoration troops" who were rested and acclimatized after nearly two months in the valley. A couple of smaller skirmishes followed, and the two armies finally met on January 30 at the battle of Yungay.

Santa Cruz was completely defeated. The place of battle had not been well chosen, and his most trusted lieutenants were absent. In the wide valley known as the Callejón de Huaylas, Santa Cruz had tried to corner his enemy on one side of the river by destroying all the bridges. Initially, it seemed Santa Cruz had led his enemies into a difficult position, but in reality he had done nothing but render his situation more precarious, and he was forced to give battle at a disadvantage.

Each side had approximately 6,000 men. The highly trained Con-federate army included recruits from Bolivia as well as from Northern and Southern Peru. Although they had much experience, the men were exhausted from the long marches, because they had traversed nearly the whole country on foot. The "United Army" had traveled by sea, which brought its own problems, but they had been on land for nearly four months, for two of which they had been camped in this very valley, adapting to the altitude. This army included 800 Peruvians and all kinds of recruits from Chile – even Indians from the southern provinces not yet incorporated into the Chilean nation, who fought as mercenaries. A whole new mounted regiment had been put together by General Ramón Castilla, another veteran of the wars of independence, who made his name during this campaign. In his final charge he took control of the hill where the Confederates had their camp. This was the main reason why the victory of the "Restoration" was so complete.

Miller, Riva Agüero, and Santa Cruz were able to escape after the battle, and a week later they arrived in Lima. The war had not been completely lost, and the Protector hoped that he would be able to regroup and fight from the south, where he thought he had much more strength and support. In order to continue fighting from a more secure base, Santa Cruz abandoned the capital and traveled farther south. He asked Consul Wilson to once more attempt to obtain a peaceful solution with Chile. Santa Cruz was more open to the possibility of peace if Peru was to be permanently divided. He thought peace could be obtained in exchange for the permanent cession of the port of Arica to Bolivia. He was prepared to fight if his conditions were not accepted by the Chileans. In his letter to Wilson, it was evident that Santa Cruz was not sure of his ability to succeed: he asked Wilson to send a British vessel to travel along the coast ready to rescue him, in case his situation became untenable.[34]

---

[34] Letter from Santa Cruz to Wilson, Lima, 27 January 1839, in FO 61/58, p. 86r.

Santa Cruz traveled to Arequipa, where he had a strong garrison and was preparing to force the Chileans onto the punishing march south. The same people who had been invaded only eighteen months before were still behind his project. Nevertheless, the Confederation lay in ruins. At this point, Santa Cruz was still more preoccupied with salvaging what he could than with rebuilding the failed union. He wanted to retrench in his traditional space. This, he believed, would allow him to negotiate from a stronger position. During his trip overland, he was greeted in every town, even in Lima, with much support. According to British Vice Consul Crompton, backing for Santa Cruz in Arequipa, particularly from the lower classes, was "beyond all expression"; the National Guard volunteered to fight for him.[35] Santa Cruz continued his journey to Puno, where he was forced to reevaluate his situation when he heard news of an uprising in Bolivia.

His beloved godson Ballivián, who had taken part in the rebellion against the Confederation, was the one to inform him. Santa Cruz later claimed to have known about the brewing uprising long before it actually happened. He explained that all of his actions during the second Chilean campaign had been informed by this threat: he had hoped that a decisive victory would prevent the rebellion, which was why he had taken so many chances. It is impossible to know whether this was true. His defeat in Yungay was so complete that the rebellion in Bolivia was a reaction, taking place just days after the news arrived in the Altiplano.

The uprising had been carefully planned and was executed efficiently. It began in the southernmost garrison town of Tupiza, where General Velasco issued a proclamation rejecting the Confederation well before news from the defeat of Yungay arrived. Santa Cruz had replaced Velasco as president in 1828. The high-ranking officers in command of troops in Oruro and Chuquisaca had already backed the revolution. The *pronunciamientos*, the written texts that accompanied the military uprising, declared that they were breaking away from the Confederation because it brought no benefit to Bolivia. Velasco took over the presidency, and Ballivián was sworn in as vice president. This stung Santa Cruz, because he had treated Ballivián like a son, protecting and promoting him on every possible occasion. Ballivián's escape from the Chileans

[35] Letter from Crompton to Wilson, Arequipa, 17 February 1839, in FO 61/58, p. 95r.

had already raised eyebrows because it was seen as too fortuitous, and many thought that he was collaborating with the enemy. Even Santa Cruz's wife had warned him, as early as April 1838, not to trust Ballivián. In any case, there seems to be little doubt that there was communication between the rebels and the Chileans. They had been working together to ensure the fall of the Confederation and the end of Santa Cruz's political career.

Ballivián suggested that Santa Cruz go into exile, now that he had been totally defeated. Without options, and not wishing to needlessly prolong the agony, or to provide the Chileans with more excuses for intervention, the Protector resigned his post. He then recommended that Ballivián take over the uprising, in order to take control of the country and eventually continue Santa Cruz's legacy. He begged him to bear in mind the importance of maintaining the legal framework Santa Cruz had created and the new laws he had enacted during his presidency. He suggested that Ballivián be the next presidential candidate, as soon as elections were called for. The fallen Protector was anxious for passions to be kept in check to prevent the country from becoming engulfed in anarchy.[36] Santa Cruz wrote to Velasco renouncing his post both as Protector of the Confederation and as president of Bolivia, and in his letter defended his project of union once more. He said that the Confederation had been advantageous for both countries; he maintained that he had never had any personal ambition and that his only desire had been to serve the countries to which he felt so closely bound. He declared, at the end, that his only desire was to see legal order reestablished and that he felt no bitterness abandoning public life. He did not want the ten successful years over which he had presided to be quickly obliterated.[37]

Santa Cruz's situation soon became even more precarious when a group of young lawyers from Arequipa led a crowd to his residence and threatened him if he did not remove the Confederation flag. Santa Cruz complied, and then asked for a commission to be formed so that he could negotiate his withdrawal from Arequipa. The new prefect called for the separation of Arequipa from the Confederation and for the

---

[36] Letter from Santa Cruz to Ballivián, Arequipa, 20 February 1839, quoted in Parkerson, *Santa Cruz*, p. 299.

[37] Letter from Santa Cruz to Velasco, Arequipa, 20 February 1839, quoted in Parkerson, *Santa Cruz*, p. 300.

province to accept Gamarra as president. Santa Cruz was able to evade the angry mob and escaped to Islay, taking refuge at the residence of the British vice consul. He was forced to remain on land for a couple of days before he could board the *Samarang*, and during that time he had to be protected by the British marines against his own guard. When he finally boarded the ship, he was received with a twenty-one-gun salute: he was still recognized by the British as a head of state. Only a month had gone by since his defeat in Yungay, and in that time his entire power base had violently crashed into pieces.

## THE AFTERMATH OF THE CONFEDERATION
## AND THE LONG YEARS OF EXILE

Defeated and with few prospects, Santa Cruz went into exile in Guayaquil. Nevertheless, he was still a force to be reckoned with. A measure of his power was the fear he continued to instill in his enemies. The fallen leader had much support, especially in southern Peru and in northern Bolivia. The president of Ecuador, General Flores, provided him with hospitality, honoring the unwritten pact between the erstwhile supporters of Bolívar to always look out for each other. Santa Cruz remained close, so the leaders in power in Peru, Bolivia, and Chile had to consider him in their political calculations. When he wrote his 1840 manifesto, outlining his plans to continue fighting for the union of the countries he had managed to bring together, however briefly, he had this in mind. In his manifesto, he denounced those who he felt had betrayed him.[38]

In the aftermath of an expensive war, Santa Cruz's enemies in Peru and Bolivia organized what they described as the "Restoration." They chose this name because they wanted to implement reform and "restore" what they considered the authentic spirit of the republics. Gamarra had promised the Chileans to get rid of the liberal trade codes introduced by Santa Cruz. Although he did abolish several laws introduced during Confederation, he kept some of the more progressive ones. The Constitution was, however, changed to give Gamarra's regime a veneer of legality. With Lima still occupied by the Chileans, Gamarra called for a

---

[38] Andrés de Santa Cruz, *El General Santa-Cruz explica su conducta pública y los móviles de su política en la presidencia de Bolivia y en el Protectorado de la Confederación Perú-Boliviana*, Quito: Imprenta Alvarado, 1840.

Constituent Assembly to meet in the small Andean town of Huancayo. This constitution was heavily influenced by the conservative Chilean Constitution of 1833. It centralized power in the hands of the president and curtailed devolution to the provinces, something that had been a hallmark of the Santa Cruz regime.

Gamarra's policies on territorial changes as well as on taxation were flexible. He kept the southernmost provinces of Arequipa as an independent department. The Constitution of Huancayo, however, changed the name to Moquegua. This was somewhat of a recognition for the city's desire for independence, but the capital remained in Tacna. Gamarra understood that it would have been counterproductive to further antagonize an area that had been such an active supporter of the Confederation. His instinct told him that if he reincorporated these provinces into the department of Arequipa, they might easily provoke the people there to once again attempt to join Bolivia, just as they had done in the early days of the Confederation. In the south, many had not abandoned the ideals of the Confederation, and Santa Cruz still had many followers.

In Bolivia, President Velasco worked hard to dismantle Santa Cruz's legacy. He was eager to prove to the world that neither he nor his country had supported the Confederation. He went as far as to congratulate General Bulnes for his victory in Yungay. This was not a particularly patriotic gesture, considering that most of the defeated troops were actually Bolivian. Velasco normalized relations with the Argentine Confederation and returned the piece of land that had declared for the Confederation, claiming that because it had been obtained illegally, it could not be kept. With Peru, however, it was much more difficult to regain normal engagement because Gamarra wanted to annex Bolivia to Peru. He had wanted to do so since at least 1828, when he had first intervened to help oust Sucre. Now Gamarra felt that he had the appropriate excuse, making it clear to Congress in Peru that Santa Cruz and his followers continued to be a threat.

Santa Cruz, in exile in Guayaquil, remained in touch with Peruvian events and could easily return. In 1840, he traveled to Quito with his family. There he wrote a long manifesto explaining his political choices. He took this opportunity to criticize the "restoration" government in Bolivia and accused his enemies of having caused their own problems. He believed that they were to blame for Gamarra's 1828 invasion, and he held them responsible for the pervasive climate of instability and the enduring fear of a possible Peruvian invasion.

After a couple of years of tense calm, southern Peru saw a large uprising at the end of 1840. It initially broke out in Ayacucho, but then
spread to Puno, Arequipa, Moquegua, and Cuzco.[39] Of the provinces
that had once been part of the Southern Peruvian state, only Tacna
remained loyal to the authority of Lima, because the prefect there was
close to Gamarra. The uprising was quickly put down, but it had important repercussions and showed that the whole area was still open to the
idea of separating from Northern Peru. This uprising brought into focus
not only the danger of secession in the south, but also the possible rees-
tablishment of the Confederation. Gamarra was confident that he could
maintain order in Peru, but he had little or no power to stop rebellion
in Bolivia.[40]

Hearing of the trouble in Peru, the ousted Protector increased his
efforts to return to power. He planned to invade the north or to take
a ship to the port of Cobija. In February 1841, when a revolution
proclaimed Santa Cruz president of Bolivia, he asked the British Navy
to allow him to board one of their ships so that he could reach his
country. The British Consul General in Lima, Belford Hinton Wilson,
his former friend and ally, wrote to Lord Palmerston that Santa Cruz
was determined to accept the constitutional presidency of Bolivia and
had officially requested transportation to Cobija. Wilson, was already
in a difficult position with Gamarra's regime, and could not request the
British to help so he had to inform Santa Cruz that he was unable to aid
him on this occasion.[41] Without British backing, Santa Cruz could not
travel.

To further counter the threat from Bolivia, Gamarra gave Ballivián
asylum and support after his failed rebellion against Velasco. The
Peruvian president obtained extraordinary powers from Congress in
July 1841 to wage war against Santa Cruz, if his name was proclaimed
in Bolivia. The permission to go to war was to last until assurances were
obtained that the tranquility, independence, unity, and liberty of Peru
would not be affected.[42] Gamarra marched south, and by October he
had crossed the border. Ballivián, who accompanied the invasion, abandoned his Peruvian backers once in Bolivia and joined his compatriots,

[39]  Proclama by Valentín Boza, Cuzco, 31 December 1840, published in *El Rejen-*
      *erador Peruano*, Cuzco, 6 January, 1841.
[40]  Jorge Basadre, *Historia de la República del Perú*, Lima: Historia, 1961, vol. I,
      p. 460.
[41]  Letter from Wilson to Palmerston, Lima, 6 September 1841, FO 61/79.
[42]  *El Comercio*, 15 July 1841.

claiming that he did not want to be the Bolivian Orbegoso. Ballivián was proclaimed president and asked Gamarra to leave Bolivia, making it clear that since Santa Cruz had failed to disembark in either Peru or Bolivia, Gamarra had no reason to remain.[43] Ballivián claimed to have tried every possible avenue to have Gamarra agree to abandon his ambition of taking over Bolivia. However, because the Peruvian president had not acted reasonably and had continued with the invasion of his country, Ballivián was forced to attack.[44] Against the advice from his closest generals, Gamarra decided to continue the unpopular invasion of the province of La Paz.[45] After a small victory, enemy forces met in the battle of Ingavi. Peruvians were deeply divided, and many were against continuing in Bolivia. The battle was extremely disorganized, and not only were the invaders defeated, but General Gamarra was killed.[46] One of the Peruvian generals abandoned the battlefield and, after retreating over the Desaguadero, burned the only existing bridge to prevent the enemy from crossing into Peru, leaving many of his own troops stranded.

Gamarra's death left Peru in anarchy. The discontent that had simmered during his short government, and erupted briefly during the "Regeneration," now came to the fore. The specter of the Confederation still loomed, and the various power centers in the south wanted to gain as much power as possible in this time of political turmoil. When Ballivián and his troops invaded Peru, a new army was hastily put together, bringing back into service many of the Peruvian generals who had supported the Confederation. The president of the State Council in Lima was nominally in charge of the country, but in reality each provincial prefect controlled his own territory. According to law, elections were to be held within the first ten days of the provisional government, but these could not take place while the country was being invaded.[47] Peru descended into such chaos that, for a brief period in 1842, there were as many as four simultaneous governments that claimed to be legitimate.

---

[43] See *El Restaurador*, Sucre, October 1841, especially "Bando dado por José de Ballivián el 1 de octubre 1841, en La Paz de Ayacucho," in FO 61/84.

[44] "Bando ¡Viva la Patria! ¡Viva la Restauración!" Sicasa, 2 November 1841, printed in *El Restaurador*, Sucre, October 1841, in FO 61/84.

[45] Manuel de Mendiburu, *Memorias*, booklet 9, f. 3.

[46] Some authors note that he could have been killed by his own forces. On this see Alfredo Gonzáles Prada, *Un Crimen perfecto, el asesinato del Gran Mariscal Don Agustín Gamarra Presidente del Perú*, New York: H. Wolff, 1941.

[47] *El Restaurador*, Cuzco, 11 December 1841.

Given the situation, the borders became more porous, and Santa Cruz attempted to return to Bolivia by sea in September 1843. Months before, an expedition sponsored from Ecuador had tried without success to enter Peru from the north. Santa Cruz had the backing of President Flores, and there was talk of implementing a possible larger federation following on Bolivarian ideals. The details of how this would have unfolded remained sketchy at best, but Santa Cruz now had full backing from Flores, and with it he hoped to lead a rebellion against Ballivián.

In October, Santa Cruz tried to reach the Bolivian border through southern Peru. News of his impending arrival had been received, and he was captured by Ramón Castilla and Nieto's followers. Given the civil war raging in Peru, the former Protector was fortunate to have fallen into the hands of men with whom he had at least collaborated, instead of his sworn enemies. Because his captors were occupied with their own internal difficulties, and given the civil war in Peru, Santa Cruz was handed over to the Chileans, who agreed to take charge of his confinement. He was sent to Chillán, where he remained incarcerated until 1845, in spite of efforts by the British, the French, and even the Ecuadorians to have him freed.

After much negotiation, and once the political situation in both Peru and Bolivia was more stable, it was finally agreed Santa Cruz would travel to Europe and remain in exile for a minimum of six years. The Bolivian government would provide him with a pension of 6,000 pesos while he was away, and all his confiscated property was returned to him and his family. Santa Cruz had little room to maneuver, so he accepted the terms and vowed to retire from public life, dedicating all his energy to the education of his children and caring for his wife.

Santa Cruz was a family man, and during his years in exile he dedicated himself completely to educating his large brood. He had married his cousin, an orphan, because he considered it his responsibility to care for her. In contrast to his mentor Bolívar, Santa Cruz was never known for taking lovers, and his private life remained private. He referred to his wife in some of his letters to his friends and political allies, especially when he had to spend long periods away from her and she was with child. There is, however, little information on any political role she might have played, or on her relationship with Santa Cruz. Although most of his correspondence has been published, none of the letters to or from his wife have been included, even though some letters remain in the family archives.[48] The lack of letters, however, is not enough to support the claim that she had no major political role. In the case of Francisca Gamarra, the famed *Mariscala*, there is only one short letter that survives in her husband's published epistolary, where he calls her "dear child."[49] This short missive, however, shows how involved she was in fighting and in the organization of the civil war of 1834. Of course, there are also the numerous reports of her participation in all the major campaigns of the time and of the important role she played in the politics of the time. Her namesake Francisca Cernadas was different and remained very much a silent companion to her husband. She accompanied him faithfully during his time in power as well as in exile and brought up a large family with him.

Santa Cruz and his family traveled first to France and established themselves in Paris. Although Santa Cruz was happy in his new, more peaceful surroundings after two years in prison, he still thought about his homeland. In a letter written in 1847, he declared that if it were not for the insecurity that plagued his native land, he would happily leave the "charms" of Europe. He claimed that having had the opportunity to know such comforts, he had come to love his own homeland even more.[50]

Soon enough, it was possible for him to be of service to Bolivia. President Manuel Isidoro Belzú ousted Ballivián in 1848. Belzú had begun his military career fighting for Santa Cruz in the battle of Zepita in 1823, at the age of fifteen. He had risen through the ranks during the Confederation, and after defeating Ballivián, he installed a government often described as populist. In 1848, Belzú, who embraced his heritage as a mestizo, appointed Santa Cruz Plenipotentiary Minister to the courts of France, Belgium, Great Britain, Spain, and the Vatican. This was to a degree a political rehabilitation, because it gave the former Protector the opportunity to once again walk the corridors of power, although

---

[48] The *Archivo del Mariscal Santa Cruz*, originally with two volumes, now with six, has been published as a result of the efforts of his descendants, particularly his grandson General Andrés de Santa Cruz Schuhkrafft. Phillip Parkerson has had access to the family archives and quotes some letters by Santa Cruz's wife.

[49] Letter from Agustín Gamarra to Francisca Gamarra, Tacna, 13 May 1834, in *Epistolario*, p. 257.

[50] Letter from Santa Cruz to Francisco Marcos, Paris, 13 September 1847, in Parkerson, *Santa Cruz*, p. 312.

in a different role. Santa Cruz was successful in signing a treaty with France, and a Concordat with the Vatican. In 1850, when he traveled to London on official business, a long biographical article appeared in the press, highlighting his important services to his country and his close ties to Great Britain.[51]

His greatest achievement was to sign the Concordat with the Vatican in 1851. Santa Cruz had remained close to the Church, and indeed during the Confederation, the representative of the Pope in the region had sent several dispatches to the Holy See with a favorable assessment of his administration. Santa Cruz had been described in the 1830s as one of the only presidents in the new republics who was not ashamed to call himself a Catholic. The Bishop of Bagnovo had also noted that Santa Cruz was accused of trying to make himself king. Even as he doubted the veracity of these claims, the nuncio was convinced that this would be a great advantage for the countries under his control.[52] There were high hopes that Santa Cruz would be able to have a Concordat passed without having to have it approved by Congress, which according to the pope's representative were made up by young, unbelieving, and libertine men. The Protector had gained much of their respect by appointing a representative of the Church to the Assembly that met in Tacna to decide on the creation of the Confederation. This initial enthusiasm subsided when it became apparent that the main secretary of the union was none other than Spanish liberal José Joaquín Mora, who had made his name writing on the natural rights of man.

The Concordat was finally signed more than a decade later by Santa Cruz himself, who had negotiated directly with the representatives of the Pope in the Holy See during 1851. The document, written in Latin and Spanish, begins with an invocation to the Holy Trinity, and in its first article declares that Bolivia is a Catholic country. In the following articles it gave the Church far-reaching rights over education and control over publications: the Curia was given the power to censor what they considered offensive. In administrative matters, the Concordat gave the Pope and not the president the prerogative to name bishops. In exchange, the ecclesiastical court, the *fuero*, was limited to matters

---

[51] *The Illustrated London News*, vol. 1, no. 2, London, 8 July 1850.
[52] Letter from Gaetano Bishop of Bagnovo to the Pope, Bogotá, 25 August 1837, in *La Confederación Perú-Boliviana*, p. 60.

concerning the religious aspect of their mission, and all other offenses were to be dealt with in the normal courts.

This was a great victory for the new state and was achieved without fighting, in contrast to many of the neighboring republics where the issue of the corporate courts had led to confrontations in civil wars. Special invocations for the republic and the president were included in each mass, and all those serving the state had to swear allegiance to it over a bible and making reference to God.[53]

In spite of Santa Cruz's great success in reaching this agreement with the Holy See, his relationship with Belzú slowly deteriorated, even over the great distance that separated them. So, after serving for nearly five years, Santa Cruz was dismissed from his post. Santa Cruz later made it clear that he had been relieved, because he no longer desired to represent a repressive and dictatorial government. He stressed the fact that he had helped Belzú only at the start of his regime, when it had been democratic, and stated that he hoped the president of Bolivia would soon return to the path of legality.

Santa Cruz was soon again engaged as plenipotentiary minister, this time representing the Republic of Guatemala in the French court. He refused pay, however, because this was a service for a country that was not his own. He even looked after some of Peru's interests in France, and with time and distance he began to be viewed with sympathy even by some of his former enemies. Even though it was sometimes difficult to be paid all of his retirement money by the Peruvian and Bolivian governments, he did live off these pensions.

In 1855, after a decade in Europe, Santa Cruz returned to America as a presidential candidate, but he was not allowed to travel to Bolivia; clearly he was much easier to accept at a distance and was forced to campaign from neighboring Argentina. He settled in the city of Salta, until the Bolivian government was able to have him expelled. Santa Cruz moved to Entre Ríos, invested in land, and saw his eldest son Simón marry the daughter of the Argentine president, Justo José de Urquisa. After his electoral defeat, and still unable to enter Bolivia, Santa Cruz returned to France. In 1863, he offered mediation to try to prevent Chile from taking control of Bolivian territory at Mejillones. He was adamant that Bolivia needed to take a strong stance or would

---

[53] *Concordato Celebrado entre el Gobierno de Bolivia y la Santa Sede*, La Paz: Imprenta Popular, 1851.

Figure 5. Mausoleum in La Paz – photograph by the author.

risk losing its Atacama territory. His advice was not heeded. Two years later, he died in Bougenais. He was buried at Versailles, where his body remained until it was returned to Bolivia in 1965 and interred in the cathedral of La Paz. There he rests in a mausoleum especially designed for him, permanently guarded by two soldiers in a space covered by murals that commemorate his time in power.

# The Long-Term Consequences of the Fall

## of the Confederation

The failure of the Confederation had far-reaching consequences that
continue to be relevant today. The fight for the control of the port
of Arica, as well as of the cities of Tacna and Tarapacá, has been at
the center of the difficult relationship among Bolivia, Peru, and Chile
that emerged in the western part of South America at the end of the
colonial period. These republics have all laid claim to this area, and even
today the control of Arica remains an issue of contention, discussed in
bilateral and multilateral meetings of presidents and ministers. The
vision that Santa Cruz put forward of joining Bolivia and Peru in a
confederation was for him, and for many of the people of this region,
the ideal option that would have allowed the people from the Altiplano
access to the most suitable port. His failure, caused in no small measure
by the intransigent opposition of Chile, and parts of Peru left the issue
to simmer for decades, only to resurface when natural resources made
the area ever more desirable. After the defeat of the Confederation,
Chile had been content with the assurance that Bolivia and Peru would
never be united politically. With time, as Chile's economic interests in
the region grew, this changed, and their desire for control of the area
increased.

By the time of Santa Cruz's death, it was clear that Chile had
developed an interest in taking control of the sparsely populated
Bolivian territories of Atacama, which were growing in economic sig-
nificance. They had first become economically important through the
export of guano, fertilizer made from bird waste that had made Peru
immensely wealthy after the fall of the Confederation. Later, the export
of saltpeter overtook that of guano. Chileans carried out most of the
exploitation, and their interests in the area grew greatly during the

1860s. A treaty establishing the border in this area was not signed until 1866. This was, incidentally, the year Peru and Chile joined forces to combat the attacks of the Spanish fleet that sought to take over the guano-producing islands and threatened the ports of Callao and Valparaiso. The three neighbors were temporarily united against a common enemy.

Some years after the Spanish threat had subsided; a new Bolivian government rescinded all previous agreements and negotiated a new treaty with Chile in 1874. This pact was generous toward Chile, stipulating that taxes could not be increased for twenty-five years. A year earlier, the Bolivian government had entered into contract with the Anglo-Chilean Saltpeter and Railway Company, allowing it to exploit the area for fifteen years. This was never ratified by the Bolivian Congress. Some years later, in 1878, a cash-strapped Bolivian regime, looking for ways to circumvent this limitation, pointed out that the contract still had to be finalized. They made it clear they did not consider it to be in effect, because it had not been approved. Congress passed a law accepting the contract with the Anglo-Chilean company but charging a 10-cent tax on every quintal of saltpeter exported. The Chileans, quoting the 1874 treaty, refused to pay. Exasperated, the Bolivian government decided in February 1879 to rescind all contracts and auction all the saltpeter houses owned by the Chileans to cover the unpaid taxes. Chile invaded, and Peru sent a diplomatic mission to Santiago in an attempt to prevent war.

Peru and Bolivia had signed a secret pact of mutual defense in 1873. Argentina had been invited to participate but had declined. According to the Peruvian envoy to Chile, the agreement was limited to promoting friendship between the countries, but Santiago saw it as an act of aggression and rejected Peruvian mediation. By March, Bolivia had stopped all trade with Chile, and weeks later its coastal territories were invaded. In April 1879, war was declared against Peru and Bolivia, and a naval campaign began. In spite of all the provisions set up by Chile to prevent Peru from developing a strong navy after the Confederation, Peru attempted to keep up with its southern neighbor, but forty years later it still remained unprepared for conflict. Bolivia lost its coastal territory in Atacama quite early in the war. Because it had no naval power and no further interests to defend, the Bolivian army retreated to the Andes after their defeat. Cobija, the port that Santa Cruz had worked so hard to develop, was lost forever. The department that he had considered Bolivia's only hope for an independent exit to the Pacific was now in

the hands of the Chileans. Even though Chile quickly succeeded in controlling the areas in which they had economic interests, war continued
against Peru. Until October 1879, the campaign was fought largely at
sea, but once the Chileans had defeated the last of the Peruvian naval
forces, an invasion of southern Peru followed. By 1880, the Chileans had
taken control of the cities of Tacna, Arica, and Tarapacá, even though
the allied forces defeated them in the last of the three. The cities that
had been contested by Bolivia since its inception were now in Chilean
hands. The port that was best suited for the city of La Paz was no longer
in Peruvian territory.

The first attempts to negotiate peace began in 1880, brokered by
Britain, North America, and Germany. In October that year, the representatives of Peru, Chile, and Bolivia met off the port of Arica, aboard
an American vessel. In exchange for peace, the Chileans wanted the
territories of Atacama, Cobija, Tarapacá, and Iquique to be ceded in
perpetuity. They wanted a compensation of 20 million pesos, the return
of the property of all their nationals, and the right to occupy Tacna and
Moquegua until all the conditions were met. In addition, they insisted
on a guarantee that Arica would never become a fortified port. The
most interesting condition, however, was that there would never be a
Confederation between Peru and Bolivia. So, more than forty years after
the end of the proposed union, the specter of Santa Cruz's dream still
haunted relations among neighbors. Chile was still afraid of the potential union of these two countries. These conditions were not accepted,
war continued, and Lima was occupied. Chile tried to convince Bolivia
to join them against Peru and offered the port of Arica in exchange.

Ultimately, Bolivians did not join the fray, and with the Chilean
invasion of Lima in 1881, the Peruvian government imploded. For the
third time in less than a hundred years, stronger naval forces from
the south took control of the administrative center of Peru. Just as
on previous occasions, this was not enough to control the country,
and for more than three years a guerrilla campaign was sustained from
the highlands. The Chileans were never able to control the Andean
regions of Peru. The Peruvian forces were, as they had historically been,
strongest in the south, and it was only when one of the guerrilla factions
fighting for Peru was defeated in the northern Andes that a peace
was finally negotiated. Signed at the port of Ancón, in 1883, with the
faction that controlled the north of Peru, the treaty stipulated that Chile
would gain control of Tarapacá and the provinces of Tacna and Arica
would remain in Chilean hands for ten years. After this, the people

of those provinces would decide by plebiscite to which country they would rather belong. The treaty allowed Chile the control of all the guano-producing islands off the coast of Peru until all debts had been cleared. The Chileans abandoned Peru in 1884, and civil war broke out. Although the treaty had been signed by a faction that only controlled the north of Peru, the terms for peace could not be changed even after the general in charge was defeated. Chile did not fare much better than Peru and in 1891 was engulfed in civil war. The situation in both countries was such that it was not until the turn of the century that either was prepared to return to the third clause of the Treaty of Ancón.

Once again, just as they had been during the creation of Bolivia and during the Confederation, the territories of Tacna and Arica were at the center of conflict. Chile was not keen on holding the plebiscites stipulated in 1883 because the local population remained committed to Peru. From 1901, Chile began pursuing an ever more violent strategy to try to curb Peruvian identity in Tacna and Arica. After the First World War, some in Peru began campaigning for rescinding the whole treaty, claiming that, because the plebiscite had not taken place, Chile had not complied with their side of the agreement. The United States, at the time the main mediator, rejected this option as lacking sufficient merit. President Calvin Coolidge ordered in 1925 that the plebiscite should be implemented.

A commission was set up and work began the same year to carry out the process. It quickly became apparent, however, that it was going to be difficult to implement the plebiscite fairly. Chileans, according to their own representatives, were convinced that they would lose because even Indians, and foreigners who had lived in the area since 1920, had been given the right to vote. To counter this, the Chilean government stepped up its strategy to ensure that the plebiscite was favorable to them. So blatant were these strategies that the U.S. observers were unable to allow the process to continue. A new solution was considered, which would have granted Bolivia control over Arica, given Tacna to Peru, and awarded Tarapacá to Chile. Although it seemed to be the most equitable solution, the Peruvians insisted that they would not accept this option. They were open to the possibility of Arica being neutral, similarly to Danzig, or administered by the United States, but Peru did not want to grant Bolivia control of the port under any circumstances. Once again, after so many years, the dispute over Arica was at the heart of the debate and the difficulties among the three countries of the southern Pacific. Arica continued to be the most important port for

La Paz, and a railway had been built joining the Bolivian city and the port.

More than a hundred years after independence, the question over who had the right to control Arica was still as central as it had been when Santa Cruz was one of the chief actors involved. By 1926 it was clear that there would be no plebiscite, and long-term solutions continued to be elusive, because it was also clear that neither Peru nor Chile was prepared to cede the territory to Bolivia. The Americans were increasingly frustrated with their lack of progress, and the situation remained locked until 1929, when negotiations started again and a compromise was finally agreed on. This time the idea championed was that of a partition: Tacna would go to Peru and Arica to Chile. A railway to the sea was to be built to allow Tacna access to the port of Arica. Peru would be given use of the port facilities in a special Peruvian-controlled area. Bolivia once again remained outside the treaty and without access to the sea. The implementation of this 1929 Treaty of Lima took a very long time. Tacna was returned to Peru in 1930, but the work on the railway and the final access to the port was not finalized until 1999, 70 years after the treaty was signed and more than 100 years after the war. Today not all the issues between Peru and Chile have been resolved. Conflict is now over the control of the seabed in the long-disputed area. There is at the time of writing a motion at the International Court in The Hague that seeks to find a solution to this difference.

Bolivia still demands its right to have access to the Pacific Ocean. Some of the reasons that led Santa Cruz to fight for a Confederation between Peru and Bolivia are still current. The relationship among Peru, Bolivia, and Chile remains fraught, after nearly 200 years of friendship and confrontation. Today there is no real interest in creating a political union between Peru and Bolivia, which still alternate between friendship and enmity. Arica, as the most important port of the region, has remained at the center of the issue. Santa Cruz understood from very early on that Cobija and the coast of Atacama were too distant from the main cities of Bolivia to become a successful port. The war of the Pacific made this evident – indeed, so clear that the conflict over Bolivia's access to the sea is seldom discussed in terms of regaining the territory it lost, but centers over the control of the port of Arica.

The defeat of the Confederation had other important long-term consequences. Santa Cruz was excluded from the politics of the region and remained in exile until his death. Even his memory continued to be so contentious that his remains were not returned to Bolivia until a

century after his death. The relationship with Peru and Chile continued
to be problematic and indeed, it remains so today. It is important to
note that, in spite of the lack of any attempt to rekindle this project,
subsequent Chilean governments continued to be afraid of a possible
union between Bolivia and Peru. This was clearly illustrated in their
demand during the War of the Pacific that these countries were never
to be joined in a confederation.

The Confederation was not able to survive the attacks from its
internal and external enemies. As a result of its failure, Santa Cruz was
exiled. Although the question of access to the Pacific and the potential
benefits of uniting Peru and Bolivia continued to be great, there were
no further attempts to unite Peru and Bolivia, outside of the brief and
unfortunate one led by Gamarra in 1841, and Santa Cruz's and Flores's
failed expeditions of 1843. After the borders were finally settled in the
1840s, a new generation of leaders took hold of the political space and
spent most of their time and energy fighting to establish stable governments instead of dabbling with a possible union between republics.
*Caudillos* tended to intervene in the politics of neighboring countries,
which often provided exiled leaders a place from which to launch their
comeback campaigns, and which had keen interests in gaining some
territory on disputed border areas. However, there was no longer any
desire to create political unions. By the 1840s, national identity ties
had become much more consolidated, even as the issue continued to be
contested, and individuals had taken sides and come to terms with their
nationalities. There were far fewer men like Santa Cruz, torn between
various competing national identities.

The matter of Bolivian access to the Pacific was not contentious in
the 1840s, and the port of Cobija continued to be developed. With the
discovery of guano, matters seemed to be settled, and Cobija began to
grow in importance. After the exploitation of the saltpeter deposits in
the region grew exponentially in the 1860s, the barren desert coast surrounding the port became increasingly valuable, and Chilean capitalists
established themselves there to exploit it. The Pacific Coast remained
distant from the centers of power, and, in spite of its growing economic
importance, there was little interest in its development until it was
seen as a possible source of income through the taxation of Chilean
enterprises. War erupted over the control of the natural resources, and
it escalated to a full-blown international conflagration. Once again, it
resembled the previous confrontations between the neighbors on the
Pacific: Chile successfully occupied Lima, as well as all the coastal towns.
The highlands, as before, remained impenetrable, and irregular guerrilla

forces kept the enemy at bay. Peace was finally negotiated, and it is telling that the most enduring issue within the treaties was to be the control over the port of Arica and the city of Tacna. Even this long after the end of the Confederation, it remained the central issue of contention. The fact is that even today, when the agreements have finally been honored and there is no more debate on who owns the land, it is still possible for Chile and Peru to disagree over the ownership of the seabed, and for Bolivia to demand to regain access to the Pacific.

Although today no one is advocating a close political union between the states of Peru and Bolivia, and a confederation as imagined by Bolívar and Santa Cruz is even less of a possibility now than nearly 200 years ago, the people who live on the border continue to be the Aymara, who have for centuries occupied these lands over which so much blood has been spilled. They live, as they have done since independence, in constant transit among the three countries, not particularly concerned by which nation-state they are in. To them there is little difference whether they are in Bolivia, Peru, or Chile, and they often divide their daily lives between the countries. The border between Peru and Bolivia at the Desaguadero is still a bridge, where today women sell their wares: fruit, vegetables, oil, rice, and beans. People move from one side of the border to the other without any difficulty, some on rickshaws, most of them walking, and border control is optional. People who live in this area do not really see a difference between being in one country or another.

This inability to see differences is echoed in a larger arena, as in the case of the recent James Bond movie set in Bolivia. The producers chose to portray the country as a barren desert and filmed entirely in Chilean locations. This is of course a standard procedure in the global film industry, but there was public outcry on the part of the local municipal authorities, who were infuriated by the idea that Chilean citizens were to be disguised as Bolivians. To the representatives of the state, the idea that the differences between Chileans and Bolivians were so minor that Chileans could be disguised as Bolivians was shocking. Santa Cruz would undoubtedly not have been surprised by this possibility: he himself lived in the border and was forced to acquire a national identity during his lifetime because of the circumstances in which he lived.

## Reconsidering Caudillismo in the Andes

Santa Cruz epitomized the Andean *caudillo*. He strongly believed that the armed forces should be the backbone of the state and considered that

the best way to achieve stability was to have a well-paid and contented
military and a system of national guards who would defend their home
provinces. During his career, spanning thirty years in active service and
nearly twenty-five in retirement, he remained loyal to the ideals of the
military institution. He took much pride, even when in exile, in his rank
as general of the Colombian, Peruvian, and Bolivian armies and chose
to be depicted in portraits and photographs in full military uniform. He
was always referred to as Marshall Santa Cruz. In contrast to *caudillos*
in other regions, Santa Cruz was never an important landowner, and
his power did not arise from his peons or from his employees. Instead,
his strongest backing came from within the army, and he did much to
cultivate this relationship. The men who rose in the ranks under his
command, first in the wars of independence and later in the wars of
the Confederation, were socialized in this way. Yet it was one of these
men – one of his closest protégés, a man he described as his godson, José
de Ballivián – who ultimately unseated him from power.

The colonial militia and the first army organized in the southern
Andes were formative for Santa Cruz. His father and grandfather had
served the king during the Túpac Amaru and Túpaj Katari rebellions
and had both risen to the highest rank of *Maestre de Campo*. They had
seen action in the convulsed last quarter of the eighteenth century in
the period when the Bourbons aimed to reform the military. Santa Cruz
had begun his service in 1809 under the command of his father, as a
member of the local militia. Family connections made it possible for
Santa Cruz to become an *alferez* under the command of Goyeneche, in
preparation for a military career similar to that of his father. Circumstances, however, were very different in the period of the king's captivity
under Napoleon, and a long and intensive war raged in the southern
Andes in the highland provinces of the Viceroyalty of Río de la Plata.
The realities of this conflict marked Santa Cruz's understanding of warfare, as did his exposure to Creole militia members such as Goyeneche,
and the Tristán brothers who had formally trained in the peninsula and
who were veterans of the wars against the French republic.

During this conflict, the Bourbon militias were transformed into a
structured army. It was no longer a matter of merely wearing uniforms
and parading every Sunday after mass. These were long campaigns where
thousands of men were mobilized through mountainous terrain. Santa
Cruz learned then how crucial it was to have the support of the local population, which the royalists did not always have where they traveled.
It also made it clear that keeping men contented was of paramount

importance, because having a smaller, more disciplined corps could ultimately lead to greater success than having large numbers of auxiliaries who could not be coerced into fighting when necessary. Santa Cruz put this lesson into practice with much success when he fought against Gamarra in 1835. In this campaign the superiority of his army was not always numeric, because his enemies often had more auxiliary forces. By providing for his soldiers, however, Santa Cruz had made sure that they remained loyal to him. He also endeavored to minimize the disruption his troops caused to local populations, once again by making sure his men were properly fed, clothed, and paid.

During the decade that he spent fighting for the king, Santa Cruz also had the opportunity to serve under commanders who came from the Spanish peninsula and who had different experiences that further enhanced his knowledge of war. One was Joaquín de la Pezuela, who, as an artillery specialist, placed much emphasis on the targeted use of cannons and the importance of choosing the most strategic locations. Santa Cruz benefited from this experience and put it into practice by maintaining an arsenal in the town of Oruro during his time as president. He remained a keen tactician who prided himself on his knowledge of both the art and the science of war, although he had not been trained in the academy and had served his apprenticeship on the battlefield. Pezuela observed the importance of women in the camps, and how they accompanied their men all throughout the campaigns. Travelers who visited Peru at the time of the Confederation often remarked on this practice and were as surprised by it as Pezuela had been twenty years before. For Santa Cruz, however, this was a normal practice of the armed forces in the Andes, and he did not consider it an anomaly: he understood the role these women played in providing for the army in war.

By the same token, Santa Cruz had an acute understanding of the needs and desires of Indian communities. After his many years of campaigning, he realized that tribute in itself was not seen negatively by communities. What they objected to was not knowing what use was made of their payments. Santa Cruz had seen the failure of many of those who abolished tribute. When Bolívar left him in charge of preparing the new tax records in the department of La Paz in 1826, Santa Cruz stopped the inspections that made Indians resentful of the new regime because they feared these lists would lead to further taxation. Santa Cruz chose instead to negotiate with the communities and work from the existing records. When he was in power in Bolivia, he worked hard to ensure that Indians benefited from his policies, and he was convinced that the best course of action was to maintain some traditional forms of taxation and communal land ownership. Santa Cruz was therefore not an ideological liberal, but a pragmatist who advocated free trade. He wanted to continue with some of the more traditional systems favored by Indians in order to retain their support.

Santa Cruz was successful in negotiating with Indian groups, and in his official speeches he highlighted how much he valued them. In Bolivia he was able to utilize some of their traditional systems of governance and link them to the structure of the state. In Peru he found important allies among Indian groups such as the so-called Iquichanos, who provided him with crucial backing during the Confederation. At this time Santa Cruz showed his pragmatism once again, because he was prepared to provide these communities with exemptions to the Indian tribute in exchange for their support. He did not, therefore, have a blanket belief in the Indian head tax, but instead saw it as a tool that could be used to foster cooperation, providing exemptions whenever needed. Santa Cruz had learned from commander Álvarez de Arenales, who had organized militias and *montoneras* in all the Andes, how useful this measure could be. Arenales was instrumental in gaining the support of Indian communities for the cause of independence in areas as distinct as the province of La Paz, the low-lying valleys of present-day Bolivia, and the high valleys east of Lima, most of which were never under the control of the Spanish authorities after his incursions there. Arenales was a man who knew how to reach compromises, and when he captured Santa Cruz after the battle of Cerro de Pasco in December 1820, he offered him a career fighting for independence.

It was after changing sides that Santa Cruz discovered the usefulness of constitutional discourse – although even as he embraced it, he favored limiting what he saw as its possible excesses. He had already served under a constitutional regime when the Cádiz charter was put into practice in 1812. On this occasion he had seen how elections had led to a volatile situation in the southern Andes that culminated in 1814 in the largest uprising of the period, during which his father had been killed. Santa Cruz had witnessed the way in which the introduction of the constitution for the second time, in 1820, had weakened viceroy Pezuela, and three years later he saw firsthand how difficult it was to govern under the first independent constitutional regime in Lima. All this led him to favor charters that gave the executive greater power and sought to limit the participation of the masses. Santa Cruz was involved in the first coup of the republican period when he led the movement that made José de la Riva Agüero president. Five years later, when Bolívar left him in charge of the government of Peru, Santa Cruz did not think twice about in interrupting the constitutional system after the mutiny of Colombian forces, because he considered it more important to maintain order.

In spite of his measured relationship with constitutionalism, Santa Cruz was convinced that for a government to be legitimate, a charter was needed. Following Bolívar's lead closely, he believed that a constitutional agreement was the best possible way to create a durable union, even as he witnessed the failure of a federation based on the 1826 lifelong charter. *Caudillos* in the Andes saw constitutions as the basis for the legitimacy they desired. This was the belief not just of Santa Cruz or Bolívar, but of all the others who sought to govern in this region. Men like Gamarra and Salaverry who opposed Santa Cruz also believed this, and as soon as they took power, they endeavored to find the constitutional arrangement that best suited them. Gamarra, in fact, left power in 1834 because the constitution did not allow him to be reelected and he was unable to control the Congress, which was in charge of making the changes mandated by law.

In spite of this desire to couch their regimes in legality, often by calling for elections after having taken power by force, *caudillos* saw constitutions as instruments for government that could be changed to better suit the needs of the regime. Santa Cruz had no qualms in enacting a new constitution in 1831 and reforming it in 1834. He considered that one of his greatest successes with this reform was to limit Congress to meeting every two years. One of the reasons he was swayed toward Orbegoso during the Peruvian civil wars that resulted in the Confederation was that Orbegoso could claim more constitutional legitimacy than any of his opponents. By the same token, Santa Cruz was convinced that a union could be created from assemblies meeting and agreeing on the union of three independent states. In fact, he remained open to the possibility of calling the assemblies once again when his opponents questioned the legality of the Confederation.

Constitutions, however, were important not only to Santa Cruz, but also to his opponents. It is no coincidence that one of the first things that both Ballivián and Gamarra did after they unseated Santa Cruz was to enact new constitutions. They in turn were also challenged by other *caudillos* who questioned the legitimacy of these charters, because some argued that they had been imposed with support from foreign forces.

Santa Cruz was by no means an exception. The leaders of this period all fitted into the same mold. Indeed, even those who came after his project had ended and he was in exile bore a great resemblance to him. Although unions were never attempted again and the issues of nationality and identity had been to a great extent resolved by the 1840s, the way of capturing and exercising power remained the same. All the way to the last third of the nineteenth century, *caudillos* backed by the military were in control of the state. In Peru there was never a civilian in charge of the presidency until 1871, even though presidential elections were recurrent. The situation in Bolivia was not different with the occasional civilian filling in. Some of Santa Cruz's successors, in fact, learned much from his style of leadership. One example is Ramón Castilla, who was president of Peru between 1845 and 1850 and again between 1855 and 1862. Castilla perfected the system of government developed by Santa Cruz. He was extremely successful in taking control of the army and providing pensions for veterans, even for those who had opposed him, though he was of course fortunate to have the wealth of guano to bankroll his regime. *Caudillismo* can only be understood within the logic of each particular region that created it, shaping the diverse picture of the way in which Spanish-American republics were governed after independence.

Santa Cruz ultimately failed in his experiment of uniting Peru and Bolivia. The reasons for this were many, not just the fact that Chile was an unrelenting foe intent on the destruction of the Confederate project. It was also abundantly clear that many within Peru and Bolivia were against the union. The elites who were to lose most, in Lima and Chuquisaca, never really supported the plan, even if at times they did not openly oppose it. The core constituency of the Confederation, southern Peru and northern Bolivia, also had difficulties in completely committing to supporting the union and were more interested in advancing their own local and regional agendas than in the overall success of the plan. The elites of Cuzco, Arequipa, La Paz, Tacna, and Arica were all in accord that the union would benefit them, but they all had different expectations in terms of where the possible capital would be located and the advantages becoming the new center would bring to them. The tensions within the Confederation and the vast expanse that needed to be controlled by a tightly centralized structure were at the core of the failure of the projected union. It is possible to speculate that if the external pressure exercised by Chile had not been so great, Santa Cruz might have been able to reconcile the various parties within Peru and

Figure 6. Bust of Andrés de Santa Cruz at the Universidad Nacional de San Andrés by Marina Nuñez del Prado (1975) – photograph by the author.

Bolivia and make the union feasible. It was this combination of internal and external factors led to the ultimate failure of the Confederation.

Santa Cruz, on the other hand, remains in a strange kind of limbo. He is a hero of independence in two countries, yet neither of them has ever completely embraced him as one of its founding fathers. In the *Casa de la Libertad* in Sucre, the museum that remembers the birth of the Bolivian nation, the triad of founding fathers is Bolívar, Sucre, and Ballivián, whereas Santa Cruz is remembered with the other presidents. In La Paz, there is a mausoleum, but the only statue in honor of its native son is a small bust at the University of San Andrés. In the city of Lima, there is an avenue in a smart section of town that bears his name, although this street occupies a space once covered by a large sugar-cane producing hacienda called Santa Cruz. The avenue traverses a section of the district of Miraflores not far from the small property *el Pacajal*, where the Protector liked to live during his long sojourns in the city. In 1994, Bolivian president Gonzalo Sanchez de Losada unveiled a small monument with an image of Santa Cruz at the start of the avenue. In 2007, Evo Morales unveiled a similar but larger monument at the other end. There, overlooking the Pacific Ocean, Santa Cruz is remembered as the founder of the ephemeral Peru-Bolivia Confederation.

# Bibliography

ALJOVÍN DE LOSADA, Cristóbal, *Caudillos y constituciones. Perú: 1821–1845*, Lima: Fondo de Cultura Económica, 2000.

ANDERSON, Benedict, *Imagined Communities: Reflections on the Origin and Spread of Nationalism*, London, Verso, [1983] 1991.

ARGUEDAS, Alcides, "Los Caudillos Letrados" in *Historia General de Bolivia (El proceso de la nacionalidad) 1809–1921*, La Paz, Arnó editores, 1922; *Caudillos bárbaros, historia – resurrección. – La tragedia de un pueblo (Melgarejo–Morales) 1864–1872*, Barcelona, Viuda de L. Tasso, 1929.

BARRENA LOPETEGUI, Antonio, *Vida de un Soldado: Desde la toma de Valdivia a la Victoria de Yungay*, edited by Jorge Javier Molina Hernández, Santiago de Chile: RiL editores, 2009.

BASADRE, Jorge, *La Iniciación de la Republica*, Lima: Rosay, 1929, 2 vols.

———— *Historia de la Republica del Perú*, Lima: Ed. Huascaran, 6th edition, 1961.

BILBAO Manuel, *Historia de Salaverry*, Lima: Imprenta del Correo, 1867.

BRAUN, Felipe, *El Mariscal Braun a través de su Epistolario*. Cochabamba: Editorial los Amigos del Libro, 1998.

BÚLNES, Gonzalo, *Historia de la Campaña del Perú en 1838*, Santiago: Imprenta de los tiempos, 1878.

BURNS, Kathryn and Margaret Najarro, "Parentesco, Escritura y Poder: Los Gamarra y la escritura pública en el Cuzco," in *Revista del Archivo Regional del Cuzco*, No. 16, 2004.

CAHILL, David, *From Rebellion to Independence in the Andes: Soundings from Southern Peru, 1750–1830*, Amsterdam: Askant, 2002.

CAHILL, David, and Scarlett O'Phelan, "Forging their own History: Indian Insurgency in the Southern Peruvian Sierra, 1815," *Bulletin of Latin American Research*, vol. II, no. 2, 1992, pp. 125–67.

CALVO, Mariano, *Oposición en Bolivia a la confederación Perú-Boliviana: cartas del vicepresidente Mariano Enrique Calvo y el Presidente Andrés Santa Cruz*. Sucre Bolivia, Corte Superior de justicia, 1996.

CHAMBERS, Sarah C., *From Subjects to Citizens: Honor, Gender, and Politics in Arequipa, Peru, 1780–1854*, University Park: Pennsylvania State University Press, 1999.

CHAPMAN, Charles, "The Age of Caudillos: A Chapter in Hispanic American History," *Hispanic American Historical Review (HAHR)*, vol. 12, 1932, pp. 292–3.

*Concordato Celebrado entre el Gobierno de Bolivia y la Santa Sede*, La Paz: Imprenta Popular, 1851.

Correspondence between Luís José de Orbegoso to Domingo Nieto, in *Archivo Benjamín Vicuña Mackenna*, vol. 221, copy held at the Instituto Riva Agüero in Lima, Colección Félix Denegri Luna.

CROW, John A., "Democracy of the Oligarchy," *The Epic of Latin America* New York: University of California Press, 1992.

DE LA FUENTE, Ariel, *Children of Facundo: Caudillo and Gaucho Insurgency Suring the Argentine State Formation Process (La Rioja, 1853–1870)*, Durham, NC: Duke University Press, 2000.

DIAZ ARGUEDAS, Julio, "Trayectoria Militar de Santa Cruz, Mariscal del Tiempo Heroico" in *La Vida y Obra del Mariscal Andrés Santa Cruz*, La Paz: Biblioteca Paceña, 1976.

DÍAZ VENTEO, Fernando, *Las Campañas Militares del Virrey Abascal*, Seville: Escuela de Estudios Hispanoamericanos, 1948.

DONOSO, Carlos and Jaime Rosenblitt B. eds., *Guerra, región y nación: La Confederación Perú Boliviana 1836–1839*, Santiago: Universidad Andrés Bello, 2009.

*Exposición de los motivos que justifican la cooperación del gobierno de Bolivia en los negocios políticos del Perú*, La Paz: Imprenta del Colegio de Artes, 15 June 1835.

FISHER, John, "Royalism, Regionalism and Rebellion in Colonial Peru," *Hispanic American Historical Review*, vol. 59, no. 2, 1979.

———— *Bourbon Peru, 1750–1824*, Liverpool: Latin American Studies Series, 2003.

FOWLER, Will, *Santa Anna of Mexico*, Lincoln: University of Nebraska Press, 2007.

GAMARRA, Agustín, *Gran Mariscal Agustín Gamarra, Epistolario*, edited by Alberto Tauro, Lima: Universidad Nacional Mayor de san Marcos, 1952.

———— *El General Gamarra a sus compatriotas*, Costa Rica, 1835.

GARRET, David, *Shadows of Empire: The Indian Nobility of Cusco, 1750–1825*, Cambridge: Cambridge University Press, 2005.

GLAVE, Luis Miguel, "Antecedentes y naturaleza de la revolucion del Cuzco en 1814 y el primer proceso electoral" *La Independencia en el Perú: De los Borbones a Bolívar*, edited by Scarlett O'Phelan Godoy, Lima: Pontificia Universidad Católica del Perú, 2001, pp. 77–97.

_____ La república instalada. Formación nacional y prensa en el Cuzco 1825–1839, Lima: Instituto de Estudios Peruanos, 2004.

GONZÁLES PRADA, Alfredo, Un Crimen perfecto, el asesinato del Gran Mariscal Don Agustín Gamarra Presidente del Perú, New York: H. Wolff, 1941.

GOOTENBERG, Paul, Between Silver and Guano. Commercial Policy and the State in Postindependence Peru, Princeton, NJ: Princeton University Press, 1991.

_____ Paying for Caudillos: The Politics of Emergency Finance in Peru, 1820–1845," in Liberals, Politics and Power, edited by Vincent Peloso and Barbara Tenenbaum, Athens: Georgia University Press, 1996, pp. 134–65.

GUERRA, François Xavier, Modernidad e independencias: Ensayos sobre las revoluciones hispánicas, México: Fondo de Cultura Económica, 1992.

HAIGH, Samuel, Bosquejo del Perú entre 1826 y 1827, in Colección Documental de la Independencia del Perú, XXVII "Relaciones de Viajeros," vol. 3, pp. 41–65.

HALPERÍN DONGHI, Tulio, Hispanoamérica Después de la Independencia, Buenos Aires: Paidós, 1972.

HAMILL, Hugh, Caudillos: Dictators in Spanish America, Norman: University of Oklahoma Press, 1992.

HERREROS DE TEJADA, Luis, El Teniente General D. José Manuel de Goyeneche primer conde de Guaqui, Barcelona: Oliva de Villanueva, 1923.

IRIGOIN, Alejandra, "La fabricación de moneda en Buenos Aires y en Potosí entre 1820 y 1860 y la transformación de la economía postcolonial en el Río de la Plata" in Moneda y Mercado. Ensayos sobre los orígenes de los sistemas monetarios latinoamericanos, Siglos XVIII a XX, edited by A. Ibarra and B. Haubserger, Mexico: UNAM (forthcoming).

La Confederación Perú-Boliviana, el Mariscal Santa Cruz y la Santa Sede, documentos inéditos, La Paz: Banco Central de Bolivia, 1977.

LECUNA, Vicente, (ed.) Documentos referentes a la creación de Bolivia, Caracas: Litografía el Comercio, 1924.

_____ Bolívar y el Arte Militar, New York: The Colonial Press, 1955.

LUNA PIZARRO, Francisco Xavier de, Escritos Políticos, edited by Alberto Tauro, Lima: Universidad Nacional Mayor de San Marcos, 1959.

LYNCH John, Caudillos in Spanish America 1800–1850, Oxford: Clarendon, 1992.

MÉNDEZ, Cecilia, "Incas Sí, Indios No: Notes on Peruvian Creole Nationalism and its Contemporary Crisis," Journal of Latin American Studies, vol, 28, no. I, 1992, pp. 197–225.

_____ "Tradiciones liberales en los Andes: militares y campesinos en la formación del estado peruano," Estudios Interdisciplinarios de América Latina y el Caribe, vol. 15, no. 1, 2004, pp. 35–63.

_____ The Plebeian Republic: The Huanta Rebellion and the Making of the Peruvian State 1820–1850, Durham, NC: Duke University Press, 2005.

MENDIBURU, Manuel, Manuscript Memoirs, Lima: Archivo Instituto Riva Agüero Colección Félix Denegri Luna.

MILLER, John, Memoirs of William Miller in the service of Peru, London, 1828, 2 vols.

MORSE, Richard "Towards a Theory of Spanish American Government," Journal of the History of Ideas, vol. 15, 1954, pp. 71–93.

NIETO, Domingo, Memoria de los hechos que justifican la conducta pública que como general del ejército peruano ha seguido en la época que comprenden los años del 34 al 39, Lima: Imprenta el Comercio, 1839.

OLAÑETA, Casimiro, Manifiesto del Ciudadano Casimiro Olañeta, Ministro Plenipotenciario de Bolivia cerca del Gobierno del Perú, Paz de Ayacucho: Imprenta de Educandas, 1831.

O'CONNOR, Francis Burdett, Un irlandes con Bolívar. Recuerdos de la independencia de América del Sur en Venezuela, Colombia, Bolivia, Perú y la Argentina por un jefe de la legión Británica de Bolívar, 3rd edition, Caracas: El Cid, Editor, 1977.

O'LEARY, Daniel F., Detached recollections, edited by Robin A. Humphreys, London: Athlone Press, 1969.

O'LEARY, Daniel F., editor, Cartas de Sucre al Libertador (1820–1826), Madrid: Editorial América, 1919.

O'PHELAN GODOY, Scarlett, La gran rebelión en los Andes: de Túpac Amaru a Túpac Catari. Cuzco, Peru: Centro de Estudios Regionales Andinos Bartolomé de las Casas, 1995.

_____ "Sucre en el Perú: Entre Riva Agüero y Torre Tagle" in La Independencia en el Perú: De los Borbones a Bolívar, Lima: Pontificia Universidad Católica del Perú, 2001.

_____ "Ciudadanía y etnicidad en las Cortes de Cádiz" in Revista Elecciones, vol. 1, no. 1, 2002.

ORBEGOSO, Luís José, Exposición que hace el Presidente Provisional de la República Peruana Luís José Orbegoso de las razones que le obligaron a solicitar de la república boliviana auxilios para pacificar el Perú. Arequipa: Imprenta de Francisco Valdez, 1835.

_____ Memorias del Gran Mariscal Don Luís José de Orbegoso, Lima: Gil, 1939.

ORTIZ SOTELO, Jorge, Perú y Gran Bretaña: política y economía (1808–1839) a través de los informes navales británicos, Lima: Pontificia Universidad Católica del Perú, 2005.

PARDO Y ALIAGA, Felipe, "Semblanzas Peruanas" in Boletín de la Academia Chilena de Historia (Santiago), vol. 32, 1945, p. 66.

PARKERSON, Phillip, Andrés de Santa Cruz y la Confederación Perú-Boliviana, 1835–1839, La Paz: Editorial Juventud, 1984.

PAZ-SOLDÁN, Juan Pedro, *Cartas Históricas del Perú*, Lima: Imprenta Gil, 1920.

PAZ SOLDÁN, Mariano Felipe, *Historia del Perú Independiente*, *Segundo periodo 1822–1827*, Le Havre: Lemane, MDCCCLXX.

PEREZ DEL CASTILLO, Alvaro, *Bolivia, Colombia, Chile y el Perú: Diplomacia y Política 1825–1904*, La Paz: Los Amigos del Libro, 1980.

PORTALES, Diego, *Epistolario de don Diego Portales*, *1821–1837*, 3 vols. Santiago: Imprenta General de Prisiones, 1936–37.

*Reglamento de Contribuciones*, La Paz, 1831.

ROCA, Jose Luis, *1809: La revolución en la Audiencia de Charcas en Chuquisaca y en La Paz*, La Paz: Plural, 1998.

RODRIGUEZ, Jaime, *The Independence of Spanish America*, New York: Cambridge University Press, 1998.

ROJAS, Armando, editor, *Bolívar y Santa Cruz Epistolario*, Caracas: Venezuelan Government, 1975.

SAFFORD, Frank, "Politics, Ideology and Society in Post-Independence Spanish America," in *Cambridge History of Latin America*, vol. III, pp. 347–421.

SALA I VILA, Nuria, *Y Se Armo el Tole Tole: Tributo Indigena y Movimientos Sociales en El Virreinato del Perú, 1784–1814*, Ayacucho: Instituto de Estudios Regionales José María Arguedas, 1996.

SAN MARTÍN, José de, "Respuestas a las preguntas del general Miller en carta del 9 abril de 1827 (borrador)" in *San Martín su correspondencia (1823–1850)* Editorial América: Madrid, 1919.

SANTA CRUZ, Andrés, *Mensaje del Presidente de Bolivia a la Asamblea Nacional en 1831*, La Paz, Imprenta de Educandas, 1831.

_____ *Mensaje de S. E. el Presidente de Bolivia a las Cámaras Constitucionales de 1833*.

_____ *El General Santa-Cruz explica su conducta pública y los móviles de su política en la presidencia de Bolivia y en la Protección de la Confederación Perú-Boliviana*. La Paz: Tipografía Salesiana, 1924 [1840].

SANTA CRUZ SCHUHKRAFFT, Andrés, *Archivo Histórico del Mariscal Andrés de Santa-Cruz*, La Paz: Universidad Mayor de San Andrés, 1976, 6 vols.

SARMIENTO, Domingo Faustino, *Facundo o Civilización y Barbarie*, Buenos Aires: Ed. Huemul, [1845] 1978.

SOUX, María Luisa, "Los discursos de Castelli y la sublevación indígena de 1810–1811" in *La Republica Peregrina: Hombres de armas y letras en América del Sur 1800–1884*, Carmen McEvoy and Ana María Stuven. editors, Lima: Instituto de Estudios Peruanos, Instituto Francés de Estudios Andinos, 2007.

STEVENS, Donald F., *Origins of Instability in Early Republican Mexico*, Durham, NC: Duke University Press, 1991.

STUVEN, Ana María, "La palabra en armas: patria y nación en la prensa de la Guerra entre Chile y la Confederación Perú-Boliviana, 1835–1839" in *La República Peregrina: Hombres de armas y letras en América del Sur*, pp. 407–41.

SUCRE, Antonio José de, *Mensaje del Presidente de Bolivia al Congreso Extraordinario de 1828, Chuquisaca 2 de Agosto*, Valparaíso: El Mercurio, 1828.

SUTCLIFFE, Thomas, *Sixteen Years in Chile and Peru from 1822 to 1829 by the Retired Governor of Juan Fernandez*, London: Fisher and Sons, 1841.

TÁVARA, Santiago, *Historia de los Partidos*, 1862.

*The National Archives of Great Britain*, Foreign Office 61.

THOMPSON, Sinclair, *We Alone Will Rule: Native Andean Politics in the Age of Insurgency*, Madison: University of Wisconsin Press, 2002.

TSCHUDI, Johan Jacob von, *Travels in Peru, during the years 1838–1842*, translated by Thomasina Ross, London: David Bogue, 1847.

TRISTÁN, Flora, *Peregrinaciones de una Paria (1833–1834)*, Lima: Ed. El Lector, 2003 [1838].

VALDIVIA, Juan Gualberto, *Memorias sobre las revoluciones de Arequipa*, Arequipa: Editorial El Deber, 1956.

WALKER, Charles, "Peasants, Caudillos, and the State in Peru: Cuzco in the Transition from Colony to Republic, 1780–1840," PhD dissertation, University of Chicago, 1992.

———— *Smoldering Ashes, Cuzco and the Creation of Republican Peru, 1780, 1840*, Durham, NC: Duke University Press, 1999.

WU BRADING, Celia, *Generales y Diplomaticos: Gran Bretaña y el Perú, 1820–1840*, Lima: PUCP, 1993.

## Newspapers

*El Coco de Santa Cruz*, 1835
*Eco del Protectorado*, 1838
*El Eco del Protectorado Extraordinario*, 1838
*The Illustrated London News*, 1850
*El Iris de La Paz*, 1830–1839
*La Guardia Nacional del Bolivia*, 1831
*El Rejenerador Peruano*, 1841
*El Restaurador*, (Cuzco) 1841
*El Restaurador* (Sucre) 1841

# INDEX

Brazil, 35, 36, 162
Buenos Aires, 24; British invasion, 3, 34, 39; Junta of, 17, 36, 39, 41, 147, 157
Bulnes, Manuel, 192, 196, 205

Cacique, *see* Indian nobles
Cádiz, Cortes de, 41, 43; siege of, 39
Cajamarca, 80
Calahumana, Juana Bacila, 31
Calahumana, Matías, 28–29
Callao, 49, 59, 69, 71, 79, 81, 132, 139, 163, 168, 170, 185, 196–197, 216; siege of, 82
Calvo, Mariano Enrique, 180, 188–189, 199
Canterac, José de, 78, 80–81, 88
Castelli, Juan José, 39–41
Castilla, Ramón, 8, 201, 208, 226
*Caudillo*, 3–13, 123, 143, 181, 220–222, 225–226; and Indians, 13
Cerdeña, Blas, 72
Cernadas, Francisca, 118, 208–209
Cerro de Pasco, 66, 80, 129; battle of, 51, 63, 77, 99, 160, 224
Challanta, 27
Chapman, Charles, 5
Charcas, Audiencia of, 16–18, 62, 84, 86–87, 90, 147, 151, 159
Charisma, 5, 7
Charles IV, 34–35
Chile, 16, 20, 49, 57, 73, 82, 90, 106, 108–109, 113, 123, 133, 138, 143, 149, 161–167, 169–178, 180–181, 185, 187–188, 190, 192, 194, 197, 200–201, 203, 208, 215–221, 226; Captaincy general, 17
Choquhuanca, José Domingo, 43
Chuquisaca, 16, 18, 34, 36, 39, 86, 91, 93–95, 99–100, 107, 116–117, 119, 121, 124–125, 134, 138, 158, 173, 180, 189, 202, 226; Junta of, 35, 84, 91; University of, 32
*Civicos*, *see* militias
Clausewitz, Carl von, 117
Cobija, 98, 119–120, 138, 172, 206, 216–217, 219–220
Cochabamba, 34, 39–41, 43, 48, 73, 81, 86, 94–95, 109, 189
Colombia, 15, 18, 64, 90, 97–101, 103, 108, 111, 122
Concordat with the Vatican, 186, 210
Confederation, of Peru and Bolivia, 2, 3, 10, 19–20, 115, 141, 139, 143, 146–147, 151, 154, 164, 175, 177, 179–181, 219, 224,

228; flag, 152, 155, 157, 159, 203; naval power, 166–167; trade agreements, 150, 162, 168; war against, 170–173, 178, 184–188, 190, 192, 194, 199, 201, 215, 217, 220–221, 226
Congress: of Bolivia, 98, 100–101, 107, 115, 120–121, 124, 133, 144, 138, 188–190, 216, 225; of the Confederation, 152; of Chile, 167; of Chuquisaca, 18, 89, 94; of Peru, 63–66, 68–69, 71, 74–75, 77, 89–90, 92, 98, 101, 105–106, 111, 127, 139, 144, 196, 205–206, 225
Constitutions, 2, 5, 12, 13, 224–225; of Angostura in 1819, 151; of Bolivia 1831, 225; of Cádiz, 12, 44, 46, 49, 57–58, 106; Chilean of 1833, 205; enacted by Santa Cruz, 124; Peruvian of 1823, 78, 101, 103–104; Peruvian of 1828, 106, 127; Peruvian of 1834, 131–132; Peruvian of 1839 (Huancayo), 204–205; written by Bolívar in 1826 (vitalicia), 84, 95, 97, 99–104, 225, 107, 120, 132, 147, 151, 161, 193
*Corregidores*, 25, 30
Council of Regency, 39
Creoles, 14, 15, 25, 27–28, 33, 50, 56, 58, 79
Crompton, Thomas (British Vice Consul in Islay), 175, 179, 202, 204
Cuenca, 59, 61–62, 66, 98, 105
Cuzco, 11, 15–18, 22, 24, 25, 27–28, 32–34, 37, 39, 46, 47, 50, 59, 72, 82, 87, 89, 93, 100, 102, 104, 111, 115, 118, 121, 127–128, 130–131, 133–135, 137, 140–145, 147, 150, 154–158, 169–170, 206, 226; Audiencia of 30, 33, 118, 153; as viceregal capital, 55, 81

Desaguadero, river, 39, 87, 90, 107, 127, 207, 221

Ecuador, 18, 64, 122–123, 143, 165, 181, 187, 204, 208
Elections, 12, 40–41, 44–46, 61, 63, 89, 95, 100, 107–109, 128, 133, 144, 197–199, 207, 225–226

Federations, 2, 13, 17, 18, 20, 84, 94–99, 102–103, 149, 161, 226; of Peru and Bolivia, 107–108, 111–112, 114–115, 127–129, 131–140, 142–147, 154, 157, 189, 225; of the Andes, 100, 150, 152
Ferdinand VII, 35–36, 39, 48, 79